SLINFOLD STREET

The Development of a Village in the Sussex Weald

Diana Chatwin

ACKNOWLEDGEMENTS

Many people have given help and encouragement in bringing this book to publication. Among those who deserve particular thanks are the members of the Slinfold History Group, especially Eileen Burbidge, who has written up several of the properties, and Mary Davies for producing a beautiful copy of the 1651 Map of Hayes from a photograph of the original in Horsham Museum. Thanks are also due to Gordon Simkin for permission to reproduce some of his drawings made for the book on the Timber-Framed Buildings of Rudgwick, and to Sue Rowland for the maps and plans, to Eddie Harris for his drawings (Figures 10, 11, 13 & 19) and to the late Sylvia Bright for Figure 15. Mrs. Susan Whitmarsh has been kind enough to give permission for the diary of her ancestor, Charles Knight, to be quoted. Grateful thanks are also extended to all those who have lent old photographs for use in the book.

The costs of producing this book have been met by a major grant to the Slinfold Society under the Millennium Festival Awards for All programme, supported by generous gifts from the West Sussex County Council, the Slinfold Parish Council, Cordek Ltd. and Schenectady-Beck Electrical Insulation Systems. The Slinfold Society wishes to express its gratitude for all this financial support, without which this book could not have been published.

© Diana Chatwin 2000
All rights reserved. No part of this publication may be
reproduced, in any form or by any means, without permission
from the Publisher.

Printed by Springfield Press,
Slinfold, RH13 7QP

Published by the Slinfold Society
Windalls, Slinfold, RH13 7RP
ISBN 095393080-7

Front cover: Aerial view of Slinfold Street in the 1980s, looking north-west
Back cover: Slinfold Street, looking south-east, early 1900s before the erection of the War Memorial

CONTENTS

Foreword by The Slinfold Society … iv

Introduction … v

The Development of the Village

Background	1
The beginnings of the Village	2
The Village of 1500	3
A Slow Expansion (16th-18th Centuries)	5
Local Transport up to the 18th Century	9
Village Tradesmen in the 17th and 18th Centuries	10
A Rapid Growth (the 19th Century)	11
Trades & Industries in the 19th Century	15
Transport in the 19th Century	20
The 20th Century	21
Conclusion	26

Manor and Squire

The Manor	27
Squire or no Squire?	28

The Houses of The Street

Timber, Brick & Stone (Buildings & their Construction)	32
The Influence of Manors on the Development of the Village	37
Houses on Dedisham & Pinkhurst Land	39
Houses on Bassett's Fee Land	60
More Houses on Pinkhurst Land	79
Houses on Patching Land	83
Houses on Clemsfold Land	98
St. Peter's Church	113
Houses on Wiggonholt Land	115

Appendix

Genealogical Table of the Briggs	127
Genealogical Table of the Childs	128

Glossary … 129

Bibliography … 131

Index … 133

FOREWORD

Diana Chatwin moved into Slinfold House in the centre of the village with her husband and young family in 1981. As a historian she must have been excited by the prospect of exploring the development of her own house. The influence of the Child family, members of which had lived in her house and several others nearby, on the development of Slinfold, led her to investigate their family records.

Other village residents were keen to know more about their homes and Diana crawled into roof spaces, examined partitioning, identified building styles and materials and traced the ownerships of these houses. Here was a wealth of historical information about the centre of Slinfold which was interesting to more people than just the owners. Diana led walks in the village to describe the history and many people were keen to know more. John Speed, Chairman of the Slinfold Society at the time, approached Diana on the possibility of running a History Group for the Society. In spite of the fact that, once started, such a group would commit her to a lot of work, Diana agreed to undertake the project if there was sufficient support. The idea was a success and a sizeable group meets regularly in Diana's house to enjoy a varied programme on the history of Slinfold.

As the Millennium approached, Diana suggested that the History Group might assist her in collecting the history of the Street. Obviously outlying properties and other parts of the village had interesting histories and contributed to the evolution of Slinfold, but the study needed to be focused to be manageable.

When John Speed persuaded Diana to form the History Group within the Slinfold Society, neither he nor she can have foreseen its success nor the production of this book to mark the Millennium. The Slinfold Society and all its members thank Diana for her steadfast leadership, her knowledge and her skills which have led to the production of this book with which they are proud to be associated.

The Slinfold Society

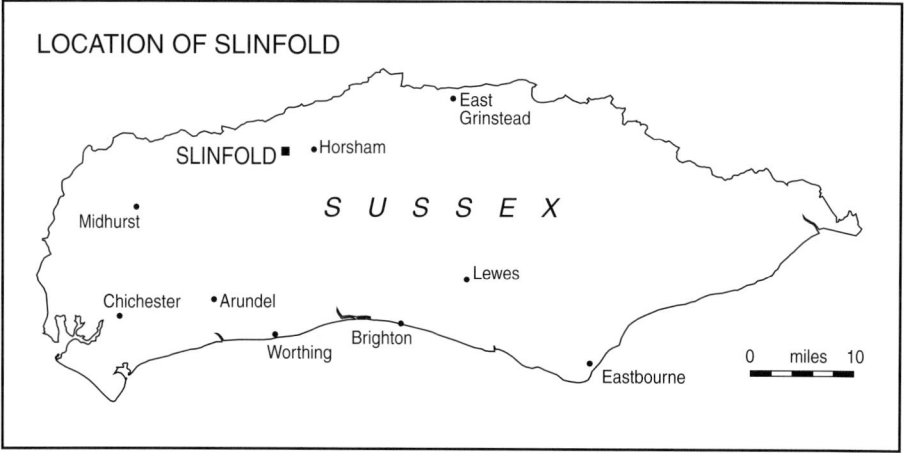

INTRODUCTION

The Slinfold History Group was set up five years ago under the aegis of the Slinfold Society. The Group has been working on the village Street for the two past years and the booklet first suggested has grown into a book as the amount of information available became clear. Members have visited the Public Record Office in Kew, gathering information from the Lloyd George's Domesday of 1910 and the National Farm Survey of 1941, and the West Sussex Record Office in Chichester, where the Tithe Map, Land Tax Returns, Census Returns, Poor Rate Valuation Lists, Trade Directories and a host of other documents have been consulted. Members have been involved with sifting and processing the information, interviewing residents and transcribing earlier interviews, and without their hard work and encouragement this book would not have been possible.

One great bonus was the chance meeting at a conference with Peter Child whose ancestors lived in my own house. His sister, Sarah, was at that time in the process of working through the family archive which had lain untouched for many years. I have been allowed free access to this archive and it has proved a rich source of information. The Childs owned a number of properties in the Street and were connected with others as trustees to wills, and they were meticulous in preserving documents related to them.

I am very well aware that local history is only the best interpretation that can be made on the basis of the evidence available at a particular time. In the light of increased knowledge and further information, students in the future may well be able to add to or amend what I have written.

The buildings included in this book are those within the Conservation Area. This has enabled the group of houses to the north and west of the church in Clapgate Lane to be within the book, as well as Padora-Nibletts, Stone Cottages and York Cottage to the south of the Street, while the three houses in the Street between Old House Farm and Park Street are outside the Conservation Area. The timber-framed houses have not been described in great detail in this book, but if anyone wishes to see a full report on a particular building they are welcome to get in touch with me. The modern names of the houses have been used throughout, with references to earlier names where appropriate.

We owe a great debt to the owners of the houses who have been unfailingly helpful in response to our demands for information and requests to examine the buildings in detail. I would like to record our thanks to them.

Diana Chatwin

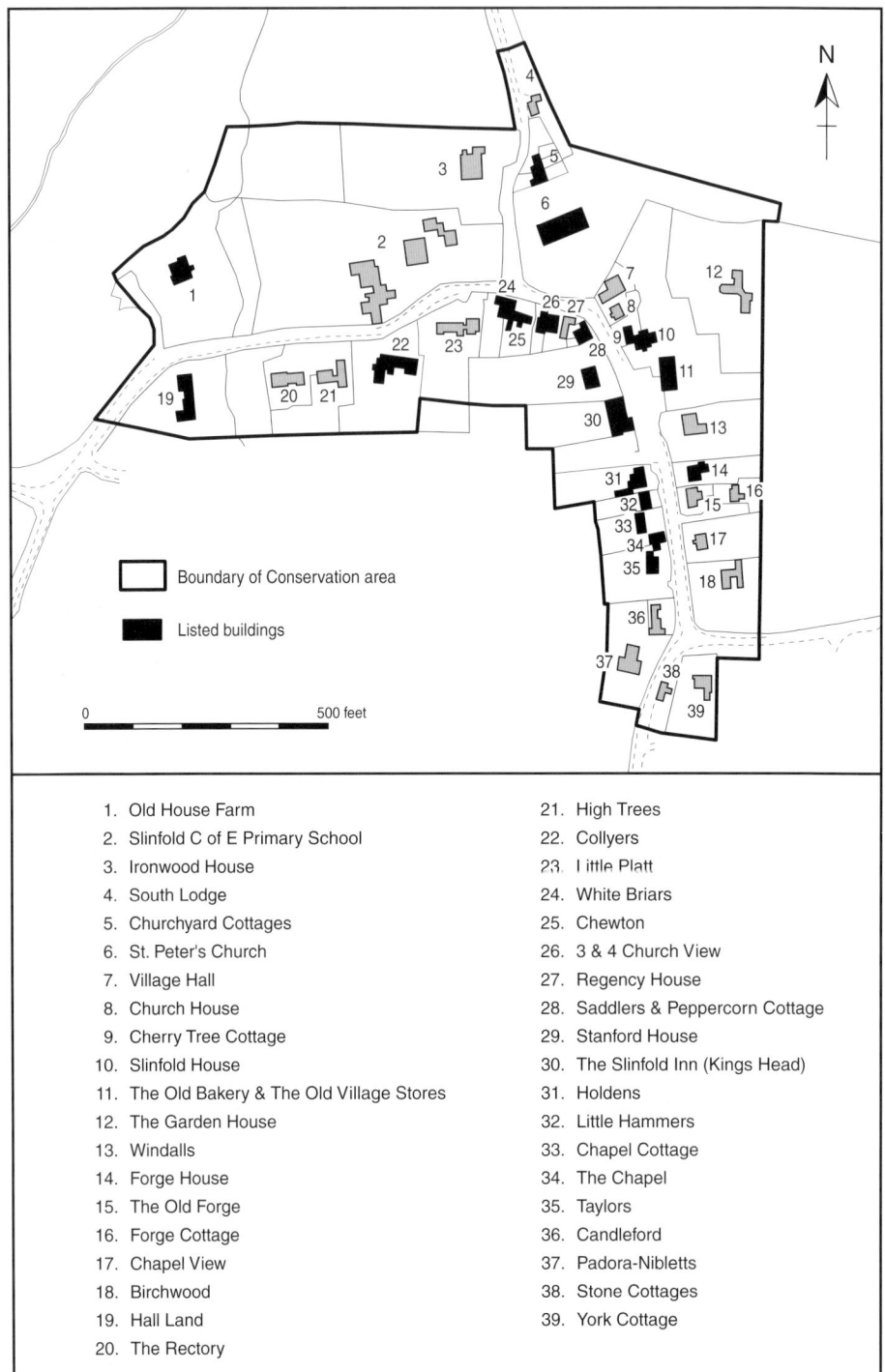

Map 1. *Slinfold Street & the Conservation Area*

THE DEVELOPMENT OF THE VILLAGE

The village of Slinfold is one of the more attractive in the Sussex Weald and contains all that is seen as quintessential to a true English village. There is a church, shop, pub, school, and village hall, and the houses of different dates, styles and materials all blend together in one harmonious whole. An additional pleasure is the curving shape of The Street, which creates a constantly changing panorama as one goes through the village. But how did the village of today come into being? What gave it its particular form and character? To answer these questions one must go way back in time.

Background

Prehistoric people had used the Weald, especially the hunter-gatherers who saw it as a vast larder, and the Romans too had made their mark in the area. Stane Street runs through the parish, with a posting station (the Roman equivalent of a motorway service area) at Alfoldean, near Roman Gate. There was also a tile-works at Itchingfield.

But the seeds of the development of Slinfold were sown by the Saxons who arrived in the fifth and sixth centuries. In Sussex they first of all settled the coastal plain and the band of Upper Greensand along the scarp foot of the Downs, both very fertile areas. They also settled the Downs themselves which were more easily worked than the heavy, tree-covered, clay soil of the Weald. The Weald, however, played an important part in the Saxon economy, providing resources which were not available immediately round the settlements to the south. Groups of settlers tended to use particular areas of the Weald and some of these early connections are preserved in place-names. For instance, Clemsfold (which was earlier known as *Clympsfold*) would have been used by the people of Climping.

As settlement in the Weald increased, the large and somewhat ill-defined tracts of Wealden land which had been used by the southern estates in early Saxon times had by the ninth and tenth centuries become smaller, more precisely defined, units. Each coastal and downland settlement had its own area of the Weald to the north which provided it with woodland pasture and a source of timber and wood. These *Wealden outliers* could be separated from the parent settlements by a distance of anything up to twelve miles. Many of the earlier connections indicated by place-names were lost as patterns of exploitation changed.

The Saxon economy was based on transhumance. Animals were driven up into the Weald seasonally, especially swine who were sent to the woodland pastures in the autumn when there was an abundance of acorns and beech mast. The Saxons called their pig pastures *denns* and this word is preserved locally in Denne Park in Horsham, and Dan Farm in Slinfold. Swine were not the only animals to be driven up into the Weald, as is indicated by names such as Cowfold, Shipley and Shiprods (both meaning a sheep clearing) and Gatwick (goat farm). This movement of animals from settlements in the south into the Weald has resulted in the predominantly north/south pattern of roads in the area. Even with the creation of east/west turnpike roads such as the A281 Horsham-Guildford road or the A272 east of Billingshurst, it is still to this day easier to travel north/south than east/west.

Gradually permanent settlement occurred in places formerly occupied only seasonally by woodsmen and herdsmen. It is difficult to say exactly when any particular spot was first settled, but it is now generally accepted that the Saxons had been clearing woodland and practising some form of agriculture for at least two centuries before the Conquest. Place-name evidence suggests that there was limited settlement in this area even prior to 800. Lydwicke in Slinfold is *hlith wic* in Saxon; the wic element indicates habitation, while *hlith* means a concave hill slope, and just such a slope can be seen near Lydwicke. After 800 such topographical terms were not used so precisely.

The Normans brought with them from the Continent the manorial system under which land was held, directly or indirectly, from the Crown. Many of the elements of this system had already been in place under the Saxons. Although the *Wealden outliers* were physically detached from the parent manor, they were nevertheless an integral part of the manor and were subject to the jurisdiction of the manor courts. It is this system of outliers which explains why so few places in the Weald are mentioned in the Domesday Book. The outliers were contained within the entry for the parent manor and it is only possible in very few instances to say with certainty that a particular part of an entry refers to a specific outlier. Because a place in the Weald is apparently not mentioned in Domesday, it does not mean that there was no settlement there in 1086.

The system of detached outliers also explains why parishes in the Weald have parts of a number of manors within them. There were at least ten different manors within the parish of Slinfold, a marked contrast to parishes on the Sussex coast which had only one or two manors within them. The parishes in the Weald were larger than those on the coast as they were less densely settled. Also the Wealden parishes were not created until around the 12th century and were superimposed on the already existing manorial system. Some of the outliers remained attached to their parent manor as long as the manorial system lasted. The outlier which included Old House Farm was always a part of the manor of Wiggonholt. Other outliers, such as Dedisham and Pinkhurst, became independent manors in their own right.

The pattern of land use in the Weald, with permanent settlement gradually taking place in the wood pastures from late Saxon times onwards, meant that farms in the area were each surrounded by their own separately enclosed fields. The open-field system of the Midlands, where farms were all situated in a nucleated village with each farm holding strips of land scattered throughout the surrounding arable fields, never evolved here, though a less well-developed form of the system did exist round the coastal and scarp foot settlements.

Since settlement took place in a piece-meal fashion over time, in many areas large tracts remained as commonly-held wood pasture, and these were used by the tenants of the neighbouring manors as a place to pasture their animals and also as a source of fuel. These commons were encroached upon and enclosed over the centuries until very few now remain.

The Beginnings of the Village

The land of Slinfold parish was all settled at a fairly early date, and there appears to have been very little common land left by the 14th century. But it would seem that in Norman times there was a swathe of common land running from south of the present village up to the river Arun. Much of this was enclosed before the church was built. It appears that the landholdings to either side of this swathe, Old House and Hill to the west and Rowfold to the east, added some of the common to their holdings, and a small, completely new farm called Windalls was created.

By the time the church was built in the 12th century, there was only a fairly small area of common land left open (Map 2). Two roads came into this common, the present Park Street from the west and Lyons Road from the east, both having roughly the same alignment. The Tithe Map of 1839 shows a line of field boundaries running from Park Street across to Lyons Road (Map 7) and it is most likely that there was a track here connecting the two roads and also defining the southern edge of the common. There is now no proof of this as all trace of the boundaries has vanished.

The development of the village

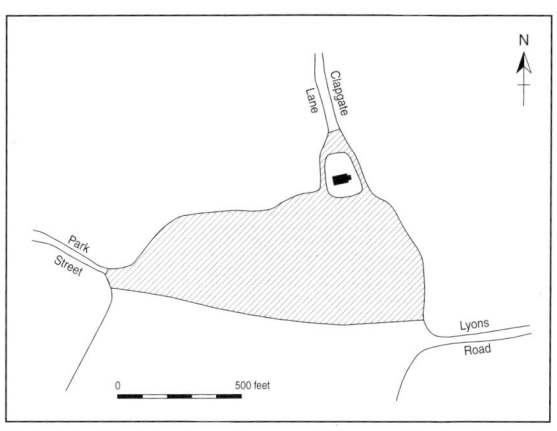

Map 2. *The hatched area is the presumed extent of common land when the church was built*

There was, however, a third track coming from the north, the present Clapgate Lane. This opened out into a funnel, which is a typical feature of a road entering common land. It was on this funnel-shaped piece of land that the original church was built.

The building of the church encouraged the manors with rights of commoning to enclose much of the remaining common. An area of some seven acres to the north of the southern track, and extending as far west as the stream, became the holding called Nibletts. Immediately to its north the manor of Dedisham enclosed a long strip which was divided into two: Collyers to the west and Stanford House to the east. Medieval houses were built on all three of these enclosures. The land to the west of the stream was enclosed and taken into the farm called Hall Land, which belonged to the manor of Pinkhurst.

Gradually the track which ran across the south of the common land between Park Street and Lyons Road fell out of use as it was replaced by a curving road skirting the newly enclosed land. This became The Street and, apart from some encroachment, it has remained the same ever since.

The church was at first a chapel of ease dependant upon the church of Steyning and did not become a parish church until it came into the hands of the Bishop of Chichester in 1231. The parish of Slinfold would have been created once the church came under the patronage of the Bishop. The parish is almost circular in shape with a long pan-handle of Rudgwick parish stretching round the north-west of Slinfold, and there was until recently a narrow section of Warnham reaching down to Slinfold Mill on the north-east side, ensuring that Warnham did not loose its rights over the mill. These facts all point to the parish of Slinfold being carved out of already existing parishes. The name Slinfold, which means fold on a slope, earlier referred to a tithing which was somewhere within the present parish. As with most villages in the Weald, the name is much older than the village itself.

The Village of 1500

The village of around 1500 is shown on Map 3. It was predominantly a farming community with, surrounding the church, a cluster of small farms, Nibletts, Rowfold and Windalls, and one larger farm, Old House. The farmhouse for Nibletts became the Kings Head (now the Slinfold Inn) and the site of the original Windalls farmhouse is Clapgate Cottage, which was rebuilt in the 1860s as cottages for farm labourers. This is just off the map, up Clapgate Lane, but is close enough to be part of the village. The Old Bakery/Slinfold Stores was the farmhouse for the third small farm, Rowfold.

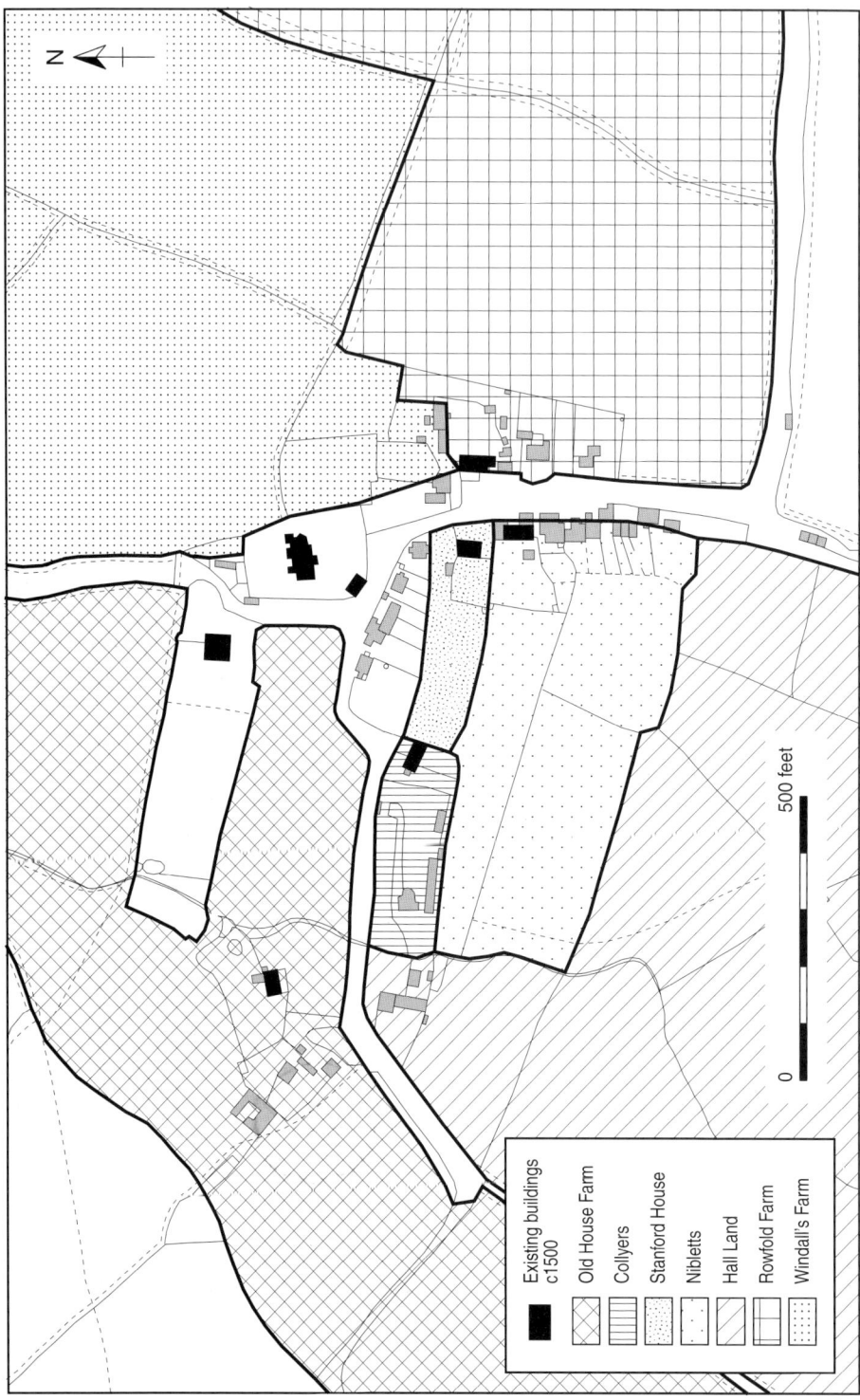

Map 3. *The Village c. 1500. All the buildings shaded grey were not in existence at this time. There was thus a large open space in front of the church*

There were also two artisan's properties, Collyers and Stanford House, each with about one acre of land attached to the house. These would have been occupied by craftsmen who supplemented their income by growing a crop of hay or corn upon their plot of land and possibly keeping an animal or two.

Near the church was the Rectory, and at the edge of the churchyard next the Street there was a church house. This was the pre-Reformation forerunner to the village hall and would have been used for church ales, which were money-raising parish jollifications. Church ales were officially disapproved of after the Reformation and many church houses developed into taverns, while others became poor houses. There is no record of the Slinfold church house later than 1590 and it is not shown on a map of 1651 (see Map 5).

A Slow Expansion (16th-18th Centuries)

One feature of the village of 1500 was the large open space in front of the church (Map 3). This was enclosed in the late 16th century. The plot opposite the church, to the north of the land belonging to Stanford House, was described in 1576 as a croft containing one acre belonging to the manor of Dedisham. Chewton, the first building to be erected on this plot, is a smoke bay house of around 1580. Another plot, on the east side of the Street running south from the church, was also enclosed at around the same time and the remains of the house built on it is encased in Cherry Tree Cottage. This was held of the manor of Clemsfold.

Further late 16th century development took place on the Street frontage of Nibletts. The landholding of Nibletts was very small which meant that the occupier needed to diversify to survive. The farmhouse itself doubled as an inn, and allowing building along the Street was another way to increase income. One of the two properties later replaced by Holdens dates to this time, as does Little Hammers, which started life as an outbuilding.

Another plot, this time very small, which was enclosed around 1600, was the land immediately to the north of the church on which stand Churchyard Cottages. The earliest part of the building here is a smoke bay house of good quality, which was most likely built for the curate of the parish. Many of the rectors either had more than one living, or had other duties as prebends of Chichester Cathedral, so that the day-to-day running of the parish fell to the curate. A dwelling opposite the rectory and right next to the former north gate of the churchyard was an ideal location for him.

In the early 17th century a small smoke bay dwelling was built against Cherry Tree Cottage. This cottage, now Slinfold House, was sideways on to the Street and faced the village green. This area had been left open for communal village activities and at one time had the village stocks on it. Nowadays it is hard to imagine that there was ever enough space for a reasonable green here, but it has to be remembered that the later extensions in front of the timber-framed ranges had not yet been added to the houses fronting on to the green, nor were there any gardens in front of the houses.

Further development took place through the 17th century, but the pace of expansion was slow and by the end of the century Slinfold was still only a hamlet. In the early 1600s Reginald Gilbert, the blacksmith, built another property on his land, which he leased out. This was the other house which was demolished to make way for Holdens. Chapel Cottage, further south along the Street frontage of Nibletts, appeared in the second half of the 17th century.

Old House Farm was rebuilt circa 1640, replacing a farmhouse which must have been of considerable antiquity to have merited the name Old House. The new house was constructed in the very latest style for Richard Naldrett, a member of the gentry family of the Naldretts of Rudgwick, and it must have been the cause of much comment among the people of Slinfold.

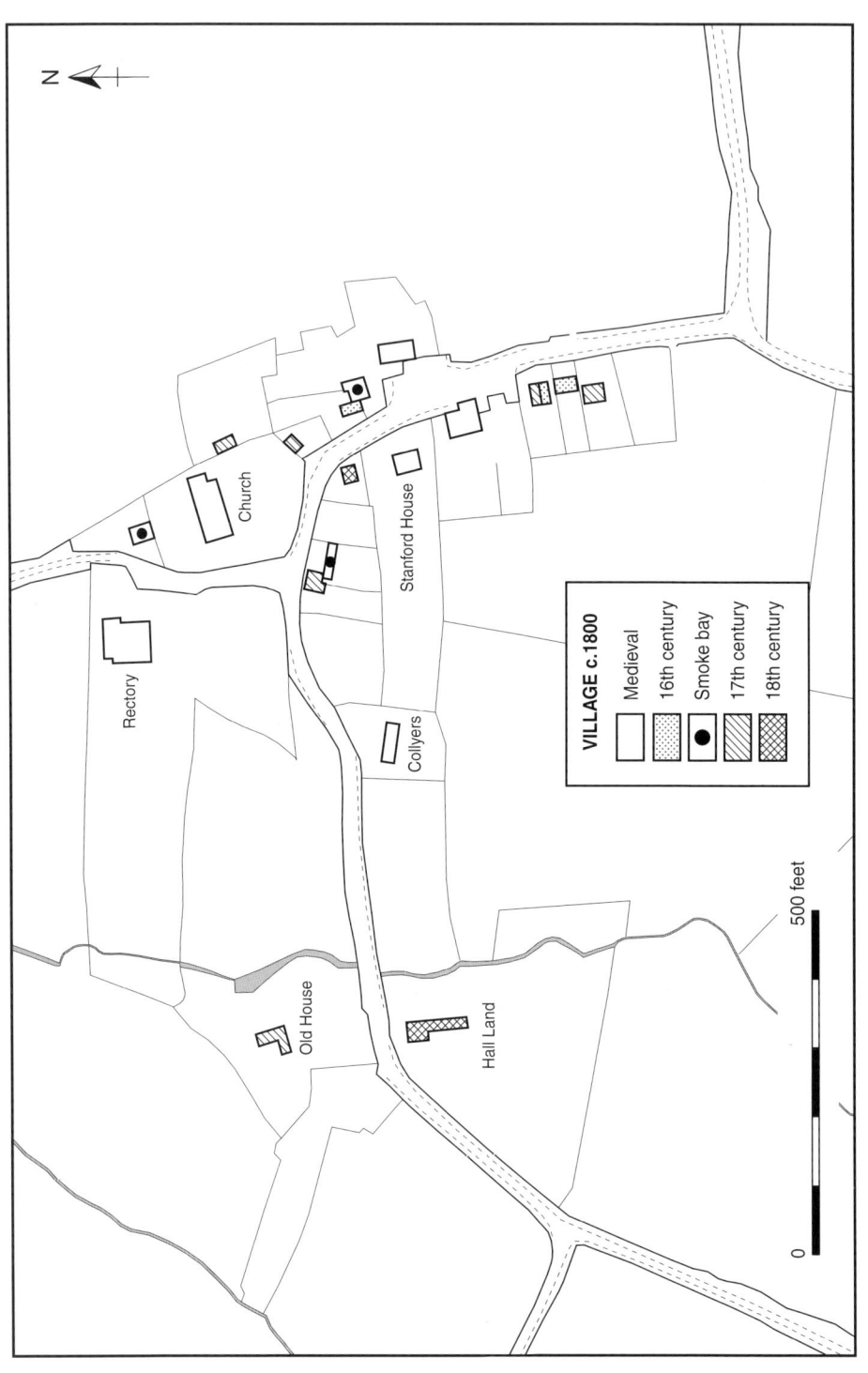

Map 4. *The Village c. 1800*

The development of the village

Plate 1. *The Centre of the Village today. The Kings Head to the left, Slinfold House centre & the Shop to the right*

Another fine house was White Briars, purpose-built as the Weeping Eye alias the Star around 1680, and taking over from Chewton which had up to then functioned as an alehouse of the same name.

Two other small cottages probably came into existence in the 17th century, although there is no record of exactly when they were built. These were next to the south and east wall of the churchyard and were parish cottages used to house the poor. They had become dilapidated by the 1830s and were replaced by The Barracks and Stone Cottages.

The village remained remarkably static from around 1680 for the next hundred years and no new building occurred during this time. After the years of the Civil War in the 1640s when large quantities of food were needed to supply the combatant armies, farmers suddenly found themselves with large surpluses that were no longer needed and farming went through a long period in the doldrums. This lasted until the mid-18th century, when two trends brought about change. The country's population began to rise markedly after 1750, and cereal prices increased from 1750 through to 1815.

The rise in population was in many instances met by subdividing houses for multiple occupation. This happened in the case of Cherry Tree Cottage, Chapel Cottage, Little Hammers and Chewton, all of which were divided in the late 18th or early 19th centuries. One small new building, Saddlers and Peppercorn Cottage, was erected around 1780. Interestingly, although these are now a semi-detached pair of cottages, they were not built as such. Only the northern end was a dwelling while the other part was a store or workshop.

The effect of the subdivision was felt by the poorer section of the community, whereas the rise in grain prices affected the better-off. The higher cereal prices, especially during the Napoleonic Wars, produced a buoyant economy which enabled them to embark on building projects, mostly in the later years of the 18th century.

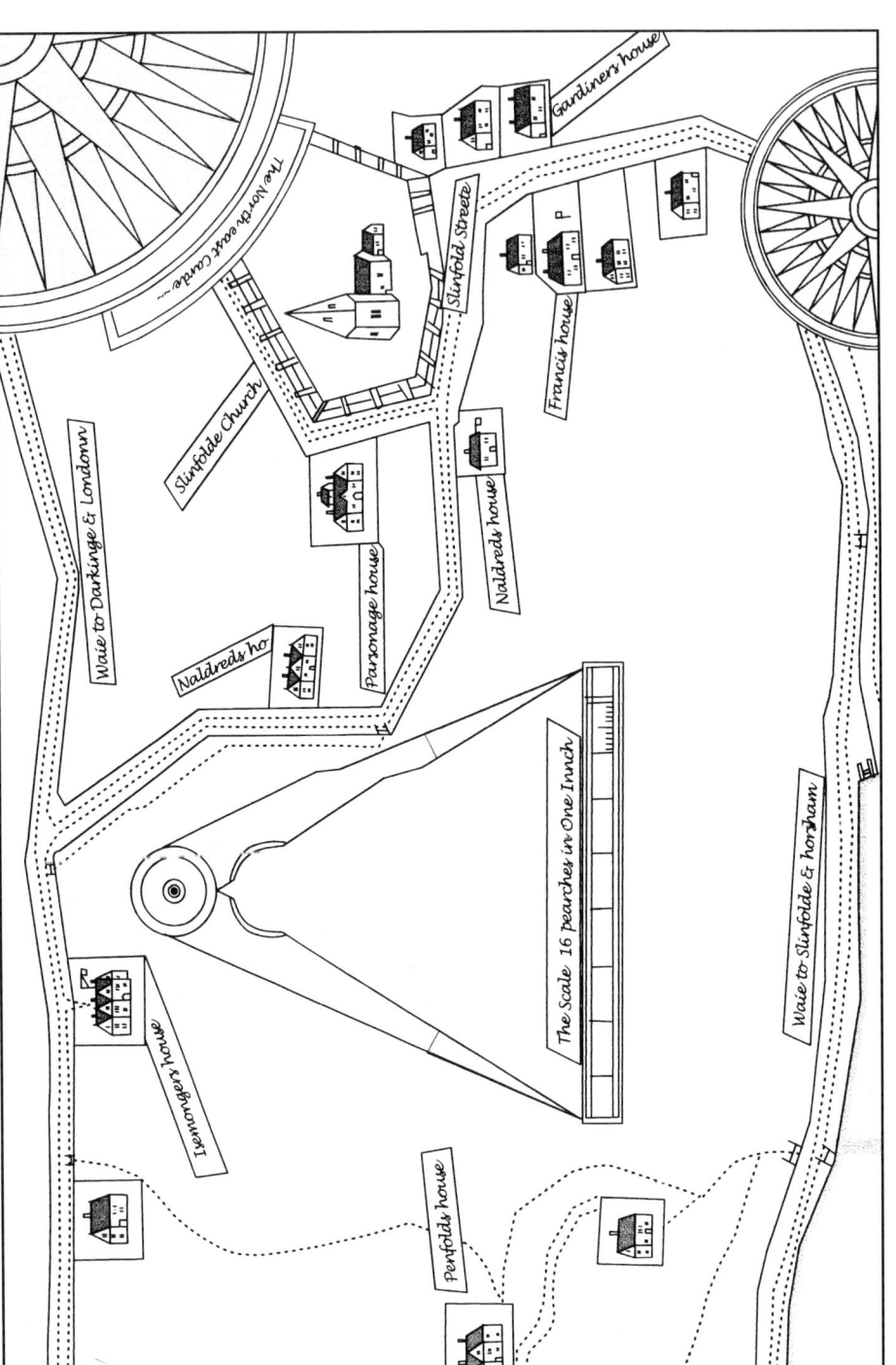

Map 5. *Detail from the Survey of Mr. Nyes land called Hayes, 1651 (Redrawn from the original in Horsham Museum)*

The map was drawn as a survey of all the land belonging to Hayes Farm, now Slinfold Manor. To place it in context the surrounding area was also shown, including, in the top right-hand corner, the village of Slinfold. The buildings are not correct in detail; the church never had a tall spire. The drawings represent the relative status of the houses. The rectory is known to have been a fairly small building, whereas the drawing shows a large house indicating the status of the rector. It is correct in showing a separate outbuilding behind. To the left of the rectory is Old House and on the other side of the churchyard is an alms house, a building representing Cherry Tree Cottage and Slinfold House and The Old Bakery, home of Gardiner the mercer. On the other side of the road, Chewton has a little flag sticking out from the eaves indicating that it is an alehouse. To its right is Stanford House, the Kings Head, also with a flag as an

The development of the village

Hall Land, which dates from 1797, was built by the Briggs who ran the tannery at Collyers, as a more fitting residence for the family, although they continued to use Collyers as well. Around the same time other properties in the centre of the village were being considerably enlarged by additions in front of the old timber-framed ranges. Slinfold House and the Old Bakery had extensions with very attractive brickwork of blue headers and red stretchers. The Kings Head was also extended, while the old Stanford House was replaced by a new brick building c.1808. Although this is into the 19th century, it is part and parcel of the same expansion fuelled by high grain prices. This changed the character of the village which, in the early 18th century, consisted almost entirely of craftsmen and labourers. Now the community was becoming more mixed, with people who could be described as *middle class* dwelling in the new or enlarged houses, alongside the cottagers.

As well as the benefit of higher cereal prices, the Napoleonic Wars also brought the downside of a genuine fear of invasion. This was considered sufficiently serious for the JPs to appoint parish officers in 1798 to deal with such an emergency. Charles Holden of the Kings Head was detailed *to take charge of the removal of women and children, especially those incapable of removing themselves, when the country is to be cleared.* Robert Jupp of Clemsfold Farm was to have *inspection, care and management of livestock of the parish that may be to be removed,* and John Stanford of Theale was to have *like inspection, care and management of dead stock of the parish that may be to be removed.* It must have been a great relief to people when the threat of invasion receded.

Local Transport up to the 18th Century

The perception of people these days is that the majority of country people in the past hardly travelled at all. While it is true that some scarcely moved out of their parish all their lives, yet there was a surprising amount of travel in years gone by.

In the 14th century, for example, the tenants of Fure, the Wealden outlier of the manor of Ferring, which included Ranfold and Farthings in Slinfold, were expected to attend the manor court in Ferring every three weeks. If they did not, and had no valid excuse, they were fined. The tenants were also expected, as part of their duties to the Bishop of Chichester, their Lord of the Manor, to cart wood and nuts to Ferring, to fetch timber from Pephurst in Loxwood and take it to Aldingbourne to repair the park paling, and to drive pigs to Ferring, Amberley, Chichester or Dorking. While these duties may not have taken place very often, yet the tenants could not be described as stay-at-homes. Tenants of other manors would have had similar duties.

In later centuries the churchwardens of Slinfold often had to travel to Chichester, Arundel or Horsham in the course of their duties. And in 1606 they and one other resident took the tenor bell on a cart pulled by four horses up to Whitechapel in London to be recast.

Nevertheless, the Weald clay was a considerable hindrance to travel and, throughout the country, Sussex was synonymous with bad roads. It was said that men and beasts in Sussex had legs longer than the average from the constant pulling of them out of the mud!

In medieval times not only did monasteries contribute to the repair of roads and bridges, but people were encouraged, for the good of their souls, to leave money in their wills for the upkeep of the highways. These bequests continued on a lesser scale in later centuries. In the early 1600s the interest of £10 left to the parish by William Smith was used each year to spread 20 loads of cinder, or iron slag, upon Park Street. At that time Stane Street was called Park Street, and the present Park Street was considered to be part of the Street.

With the dissolution of the monasteries there was no longer anyone in charge of road repair and with the worsening climatic conditions of the time, the state of the roads began to cause concern. In 1555 an act was passed which transferred responsibility for the upkeep of roads to the parish. Each parish had to elect one or more overseers of the highways and every householder had a statute duty to perform four (later six) days' labour upon the roads under the supervision of the overseers. The Slinfold Vestry Minutes for 1665 record:

> *That upon the nine and twentyeth of March Anno Dni. 1665 the Churchwardens & parishioners of the parish of Slynfo(l)d did nominate and chouse Stephen Humfrey and John Hayler to be survayors of the high wayes within ye parish of Slynfold for this present yeare 1665. And did li(ke)wise the appoynt six dayes for those that keepe teemes and for the Labourars to worke to amend the sayd highwayes accor(d)inge to the Statute in that case provided That is to say wensday and friday in ye second weeke in May And wensday and friday in ye third week in May And wensday and friday in ye fourth weeke in May next.*

This system was open to abuse and evasion. Nevertheless, 'statute labour' formed the basis of road maintenance until 1835.

Before the late 17th century traffic consisted mostly of pedestrians or beasts of burden. The increase of wheeled traffic from then on contributed significantly to the poor state of the roads and there were frequent complaints. In the late 18th century Horace Walpole wrote to a friend:

> *If you love good roads.....be so kind as never to go into Sussex.....Coaches grow there no more than balm or spices.*

Roads only improved with the coming of turnpikes from the mid-18th century onwards.

Village Tradesmen in the 17th and 18th Centuries

Although still not very large, the Slinfold village of 1700 had changed considerably in character from the village of 1500. It was no longer a small farming settlement, but had become a community of tradesmen and craftsmen. There would have been a butcher, tailor, weaver, cordwainer or shoemaker, carpenter, blacksmith, and wheelwright, providing for all the immediate needs of those in the parish. The property in which these tradesmen were living is in many cases unknown.

The Old Bakery/Village Stores was a mercers in the 17th century and, after a short break in the early 1700s, it continued as a mercers throughout the 18th century. A mercer dealt in fabrics and many mercers were also tailors, making up the fabrics into clothes. Walter Knight was both mercer and tailor in the 1740s. Mercers very often developed into general stores, which is what happened in the case of the Old Village Stores by the 19th century.

Much of the cloth used by the mercer would have been bought in from outside, but woollen cloth and linen would have been woven locally. In the mid-17th century there was a weaver, Peter Fish, living in part of Collyers.

Shoemakers were obviously a very necessary part of village life and it would seem that there was often more than one at work in the village. John Groombridge was in Little Hammers in the early 1700s, in the mid-1700s John Knight and David Worsfold were in Cherry Tree Cottage/Slinfold House and, prior to his death in 1777 John Gardiner had worked as a cordwainer at 1 Churchyard Cottages.

Craftsmen such as carpenters would have been much in demand and although there were several in the parish, the only one that can be linked with a property is Charles Child who was in White Briars in 1780. The blacksmith and the wheelwright were also essential elements in the village economy. From the late 16th century the blacksmith had his forge in a workshop tacked on to the front of the property to the north of Little Hammers. The wheelwright lived in Chapel Cottage from the mid-18th century and had a workshop on the site of the chapel. With the building of Holdens in 1841, the blacksmith of the time, David Holden, moved the forge to the other side of the Street, and by 1859 the wheelwrights was also in what is now called The Old Forge.

Another trade in the village was that of tanning which was carried on at Collyers from the mid-18th century until the mid-19th century by the Briggs family. It is likely that the tannery had been in operation before that as Thomas Weale was described as a tanner in the parish registers of 1707. The pungent smell of tanning must often have hung over the village in the hundred years or more that the tannery was working.

Beer was much the safest drink in the past and brewing frequently took place in the home, many houses in the parish having a separate brewhouse where this was done. The will of John Freeman of 2 Churchyard Cottages left to his grandson *one brass furnace* which would have been used in the brewing process. Nevertheless, men have always enjoyed having a public place to meet and have a drink in company. Both the Kings Head and the Weeping Eye supplied these needs. The Kings Head was an alehouse by the early 17th century and, as mentioned above, the Weeping Eye or the Star began as an alehouse in Chewton and then moved to the purpose-built property now known as White Briars. In these establishments people would have been able to drink beer, home-made wine and perhaps a drop of smuggled brandy! The Kings Head has continued through the years as a pub, whereas the Weeping Eye ceased to be an inn sometime prior to 1780. Several of the 18th century innkeepers combined blacksmithing with running the Kings Head.

Not all the houses in the village would have been occupied by tradesmen or craftsmen. There would have been a number of men in the village working as agricultural labourers on the surrounding farms. And one man in the 17th century, George Hearsey in Little Hammers, earned his living as a gardener.

Tradesmen were often described as shopkeepers. In the past, however, a shop meant a *workshop* rather than a *retail shop*, but since tradesmen both made and sold goods in their workshop the word gradually took on its present meaning. Sometimes the shop was within the house, but in many instances it was in an outbuilding and often it would have been no more than an insubstantial shed. Although the housing stock of the village has been quite stable, these outbuildings have come and gone over the centuries, and because of their ephemeral nature very little is known about them. There was a weaver's workshop at Collyers which was mentioned in the will of Peter Fish in 1676, and a slaughter house was sited somewhere between the village stores and the corner of Lyons Road in 1789. The Tithe Map of 1839 shows an outbuilding at Chewton and another adjacent to the churchyard by Churchyard Cottages. The one at Chewton was variously described as a shop or a store/cart shed and may have been used by George Read who was a carpenter and joiner. The other was called a shop in 1856 and had been used by Richard Jayes, a shoemaker who lived in 2 Churchyard Cottages and later in 3 Church View. Both these outbuildings had disappeared by 1876.

A Rapid Growth (the 19th Century)

There was a rapid expansion in the 19th century, and during the hundred years from 1800 to 1900 Slinfold grew from a hamlet into a village. In 1800 there were 18 houses in the Street, of which eight were in multiple occupancy, and by 1900 there were 27 dwellings, still with 8 occupied by more than one family.

The growth spanned the whole of the century, one of the additions being the small semi-detached pair of cottages known as 3 and 4 Church View. These date to around 1800 and were part of the response to the rising population mentioned above.

The parish had previously had two alms houses situated just outside the churchyard. By the 1830s these had become dilapidated and, rather than repair them, it was felt better to demolish them and build anew in a more convenient situation. Money was raised by subscription and the amount collected was sufficient to build not only the Red Cottages, or the Barracks as they are better known, but also Stone Cottages. These latter were originally a terrace of three small cottages, standing on a plot of land enclosed from the roadside waste at the entrance to Hayes Lane.

In 1833 the present Taylors was erected on land belonging to Chapel Cottage by Thomas Sturt, who was connected by marriage to the owners of that property. The Street from the Kings Head southwards to Hayes Lane was in the past considerably wider than it is now. The original edge of the roadway ran on a line through the middle of the Kings Head (in front of the timber-framed rear range), past the front of Chapel Cottage and behind Candleford. Over the years the roadside waste had been encroached upon, first by outbuildings such as Little Hammers and the wheelwrights (on the site of the Chapel) which had been built forward of the houses. The land on which Candleford stands had been enclosed sometime before 1789 as an orchard for Chapel Cottage. Then the houses had all enclosed pieces of the roadside as front gardens. This was happening in the first quarter of the 19th century and there are entries in the records of the manor of Bassett's Fee of the owners having to pay annual rent for these enclosures.

Plate 2. *The roadside waste was enclosed to create front gardens in the early 19th century Little Hammers, Holdens and the Kings Head*

No development at all had taken place in earlier centuries on the roadside frontage to the south of the Village Stores. The field adjacent to the road was called Shopfield and was part of Rowfold, which had been farmed together with a group of other farms in Slinfold since the 17th century. From the early 18th century this group included Hill, Nowhurst and Windalls and they had been owned by people of some substance, many with interests in other parts of the county as well. Clearly they had not in the past been concerned to raise relatively small amounts of money by selling the street frontage. By 1828, however, it may well have been the personal influence of Edward Child of Slinfold House which was able to persuade the then owner, John Henry Ellis, Gent. to sell him a plot next to the shop. On this plot Edward built a house for his only son, Thomas, who was getting married the following year. This house is the present Windalls. The name is a source of confusion to anyone looking at the past history of the village. The house which now has the name was not so called until the mid-1860s and it does not stand upon land belonging to Windalls Farm. The original Windalls farmhouse was rebuilt and is now Clapgate Cottage.

In 1829 two further plots were sold. The first was adjacent to Windalls and was also bought by Edward Child. Nothing was built on this for a while and in 1839 it was described as a garden. The plot next to this garden was bought by David Holden, the blacksmith. This had a house, stables and garden on it by

The development of the village

1839. When the forge on the other side of the Street was demolished to make way for Holdens, the smithy moved over the road to this site; it would appear that the earlier house was replaced by the present building. What is not clear is when Forge House was built and by whom. The brickwork is rat-trap bond (see p.36) so one would not expect it to be later than the 1840s. Did David Holden build it on Edward Child's land, or did Thomas Child have it built after David and his son sold out to him in 1850? What is known is that a few years later, in 1856, Thomas built Forge Cottage at the back of the Forge to house his farm bailiff. It was not connected with the Forge until around 1915 and in the 1920s it was known as Lower Forge. In 1878 the Aylings built Chapel View next to the Forge on land owned by the Childs.

By the time the properties on this stretch of the Street were built front gardens were the norm, so the houses were placed sufficiently far back on their plot to allow for this. There was thus no roadside encroachment here as there had been on the opposite side of the Street.

Two other houses in the village are very similar in style to Chapel View, but are slightly smaller. Both Church House and South Lodge were built in the early 1880s, Church House for the Rectory gardener and South Lodge as a lodge for Hill House. Both Church House and South Lodge must have been built by Thomas Ayling, although he was not described as a builder until the end of the 19th century. Before that he was simply called a bricklayer.

Across the Street from Church House is Regency House. The name is a misnomer as it is Victorian, being erected in 1880 by John Freeman, both as a dwelling house for himself and a place to carry on his tailoring business.

The 19th century also saw the advent of public buildings. Previously the only public building had been the church, apart from the church house which was in existence in the 16th century and possibly earlier.

Plate 3. *Photo taken c. 1881. Regency House can just be seen centre right, and the new Village Hall is there, but Church House has yet to be built*

In 1845 Edward Brice Bunny of Speen Hill in Berkshire and also of Slinfold Lodge gave a piece of land to the Rector and churchwardens as a site for a School which opened in 1849. The land was in a field called Church Croft and was part of Old House Farm, which was one of several farms in the area owned by the Bunnys. The plot was very small, just 26 perches, whereas now the school and its playing fields have expanded to take in the whole of Church Croft. There must have been dame schools in the village in the past which would have been run from private houses, but next to nothing is known about these. The only information comes from the 1841 census returns; there was an elderly lady, Elizabeth Freeman, living at Saddlers whose occupation is given as schoolmistress, and another schoolmistress named Rebecca Tanner was at Windalls Farmhouse (now Clapgate Cottage).

The present Chapel dates from 1878 and was built by the Aylings of Chapel View. It was originally Congregational, but is now a United Reformed Chapel. There was an earlier chapel here and both were on the site of the wheelwright's workshop.

The Village Hall and Library was erected in 1881 as a memorial to Thomas and Caroline Child of Windalls by their children and grandchildren. Prior to that the outbuilding in the grounds of Slinfold House had been used as a Parish Reading Room for a couple of years. This was run for working men of the village by the curate, who at that time lived in Slinfold House. A lending library was also established here, which was transferred to the Village Hall when it opened.

As well as the considerable amount of new building which took place throughout the 19th century, a number of older properties were rebuilt. The rebuilding of Stanford House has already been mentioned above, and in addition the Rectory (now Ironwood House) was rebuilt on a much grander scale in 1836, Holdens replaced two earlier dwellings in 1841 and the old church was demolished to make way for new, larger church in 1861 to accommodate the growing population.

Plate 4. *The old church being demolished in 1860. Several photographs of this date survive, at a time when photography was still the preserve of the wealthy. Circumstantial evidence suggests that they were taken by Thomas or Charles Child*

The development of the village

By the end of the 19th century the village was a thriving, but mixed community. There were the poorer people, some living in the parish cottages and others cramped into small, subdivided cottages. These people were paternalistically supported by the richer members of society through such institutions as the *clothing club*, the *shoe club* and the *blanket loan club*.

Trades and Industries in the 19th Century

While a number of people profited from the boom years of farming in the early 19th century, families such as the Stanfords and the Holdens remained essentially parochial. Two families, however, the Briggs and the Childs expanded their varied interests far beyond the confines of the parish. Genealogical tables for both families are given in the Appendix on p.127&128.

The Briggs had been tanners at Collyers since the mid-18th century. The site was ideal for a tannery since Collyers had an acre of ground which was bounded by a stream to the west. The three necessary raw materials for a tannery were water, oak bark and hides, all of which were readily available locally. Indeed the timber trade in the area catered for tanning by cutting oak trees in the spring when the sap was rising and the bark was easier to flaw, or strip, in spite of the fact that the best time to fell oaks was in the winter. Hides would have been procured locally or from the cattle market operating in the Bishopric.

Three generations of Briggs were tanners; Samuel, his son William, and his grandson, another William. Tanning tended to be a profitable business and this certainly seems to have been the case for the Briggs. There would have been a greatly increased demand for leather to equip the army during the Napoleonic Wars. The Briggs had already improved Collyers, which was then known as *Tanyard House*, by rebuilding the western end, but in the 1790s the family had sufficient capital to build a completely new dwelling house. They bought a $1^1/_2$ acre plot of land on the far side of the stream where they built the house now known as Hall Land. At the time, it took the name *Tanyard House* while Collyers became *Old Tanyard House*. The family now occupied both houses, with William the father living in Hall Land, while William the younger continued to occupy Collyers and ran the tannery until his old age. This is last mentioned as operating in 1842.

William the elder started to diversify into farming with the acquisition of Park Farm in 1804. His second son, John, did not follow his brother into tanning, but concentrated on farming. By 1839 he was managing Hall Land Farm, Park Farm, Gaskins, Ranfold, Hill, Rowfold, Nowhurst and Windalls, and farmed the largest acreage in the parish. In his later life he felt able to call himself a 'gentleman'. He had presumably acquired a London residence, since his son, also John, is said to have been born in London. John junior kept the Slinfold properties and clearly spent part of the time at Hall Land, but he was always described as 'of London'. He, too, called himself a gentleman, but on occasions he was also said to be a butcher. He may have been a cattle dealer rather than a butcher pure and simple, and it would appear that he had overseas links. His son, John, died in Montevideo in Uruguay in 1869 at the age of 31 and his daughter, Elizabeth, married a civil engineer who had been born in Montevideo. Uruguay was a great cattle ranching country and exporter of hides. Is it possible that young John, coming from a family of tanners, was in Montevideo dealing with the export of hides as part of his father's business in London? Although the later Briggs were based in London, they never severed their links with Slinfold and Elizabeth came back to live in Hall Land when she was widowed.

Edward and Martha Child came to Slinfold with their small son in the early 1730s. Unfortunately this son died, but five other children were born to them and baptized in Slinfold church. Their eldest son, Charles, was a carpenter and in 1780 he was living in White Briars. He and his wife had four children and then moved to Warnham, where their last child was born. Their eldest son, Edward, who was also a carpenter, came back to Slinfold where he married Ann Holden, daughter of Charles Holden of the Kings Head. In 1808 Charles gave to his daughter and son-in-law Slinfold House, together with Cherry Tree Cottages and all the land that went with them. Edward Child had clearly made a very wise move in marrying Ann Holden! Conversely Charles must have realised the potential of Edward. Edward lived in Slinfold House for the rest of his life and ran his business as a timber-merchant from here, in conjunction with his younger brother, Charles, of Warnham. They built up a thriving concern, buying timber from a considerable radius around Slinfold, having it hewn and sawn, and then shipped, either as timber or timber products such as wattles, posts and rails, from Newbridge Wharf in Billingshurst to Arundel or Littlehampton.

At the same time Edward Child was acquiring farms both in Slinfold and in the surrounding parishes so that by 1840 he was farming a total of 576 acres, a similar acreage to John Briggs, but not all within the one parish. At the same time he owned four properties in the Street, two in Hayes Lane, a cottage in Rowhook, as well as two houses in Warnham and a cottage in Rudgwick. He had progressed a long way from the simple carpenter he was in his youth.

Edward's brother, Charles, died in 1826, by which time Edward's only son had joined his father in the business. Thomas, who lived at Windalls, diversified, becoming a coal merchant and having shares in barges on the Wey and Arun Junction Canal. He was a partner in a coal merchants at Arundel called Child & Henly, and they shipped a variety of goods up to Newbridge and sometimes beyond. Coal, gravel, salt and cheese came from Littlehampton, sand from Waltham and chalk from Houghton. The same barges that Thomas used to ship goods northwards carried Edward's timber south. Thomas was a true entrepreneur, taking advantage of opportunities as they arose. He realised, for example, that there was a ready market for coal in the area in the years around 1840 and he set about supplying that need.

Thomas continued his father's farming concerns and became very interested in stock breeding. He also acquired more property in the village Street.

In 1830 this country was the only one in the world in which society was sufficiently mobile to allow the emergence of a middle class. Thomas Child and John Briggs the younger are prime examples of this in action.

Charles Child joined his father Thomas in the family business. The original timber yard was situated in the village and it is recorded in the poor rates for 1863 and 1867 as being owned by Thomas Child and occupied by T. Child and Son.

Plate 5. *Thomas Child of Windalls*

The development of the village

There is no indication now as to where this was, but the ladies who wrote the WI Scrap Book in 1947 suggested it was close by the present chapel. Charles married Ellen Mills whose father owned Park House on Stane Street. By 1863 he was living in Park House and the timber yard moved from the Street to a site to the south of the house, the present Youngmans.

When the Act for the Horsham & Guildford Direct Railway went before the House of Commons in 1860, a Slinfold timber merchant (almost certainly Charles Child) complained that *he had to cart bark six miles to obtain water carriage to the tanning factory at Godalming and that bark could not be as conveniently loaded in and out of barges as into trains* (P.A.L. Vine, 1973). It would have been the railway which led Charles to site the timber yard where he did. The yard was served by its own private siding, which would have been a considerable advantage.

With the removal of the timber yard to the Stane Street site and the death of Thomas in 1870, the business connection of the Childs with the Street came to an end. But Charles' mother and sisters continued to live in Windalls, and the Childs' involvement with village life was as strong as ever. In this respect the Briggs differed from the Childs. Although John Briggs senior was churchwarden for one year and he was commemorated by a stained glass window in the new church, yet the family was never as committed to supporting the village as were the Childs.

In his article entitled *Slinfold Fifty Years Ago* in the Sussex County Magazine for 1932, the Rev. G.P. Crawfurd, the curate who had lived in Slinfold House, described the parish of around 1880:

> *The population when I came to it was about 800 persons, a family party, for the people were peculiarly friendly together, consisting of a few gentry, some retired agriculturists, farmers, their work-people, a carpenter and builder in a small way, a blacksmith, two cobblers, a mole- and rat-catcher, a grocer who sold everything and anything and was also postmaster, telegraphist, and tax-collector. It was, in fact, a somewhat complete and self-contained village; and as things were, none was doing badly.*

This self-sufficiency was a characteristic of village life throughout the centuries and has only come to an end over the last fifty years. Much of the information on people's occupations in the 19th century comes from the census returns. These mostly list inhabitants under general addresses, such as the Street, and it is not always possible to link individuals with a particular property. Nevertheless, the picture that emerges is that within the self-sufficiency was a very fluid society among the cottagers. There was much coming and going among the tenants and in the majority of cases there was no fixed venue for a particular craft.

There were several carpenters working at different times. In 1841 there was one at Collyers, and one in Chewton, where, by 1861 there was another carpenter who also described himself as a joiner. A carpenter with the intriguing name of Lorenzo Holland lived in 4 Church View for the last 30 years of the century, and a carpenter at Cherry Tree Cottages in 1881 and 91 was also a cleaver. Alfred Grinstead of Taylors was a master carpenter in 1861 but had expanded his business to become a builder ten years later. His widow carried on the business until the 1890s. After Mary Grinstead had ceased to trade, Thomas Ayling of Chapel View took over as the village builder. Prior to 1891 he was described as a master bricklayer. When both he and Alfred Grinstead did work for the school in 1884 the cheque was made payable to Mr. Grinstead, which indicates that the latter was considered the more important at that time. The builders were assisted by bricklayers living at Chewton and Chapel Cottage.

There was a shoemaker working in a small outbuilding adjacent to the churchyard for much of the first half of the century; he lived first in 2 Churchyard Cottages and then in 3 Church View.

Another shoemaker was at 3/4 Church View in 1861, while in 1881 a bootmaker lived at 2 Churchyard Cottages.

In the years between the shoemaker and the bootmaker, a tailor worked at 2 Churchyard Cottages, first of all John Mills and then his grandson, Henry. Henry sold up in 1856, after which there appears to have been no tailor in the Street until 1871, when young John Freeman was a tailor's apprentice. He was living with his parents and brothers at Cherry Tree Cottages. By 1880 he was a qualified tailor and at the age of 24 he built Regency House as both a dwelling house and a tailor's shop. It is interesting to realise that this was the only purpose-built shop in the Street. Charles Reader, son of the innkeeper at the Kings Head, was also a tailor; he was some 8 years younger than John Freeman. Is it possible that he worked for John at Regency House?

In 1891 George Holland of Chapel Cottage was employed as a stone quarryman. Many men over the centuries would have dug Horsham Stone from the quarries at Theale, Gaskins and the Nowhurst area. But by the second half of the 19th century new avenues of occupation were emerging. The coming of the railway in 1865 provided employment for 23-year old Charles Browning who was a porter and lived at Collyers in 1871, and William Clarke of Little Hammers who was a platelayer in 1891. The timber yard on Stane Street also provided new opportunities. Thomas and George Reed were both steam sawyers who came from Buxted. They had their own steam engine and saw bench, and travelled around the county from estate to estate sawing timber as required. When they came to Slinfold, they settled here and worked permanently at the timber yard. In 1881 George was lodging at Chapel Cottage and in 1891 Thomas lodged at Saddlers.

With the increasing interest throughout the century in gardens a number of men found employment as gardeners for the larger houses. The greatest category of employment, however, was that of agricultural labourer on the local farms. Some were employed full-time, but many were casual labourers, working whenever they were needed, and others worked seasonally at woodland trades. This explains why someone like Elias Knight of Collyers gave his occupation as a hoop maker in 1881, but called himself a labourer in 1891.

Michael Constable was a casual worker who lived in Little Hammers from 1808 till his death at the age of 78 in 1854, and in the early years at least he was working for Philip Holland on a fairly regular basis. Philip Holland farmed Gaskins, together with Ranfold, Holmbush and Wild Harrys. His account book for the years 1805 to 1814 survives, which lists payments made to Michael as well as others. There are detailed entries of all the work he did, giving a good insight into the varied tasks he had to carry out:

> *To reaping 8 acres of wheat at 12s per acre; To mowing 11 acres of oats at 2s 6d per acre; To making 370 & $^1/_4$ of fagots of all sorts at 2s 6d per hundred; To threshing 34 quarters of oats at 18d per quarter; To spreading 1 kiln lime with cart; To hedge & ditch 130 rods at 6d per rod.*

The boom years for agriculture up until 1815 were not only good for farmers, the labourers reaped the benefit too and Michael Constable's wages went up over the period of the accounts. He was also buying goods direct from Philip Holland, such as wheat, peas and oats, which would have fed both his family and the couple of pigs and poultry he almost certainly kept in the back garden. As well as the goods Michael received cash in advance, and often, after deducting his purchases and cash advances from his earnings, there was not much money due to him. Nevertheless, the impression gained from these accounts was that he was not doing badly during these years. Unfortunately, the accounts end before the beginning of the bad years for farming which followed the Napoleonic Wars and there is thus no indication of how Michael fared then. He continued to work until his old age,

The development of the village

but in 1851 when he was 75, he was said to be a *pauper, ex agricultural labourer*. The safety net of a pension did not exist then.

During the years of agricultural depression after 1815 crime became more prevalent as agricultural workers found themselves out of work and with insufficient means to feed themselves and their families. This increased lawlessness was a cause of worry and many places set up Prosecuting Societies as a means of discouraging crime. Previously people had known they could get away with theft and damage to property because there were no police and the cost of bringing a prosecution was too high for the ordinary person. The Prosecuting Societies acted in two ways: firstly as a deterrent because lawbreakers now knew that the Society would prosecute as it had sufficient funds and, secondly, through rewards which were offered for information leading to a successful conviction. Members paid an entrance fee and an annual subscription and held an annual dinner. The Slinfold *Society for the Apprehension of Felons* was established in 1825 and was still functioning at the beginning of the 20th century. There are unfortunately no records of how successful this Society was.

Typical of the crimes such Societies were intended to discourage is a case which came before the Lent Assizes in 1834. Thomas Sturt, grocer of the Village Stores and also farmer, prosecuted Reuben Sageman, a labourer who resided near Slinfold. Sageman had stolen a poke worth 1s. from Baker's Barn, which was on one of Thomas's farms, not far from Slinfold Lodge. He had been caught with the poke concealed under his round frock and unfortunately for him it was marked with the initials T.S. on its four corners. Sageman was found guilty and sentenced to three months hard labour. He was described at his trial as *a notorious poacher in the neighbourhood and of very loose character* and his spell of hard labour does not appear to have reformed him. Two years later he was reported to have been committed for trial for his part in a series of burglaries in the Itchingfield area.

The majority of people were law-abiding, however, even if life offered limited opportunities. Apart from living in as a domestic servant, there were few occupations available to spinsters or widows. Some widows were able to continue their husbands' businesses. As well as Mary Grinstead of Taylors, who ran her husband's building business after his death, Sarah Holden and Mary Reader both ran the Kings Head after their husbands had died. One thing women could turn their hand to was sewing and in the 1870s and 80s Rebecca Farley of 3 Churchyard Cottages was a seamstress. The next tenant in the cottage was a widow who worked as a needle woman.

One wife whose husband had a surprising occupation for an inland village was Miriam Blann, who in the 1871 census was described as a mariner's wife, her husband being away at sea at the time. She lived in Little Hammers in the late 1860s and early 70s; she had been born in Slinfold but had clearly lived in Shoreham for a while, where her eldest child was born.

Unlike carpenters or shoemakers, where the location of the craft changed with the different craftsmen, the location of trades such as that of blacksmith and wheelwright tended to be much more static. There might be a new blacksmith or wheelwright, but he came to the same forge or wheelwright's shop that his predecessor had used. The forge stayed at the same site in an outbuilding in front of the house to the north of Little Hammers from the late 16th century until 1841, when it moved across the road. Similarly, the wheelwright's workshop was on the site of the Chapel from the 18th century until around the 1850s when the wheelwright joined the blacksmith at the new forge.

The village shop occupied the same site almost without a break from the 17th century. It had begun as a mercers, but by the 19th century had become a true general store. In 1895 it was known as the Slinfold Stores and it was a grocers, provision merchants, drapers, bakers, corn and coal &

coke merchants, ironmongers and china & glass dealers. While most things could be bought from the village shop, milk came direct from local farms and meat from the butchers which was established in White Briars around 1840 and continued there for over 100 years.

By the 19th century there was only one pub in the village, the Weeping Eye at White Briars having ceased operating some time in the mid-18th century. The Kings Head was run by the Holdens from around 1780 until c. 1860 when Sarah Holden, a widow, retired in her late 60s. For the rest of the century the pub was run by a succession of innkeepers. Brewing must have been taking place on the premises during the 19th century as there is a malthouse attached to the south-western corner of the building. The upper storey of this appears to be weather-boarded, but in fact the walling is constructed of panels of louvres. Until fairly recently the opening mechanism for these louvres was still in place.

With the coming of the Penny Post in 1840, many more people were able to afford to send letters. It was in response to the increase in mail that houses began to be given names, to make it easier for the postman to find a particular property. Prior to that most of the houses in the village would have simply been referred to by the name of the occupier. From 1845 to 55 Sarah Holden of the Kings Head was the postmistress; when the front door of the pub was moved some years ago an old wooden post box was found in the wall. The word POST can still be seen painted on one of the bricks beside the porch. By 1859 the post office was being run from the Village Stores, where it remained until 1895 when it moved to York Cottage.

Transport in the 19th Century

Travel by road often presented considerable difficulties until the coming of turnpikes from the mid-18th century onwards. Slinfold appears to have been an early beneficiary of this type of improvement. The village was on the main route from Pulborough and Billingshurst to Horsham and this route was a natural candidate for turnpiking. There is no trace, though, of any original turnpike act for the road, nor for its later dis-turnpiking. There are, however, a number of factors, both in the landscape and documentary, which suggest that there was indeed a turnpike which came from Bury Gate northwards through Pulborough and Billingshurst and then turned east into Slinfold along Clapgate Lane. It went through the village, out via Lyons Road and thus to Horsham. This route is shown as a turnpike on more than one map of the early 19th century. It is not clear why the turnpike did not use the existing Park Street but continued further north before turning in towards the village via Clapgate Lane. Much of this lane is now merely a footpath across fields, but the western end near Stane Street is still marked by an avenue of trees.

The village would thus have benefitted from all the trade generated by passing traffic. But all this ceased when Slinfold was bypassed by the A264 Five Oaks to Horsham turnpike. The villagers of the day were not concerned about the peace and quiet they had gained. Rather, there would have been numerous complaints about the loss of trade. The Five Oaks/Horsham turnpike was a completely new road over most of its length and was opened in 1811 as a quicker route for the movement of troops and supplies during the Napoleonic Wars. The A281 Horsham/Guildford turnpike dates from 1809, simplifying east-west travel in the area. It had a short spur south from Roman Gate to connect with the former Slinfold turnpike.

Heavy goods were much easier to transport by water than by road, especially in view of the dubious state of many of the roads in the the area. The lower reaches of the river Arun had been made navigable in the 17th and 18th centuries, but it was not until 1787 that the Arun Navigation finally reached Newbridge Wharf near Billingshurst. Although this is some five or six miles distant

The development of the village

from Slinfold, it did enable timber merchants such as Edward Child to have easy access to Arundel and Littlehampton, and farmers could obtain a ready supply of chalk from the Amberley Chalk Pits. This was burnt into lime in kilns situated on most of the larger farms and spread over the fields as fertiliser. Later, in the 1830s and 40s, Thomas Child was bringing considerable quantities of coal up from Littlehampton to Newbridge.

In 1816 the Arun Navigation was connected with the Wey Navigation, allowing direct access to the River Thames. There is not much surviving evidence of goods from around here being shipped on the Wey & Arun, although there must have been some traffic. It is known, for instance, that after the Slinfold tannery had closed, bark from this area was shipped to the tannery at Godalming.

While the coming of the canals did not much affect the lives of the ordinary people of Slinfold, the arrival of the railway had a much greater effect. The railway reached Horsham in 1848, but the branch line to Guildford, which passed through Slinfold, was not opened until 1865. The railway appears initially not to have made much impression on the village. The Rev. G.P. Crawfurd, writing years later of his time as curate of Slinfold from 1877 to 1882, does not even mention the railway. Its greatest impact at first must have been to encourage the expansion of the timber yard and thus provide increased local employment. The timber yard had its own private siding and there was also a private siding which served the brickworks in Hayes Lane. Train-loads of rubbish used to come down from London to the brickworks and, after sorting, the rubbish was used in firing the bricks. Again the railway was a vital part of a local industry.

The 20th Century

After the explosion of the 19th century, there was comparatively little building in the Street in the 20th century. Only six new houses have been built, largely because there was very little land left unoccupied. Padora-Nibletts was built in 1927 on the corner of Hayes Lane for Mrs. Ruse who was farming in the area. The last vacant plot of land in the Street was on the corner by Lyons Road and Birchwood was built here to a modern design in 1959. The other houses have all been infilling on large garden plots. The land adjacent to White Briars on which the slaughter house for the butchers had been situated, was used for the building of Little Platt. This was constructed in the 1950s of traditional materials which blend well with the older houses. The site of the former tannery next to Collyers is now occupied by High Trees and the Rectory (previously Conkers), which date from the 1960s, and Garden House was built in 1979 in the orchard belonging to Windalls. These last three are all built of modern materials which make no pretence of blending with the earlier buildings. There is one other new dwelling in the Street. Candleford was converted around 1980 from the former outbuilding which had been used in connection with the basket factory in the 1930s.

There were also three new properties at the western end of the Street beyond the Conservation Area. These resulted from the sale of Old House Farm in the 1950s. Old House was separated from its land, the stables and cow byre were converted into the dwelling known as the Old Stables, and two new houses, Barn End and Fosseys, were erected.

If there was not much building, there were nevertheless profound changes in village life in the 20th century, especially in the last 50 years. One of these was the arrival of the public utilities, which came to Slinfold just before the Second World War. Mains water arrived in the village in the late 1930s, which was a great relief as many of the wells contained medicinal salts and were not suitable for household purposes. There had been a parish pump on the corner of Hayes Lane, next to Stone Cottages, but with the coming of piped water this fell out of use and was removed and sold for scrap. Electricity was installed in the houses in 1936, although there were still no street lights

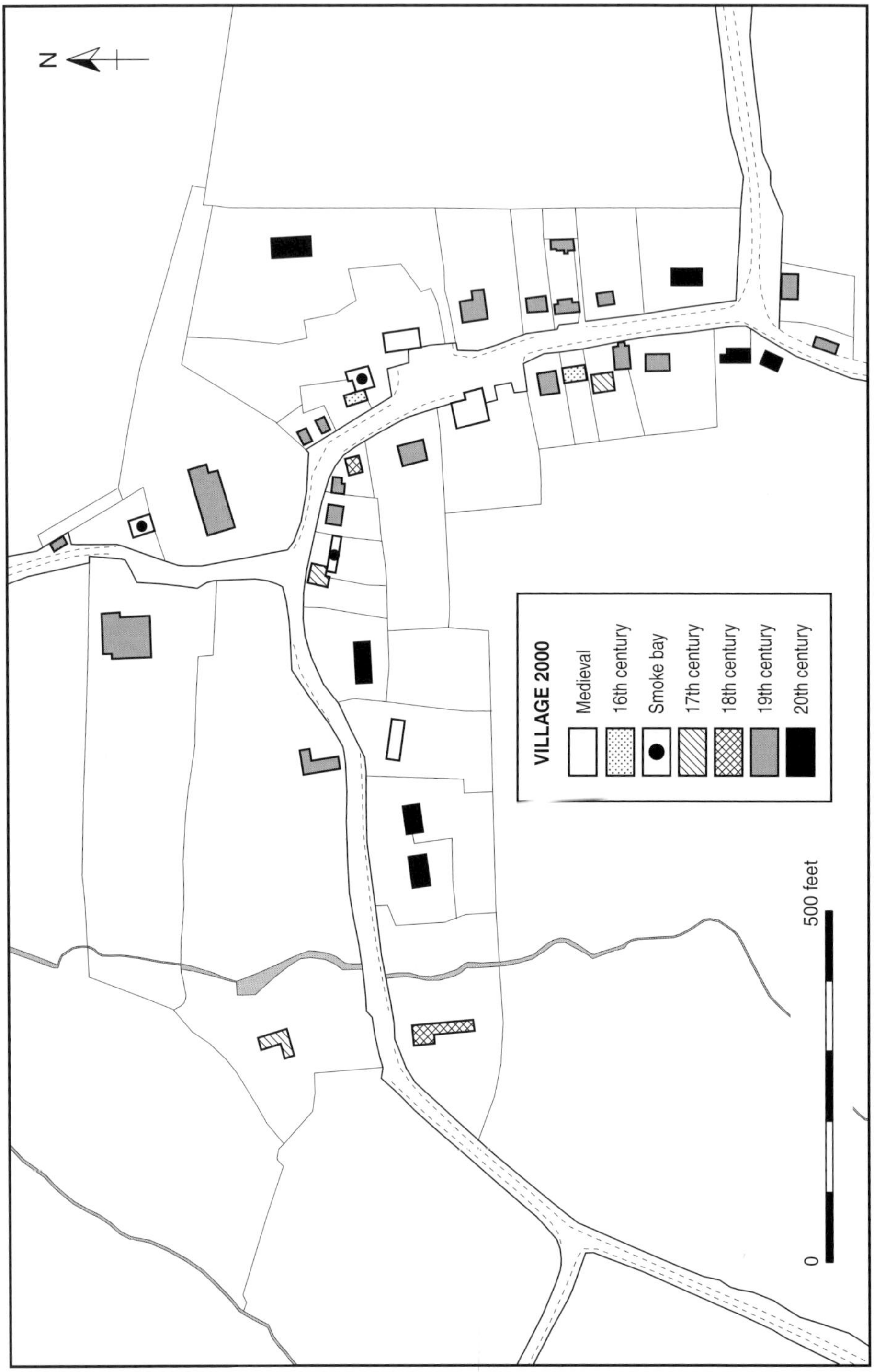

Map 6. *Slinfold Street in the year 2000*

by 1947. In fact some street lamps - White Whittle's gas-oil lamps - had been introduced in 1886 and these can be seen in some postcards of the village from the early years of the 1900s, but they apparently did not last long. Another big improvement was the treating of the roads with Tar Macadam in the 1920s or 30s, which ended centuries of struggling with mud in winter and dust in summer.

Plate 6. *The Village Centre in the mid-1920s. The girl on the left is Dorothy Hounsom of Barton Cottage, Hayes Lane, and on the right is Lena Waters of Church House*

A private bus service connecting Slinfold with Horsham commenced around 1918, and together with the railway and the increasing use of bicycles, much greater mobility was available to the general public than ever before. And yet there are tales of older residents who never left Slinfold at all during their childhood. However, the railway became an accepted part of village life and it was greatly missed on its closure in 1965. A few years later one Slinfold resident complained that, with no railway and with only a two-hourly bus service, he felt the village had 'gone backwards'.

In the past people walked considerable distances as a matter of course. In the 1840s Charles Knight, a grocer in Horsham who was born at Old House, frequently walked with his family to Slinfold or Itchingfield to visit relatives for Sunday tea. A hundred years later Slinfold mothers thought nothing of pushing their babies in prams to Horsham and back.

Now, people's travelling habits have changed completely. The culture of the car reigns supreme and no-one expects to have to walk. Among the young this is sometimes taken to extremes. One mother, doing the school run, dropped one of the children at the corner of the road, some two hundred yards from her house. Another of the children in the car complained bitterly that it was most unfair to expect the girl to walk!

Two World Wars also affected the village. In the 1914-18 War, not only were 31 men lost, including the son of the schoolmaster, William Brown, but the attitudes and expectations of those who survived were greatly altered by their experiences. Those who lived in Slinfold during the Second World War have retained very vivid memories of the period, such as cycling to Roman Gate after a German plane had crashed there, or seeing a barrage balloon which had broken loose from its mooring bobbing about in a local field. There were Canadian troops in the village, and the officers had their guard room in the Kings Head and used the outbuilding in the grounds of Slinfold House as their mess. The older residents in the village still refer to this as the *Canteen*. These Canadians were the source of a hilarious episode when they tied tin cans to the tails of Mrs. Ruse's cows and set them loose. They rushed down the Street, waking the whole village up! Not only were there troops in the village, there were also evacuees staying with several families. They attended school with the local children, except for a few Catholic evacuees who had their lessons in the Village Hall.

In the earlier years of the century there were still trades and crafts being carried on in the Street. Today, it is a matter of surprise to see someone walking along carrying a spade, but in the past it would have been a common sight to see people with their work tools. The majority of these craftsmen had gone by the end of the 1930s, but the blacksmiths and wheelwrights continued until 1951. Nevertheless, the decline in the use of horses meant they had to diversify into other areas. Already by 1925, F. & C. Wadey's printed stationery heading offered the following services:

Smiths and wheelwrights, hot water fitters, lawn mowers ground by machinery, cycle agents and repairers and estimates for pumping plants for deep wells.

Plate 7. *The Old Forge c. 1905*

In the 1920s there had been another cycle repairer, Alfred George Stemp, who worked from the outbuildings next to the Kings Head. In 1923 and 24 he advertised in the local trade directory as Motor Engineer of the Kings Head Garage. This was a time when cars and horses existed side by side, and in the same trade directory William Albery advertised his services. He was a Horsham harness maker who used to come out to Slinfold once a week to his workshop in Peppercorn Cottage.

The tailor, John Freeman, who had worked from his shop in Regency House since 1880, continued until his death in 1925. In the 1920s there was also a dressmaker, Miss Kate Kinggett, in Chewton.

At various times in the 1920s and 30s different people sold sweets from their homes. Older residents remember Miss Edwards of Chapel Cottage and Mrs. Davey, who lived in the middle cottage at Collyers and sold sweets to the schoolchildren in their dinner hour.

In the early 1930s a small-scale factory operated in the outbuildings where the dwelling known as Candleford now stands. This was a chip basket factory owned and run by Mr. Alfred Cox, who lived with his family in Hyrstlea (now Taylors) next door. It employed five or six girls and one young man. The material for the baskets came in long strips delivered by lorry. Mr. Cox used to cut up the wood in a little shed at the back. The finished baskets, which were used for soft fruit, were stored in the 'big barn' (now Candleford) at the rear of the factory and a truck called weekly to collect them. The average wage, which was partly piecework, was around £1 per week. The factory closed about 1936, when it moved to Kent.

In addition, in the early years of the century there were two people in the village who produced local postcards. William Waller lived and worked in Rowfold Lea in Lyons Road until he moved to Horsham in about 1910. The other, Clifford Money, was at Holdens which he named Kei-a-Gomeena (unfortunately no-one can discover the meaning of this). Mr. Money was responsible for the Rural England series of postcards which all have a black panel at the bottom with a distinctive handwritten inscription. He produced postcards of many events, both in Slinfold and the surrounding area, and has left a rich coverage of local life. He was in the village from 1904 until 1926 when he too went to Horsham.

Plate 8. *Wedding of Harry Anscombe, Timberyard Manager. The Rural England postcards produced by Mr. Money have a distinctive black panel with white inscription*

By 1940 the number of commercial enterprises in the Street was reduced to five: the blacksmiths, Aylings the builders, the butchers, the shop at Regency House and the Village Stores. As already mentioned the blacksmiths ceased in 1951. The butchers, which had been at White Briars from 1840, was run from the early years of the 20th century by Walter Herrington. The business finally closed in March 1952, when stricter refrigeration regulations were introduced, which old Mr. Herrington felt unable to cope with. After John Freeman's death his tailors shop became a confectioners, a tobacconists and finally a grocers run by Mr. Marley. When the latter died it ceased to be a shop as, with the increasing traffic, its position on a bend with no suitable parking nearby meant that it was no longer a viable proposition.

The Street now has only the one shop, the Village Stores, and even this has changed its character in recent years. The shop continued as a general store until the late 1970s, operating from the two southern front rooms of the building. In 1965 the Slinfold Stores stationery heading indicated that it was selling *Groceries, Provisions, Fruit & Vegetables, Wools, Stationery and Sundries*. In 1979 the property was offered for sale. It was then divided into two private dwellings and for a while there was no shop. Then in 1981 a greengrocers operated for a few months in the southern front room, and when this folded the owners of the southern dwelling opened a small food shop in this same room. This has gone from strength to strength, moving to larger, specially adapted premises in an adjacent outbuilding in 1995. Although this present shop sells a wide range of goods, it is not the general store of the past. Shopping habits have changed dramatically and the village shop is no longer the chief supplier of groceries to the inhabitants as it once was.

The post office came back to the Village Stores from York Cottage in 1904 and remained there until the premises were sold in 1979. The postmistress, Mrs. Lois White, then ran the post office from her house at 4 Lyons Road until she retired in 1987, when it once again returned to the Village Stores.

The pattern of farming has changed in recent years. In 1941 when the National Farm Survey was carried out by the Ministry of Agriculture and Fisheries there were three farms operating from the village centre. Old House farmed 92 acres, Mrs. Ruse, of Padora-Nibletts, farmed Rowfold and an area which included part of Nibletts and part of Hall Land, while the Kings Head still had 6½ acres. Now there is no property in the Street engaged in farming. Horses and tractors must once have been a common sight passing along the Street, whereas now it is so unusual as to be worthy of remark.

The character of the Street has changed beyond all recognition over the past 50 years. No longer are the inhabitants employed within the Street itself or on nearby farms as they had been for centuries past. The change had already begun in the first half of the 20th century, with a few people travelling into Horsham to work in shops. Now hardly anyone in the Street works in the parish; most commute often considerable distances to their workplace. With this change has come a change in the pattern of home ownership. In the past most houses were let and there were very few owner-occupiers. In 1839 six properties were occupied by their owners: Hall Land, Stanford House, one of the two houses replaced by Holdens, the house on the plot later occupied by the Forge, Slinfold House and 2 Churchyard Cottages. By 1910 just four houses were owner-occupied: Regency House, Stanford House, Holdens and Taylors. Now the situation is completely different and almost every property is owned and occupied by one and the same person.

The fact that the Street is no longer a working village was emphasized recently by someone who used to stay with relatives in her childhood in the 1950s. When she returned on a visit recently she commented that the village was much prettier than she remembered. She said that whereas before it had been shabby, now everything had been neatened and tidied up.

Conclusion

The whole history of the development of the village of Slinfold has been one of the enclosure of common land. The original swathe of common running up to the water meadows beside the Arun was largely enclosed prior to the building of the church in the 12th century. There was, however, an open area bounded to the south by a probable track running between Park Street and Lyons Road and having the church on its northern edge. The building of the church encouraged the enclosure of this area, but there was still a sizeable space left open in front of the church. This was largely taken into private ownership in the late 16th century, but the area bounded by the Kings Head, Slinfold House and the Old Bakery/Village Stores was retained as a village green. By the early 19th century the properties on the western side of the Street south of the green had encroached on the roadway to make front gardens, reducing the road to its present width.

Ever smaller pieces of open ground have been enclosed over the centuries until now even the remnants of the village green have been taken into private ownership and there is no public open space left in the centre of the village.

MANOR AND SQUIRE

The Manor

When the word *Manor* is mentioned, the image conjured up in most people's minds is of an attractive manor house, the dwelling of the lord of the manor, or Squire. The manor house is, in fact, only one of the elements which go to make up a manor. The manor was an estate belonging to the lord of the manor, which was held either directly or indirectly from the king, and many lords held several manors. Part of the land of each manor was directly exploited by the lord and was known as the *demesne*. The rest of the land was either tenanted or else used for common or waste. The tenants could be villeins who laboured on the lord's demesne in return for land of their own, or freemen who paid a fixed money rent.

The labour services owed by the tenants to the lord were gradually commuted to money payments and by the 16th century tenants paid a fixed annual *quit rent* which released them from manorial services. When a new tenant took over a holding, whether by inheritance or purchase, this was recorded in the court books and the tenant was given a copy of the entry. This form of tenure was called *copyhold*, the copy of the entry being the equivalent to title deeds. The conversion of copyhold tenure to leasehold occurred over a long period and different manors favoured differing conditions of lease. Some leases were for 21 years, others could be for up to 10,000 years, while another common form was a lease for three lives, where the lease held good as long as one of the three entered names was still alive. The land held by the freemen was freehold.

From the later medieval period onwards the tenant who held copyhold land was to all intents and purposes the owner, and is referred to as such in this book. Although custom dictated whether it was a man's eldest or youngest son who should inherit the property, the tenant could leave it to someone else if he went through the correct manorial procedure and paid a fee. He could also sell the land provided the transaction was recorded in the court books and the new tenant paid an entry fine. The tenant could, and frequently did, sub-let his property, again on payment of the appropriate fee. There were thus often three people involved in any one property: the lord of the manor, who let the holding to a tenant, who might in turn sub-let it to another person.

The business of the manor was dealt with by the manor courts, presided over by the lord of the manor or his steward. Though the procedure was judicial, the manorial courts considered both judicial and administrative matters, such as the transfer of property and infringements of the customs of the manor. Custom governed everything and checked the rights and duties of both the lord and the tenants. The principle was *Justice shall be done by the lord's court, not by the lord*. All the business of the court was recorded in the court books, which were at first rolled-up strips of parchment known as *Rolls*.

For 500 hundred years after the Conquest the manor was the unit of local government, while the parish, once it was established, dealt purely with ecclesiastical matters. People living as neighbours would therefore find themselves with differing allegiances. The tenants of Collyers had to attend the manor courts at Dedisham, those of Old House Farm had to travel to Wiggonholt south of Pulborough, and the tenants of Rowfold went to Patching. They would also find themselves having to obey a different set of customs and regulations. There was also another administrative division, the *Hundred*. This was a subdivision of a county dating from Saxon times, which was further subdivided into *Tithings*. There were parts of several tithings within the parish; the tithing of Slinfold belonged to the hundred of Poling while Dedisham was part of West Easewrithe. Again parishioners were looking towards different centres of authority. The church was, however, a central part of people's lives in the past and the parish exerted a strong unifying influence on the people within it.

After the Reformation the parish was vested with increasing civil authority. The Tudor monarchs found parishes a more practical instrument of local government than the manor, and during the 17th century the parish in its civil aspect gradually replaced the manor as the unit of local government. Although manors continued to operate until the end of the 19th century, no longer did people find themselves looking to various different centres of authority.

Squire or no Squire?

To many people the typical English village consists of a group of cottages huddling round the church and manor house, with the lord of the manor, or *Squire*, controlling most aspects of village life. The pattern of settlement and development in this area, as described above, means that this model is not true for Wealden villages, especially in earlier times. The manor houses were situated in the parent manor some distance away to the south, so that there was no local figure of authority. As a result, the tenants in the Weald always had much greater freedom from manorial control than those living in the parent manor itself.

The Bishop of Chichester's manor of Ferring and Fure provides a good example of this. The outlier, Fure, was a long, narrow strip of land running through Billingshurst and Itchingfield up into Slinfold, where there were three holdings, Ranfold Farm, the now vanished farm of Farthings and a small landholding called Calkett or Colgate. In the mid-14th century the tenants of Fure were able to make money payments which excused them from working on the lord's demesne in Ferring, whereas the tenants in Ferring itself had no option but to carry out the work. The only services which the tenants of Fure had to perform for the Bishop were those connected with the woodland, such as gathering nuts, carting firewood to Ferring and driving pigs from one area to another. Throughout the 16th and 17th centuries the court books of the manor of Ferring and Fure show that the lives of the Ferring tenants were being closely controlled. They were constantly being ordered to mend their fences or lay stones on the roads, they were told precisely when animals could go along the streets and roads; in fact, each court that was held recorded a list of such instructions relating to Ferring. Fure, on the other hand, was hardly mentioned. Occasionally the tenants there were ordered to repair their roads and once they had to build a new pound for stray animals. But, in general, the adage 'out of sight, out of mind' seems to have held good and the same was doubtless equally true for the inhabitants of the outliers of other manors. This lack of manorial control made for a robust and independent society in which the spirit of enterprise was able to thrive and the Weald offered significant opportunities for supplementary employment.

There were, in fact, two manor houses within the parish, those of Dedisham and Pinkhurst. Dedisham, which is thought originally to have been an outlier connected with Goring, was an independent manor by 1091. Until the mid-16th century the lord of the manor also held several other manors and was not in permanent residence at Dedisham. He would have moved from one manor to another, coming here whenever he wished to hunt for there were three medieval deer parks at Dedisham, and he would not have exerted much influence over village life. From the mid-16th to the mid-17th century the Blounts did live at Dedisham and they certainly looked after the interests of their own tenants, providing a new pew for some of them in 1649 (see p.49). Thereafter the manor house was let to tenant farmers. The most lasting influence of the manor on the parish was the Dedisham Chancel in the old church, which was filled with memorials to past lords of the manor and their families, especially the Blounts.

Pinkhurst manor was one of many belonging to the Honour of Arundel and there seems to have been no manor house on it until, in 1566, John Thornden bought Pinkhurst Farm which was considered to be the demesne of the manor. He built a fine house there, part of which remains within Ye Olde House and Doomsday Cottage. The Thorndens remained at Pinkhurst for three generations, selling in 1637 to Sir Edward Bishop of Parham. Thereafter Pinkhust became a farmhouse which was then split into labourers' cottages in the 18th century.

The Blounts and the Thorndens were part of a phenomenon taking place in Slinfold in the second half of the 16th century through to the later part of the 17th century. The parish had a considerable number of gentry residing in it, a greater number than many of the surrounding parishes. The Horsham volume of Sussex Genealogies lists only one family in Rudgwick, the Naldretts, who in fact had considerable connections with Slinfold, while five gentry families in this parish are listed, not including the Thorndens. Several members of these families were involved in county affairs. From the late 16th century through to the 1660s the parish provided no less than four JPs, one of them Ralph Cowper of Strood (now Farlington School), serving from 1620 till 1656. He and George Churcher of Hill were particularly active in the county, the latter becoming sheriff.

17th century society in Slinfold was much more stratified than that in Rudgwick. In the years up to 1680 the former had large numbers of husbandmen and there were very few yeomen in the middle ground between them and the gentry. Rudgwick, on the other hand, had more yeomen than husbandmen and the average value of goods and chattels listed in inventories for these years was considerably higher here than in Slinfold. The effect of these differences in society in the two parishes can be seen in the relative number of medieval houses surviving in the two parishes. Rudgwick has a very high survival rate of 5.5 per 1000 acres while Slinfold has the much lower rate of 3.4. The yeomen of Rudgwick were sufficiently wealthy to maintain their houses and modernise them, whilst not being rich enough to demolish them and start afresh. The gentry in Slinfold, on the other hand, rebuilt their old houses in the latest fashion, as Richard Naldrett did with Old House Farm, and the husbandman appear not to have had enough money to maintain their houses properly, let alone rebuild them. This probably explains why there are a number of fragmentary open-hall houses in Slinfold.

The 17th century yeomen in Rudgwick lived in a free and vibrant society which was creating wealth by money-lending. The impression gained of Slinfold society at that time is that the gentry were doing very nicely, but that the majority of people were being kept in their place by the gentry and did not have the same opportunities for advancement.

In the 18th century many of the gentry houses reverted to being tenanted farmhouses, Hill House, Lower Broadbridge Farm, Dedisham Manor, Old House Farm and Pinkhurst all being examples of this. The society in Slinfold was no longer stratified in the way it had been and there were opportunities for people to move up the social scale. Families such as the Briggs and the Childs took full advantage of this, especially during the economic boom years of the Napoleonic Wars.

During the 19th century the poor were housed in cramped conditions while the better-off lived in some style. Despite this, there was no segregation of society in the village. Cherry Tree Cottages were occupied by agricultural labourers, while the Childs were in the adjacent semi-detached Slinfold House.

Towards the latter part of the 19th century the gentry became increasingly paternalistic towards the lower classes. Edward Brice Bunny acquired Slinfold Lodge by marriage, but continued to live much of the time in Speen Hill, Newbury. His son, Edward John, rebuilt the house in 1870 after his marriage, and he lived chiefly in Slinfold. In 1877 he changed his name to St. John in accordance with the will of his wife's father. Edward John took upon himself the rôle of Squire. He was, among other things, a JP and perpetual churchwarden, and the curate, the Rev. Crawfurd, said that he was one of the most public-spirited men he had ever known. He exercised considerable control and influence over the village and he liked to have his own way in the parish. The curate saw nothing wrong in this at all, accepting that this was the way things should be.

Edward John's son, Colonel Edward Francis St. John, continued his father's rôle as Squire. As a JP he had the right to grant a licence for the Station Inn, now Rosewarne in Spring Lane. For many years he withheld the licence as he did not think men should be encouraged to spend their wages on drink, but should use the money to feed their families.

It was not only the Squire who felt it his duty to look after the welfare and morals of the villagers. The wealthier families such as the Childs and the Holdens saw it as an obligation to be involved in all aspects of village life from fund-raising to organising exhibitions and entertainments. At this time the parishioners accepted this as normal and did not mind that their lives were being controlled by a self-elected élite, and this continued until the Great War of 1914-18. Miss Kate Child of Windalls, who died in 1913, was one of the last examples of the *voluntary philanthropic endeavour* which had characterised lives of people of her station. The large turn-out of people from all walks of life at her funeral demonstrated how much the villagers had appreciated her efforts on their behalf.

The experience of the men of the village who fought during the Great War changed the social order for ever. No longer did they want their lives to be run by the gentry and the big landowners, they now wished to be personally involved in village matters which affected them. The provision of a war memorial after the war clearly shows that the élite expected the old ways to continue unchanged while the villagers themselves had other ideas. The gentry, led by the Rector, favoured a memorial screen in the church, while members of the Slinfold branch of the Comrades of the Great War organised a separate collection and demanded that a stone memorial should be erected in a prominent position in the village rather than in the church. The differing ideas of the gentry and the men who had actually taken part in the war are permanently commemorated in the two separate war memorials, the inscribed screen in the church porch and the granite cross outside the Village Hall.

Plate 9. *The Comrades Cross outside the Village Hall*

A further response to the commemoration of the dead was that of Mrs. Mary Cumming of Lydwicke. She founded a working men's club as a memorial to her husband, who had been chief commandant of the Church Army in France and had died as a result of his war service. Mrs. Cumming obtained an ex-Church Army hut and had it erected in Park Road, a move which reflected the influence of the social amenities which had been available to soldiers at base camps in wartime. Mrs. Cumming undertook this project without widespread consultation, but the club quickly found acceptance within the community.

In the years after the Great War the old spirit of 'voluntary philanthropic endeavour' among the better-off did not die out. Mrs. Cumming built the cottage at the corner of Park Road and Hayes Lane as a dwelling for the village nurse and set up a trust in this connection. She was also much involved in the founding and running of the Church Lads Brigade.

Major Edward St. John followed his father in acting as Squire of the village, exercising absolute control over many aspect of his tenants' lives. His gardener, Mr. Jackson, lived in tied accommodation at Brackley Burn in Park Street. The day after Mr. Jackson died his widow and two daughters were moved out by Major St. John.

But side by side with the old ways went the new. Ordinary parishioners were now much more involved in organising clubs and events for themselves.

Over the centuries the ability of the people of Slinfold to organise their own lives has ebbed and flowed. There were periods of relative freedom followed by times when the inhabitants were much more tightly controlled. But they never experienced the total control exercised in some Downland villages in the 18th and 19th centuries, where the whole parish was in the hands of one landowner who, in his capacity as Squire decided who could live in the village, and had no qualms about demolishing properties and moving people on if this was in the best interests of his farming policies.

THE HOUSES OF THE STREET

Timber, Brick and Stone (Buildings and their Construction)

Until the coming of the canals and railways, houses were constructed of local materials. Timber from woodland and hedgerow trees, underwood from coppice stools for wattle panels, daub made of clay, dung and hair or chopped straw, roofing of thatch or Horsham stone, clay for tiles or bricks, all these materials were readily available locally, so that the houses were in effect an organic part of the landscape in which they stood and blended into their surroundings.

Before the 18th century all houses in the village were timber-framed. The only stone building was the church and even that had a timber-framed tower. The type of timber-framing used in Southern England and East Anglia is known as box-frame construction. This consists of pairs of upright timbers known as principal posts connected transversely by tie-beams and laterally by wall plates at the top and sill beams at the bottom, the whole resembling a box as its name implies. The timbers are held together with mortice and tenon joints, forming a rigid structure. The space between one pair of principal posts and the next is called a bay (Fig. 1).

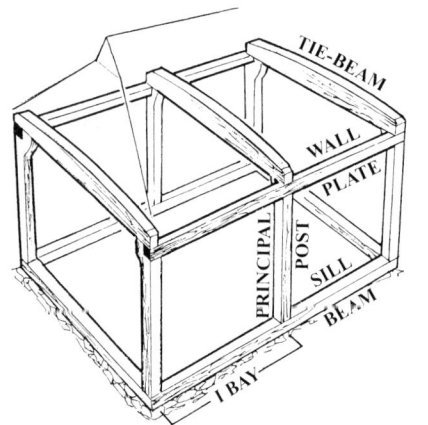
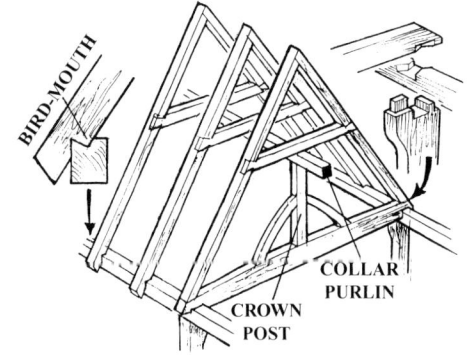

Fig. 1. *Typical Box-Frame*   Fig. 2. *Crown Post roof*

The bay is the main building block of timber-framed houses and a house could have as few or as many bays as the wealth of the owner permitted. The system was very flexible, for another range of bays could be built across the end of the building to form a crosswing, or more bays could be built abutting the house to give an L-shaped building, such as Old House Farm. Timber-framed buildings are thus normally just one room deep.

The box-frame supported a variety of roof types which evolved over the centuries. In Slinfold village medieval houses such as Collyers and the Kings Head have a type of construction known as the crown post roof (Fig. 2). The roofs of the later houses are side purlin with either queen struts or raking struts. White Briars has a special form of this roof with a dropped tie-beam (Fig. 3). Until the second half of the 18th century no roof in this area had a ridge piece at the apex. The most common roofing material in this area would have been Horsham stone, which was quarried locally at Theale and Nowhurst. Unfortunately, many of the old stone roofs have been altered to tile in recent years.

Timber, Brick and Stone

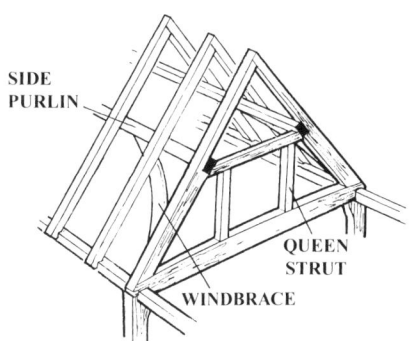 

Fig. 3. *Left: Side Purlin roof*
Right: Dropped tie-beam construction

The walls of the buildings between the principal posts were formed by horizontal rails and upright studs, the panels created by these tending to be larger in the earlier buildings. The most common infilling of the panels was wattle and daub, where a wattle framework was daubed on both sides with a mixture of wet clay and cow-dung, tempered with chopped straw or cow-hair (Fig. 4).

In the 17th century brick became a popular infill for wall panels and was used in both Chapel Cottage and White Briars. Much of the brick infill now seen in timber-framed buildings is a replacement for earlier defective wattle and daub panels, as is the case with the ground-floor walls of Chewton.

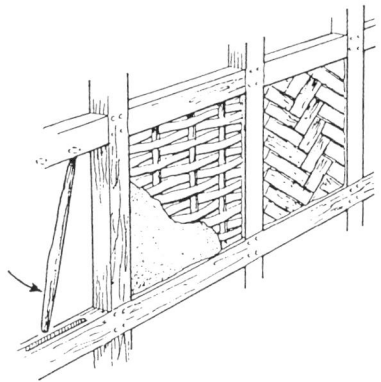

Fig. 4. *Left-hand panel: Stave being sprung into position*
Centre panel: Woven wattle with daub.
Right-hand panel: Brick infill

Timber-framed buildings were prefabricated at a framing ground. Sections of the building were fitted together on the ground and the timbers were marked with carpenters' marks to ensure that they were correctly assembled when the building was erected on site. There are good examples of carpenters' marks in White Briars.

The medieval houses in the village are of a type known as the open hall house. Here the hall, two bays in length, was open from floor to rafters. A typical hall house had a floored bay at either end of the hall (Fig. 5), but both the Kings Head and Collyers have a floored bay at one end only. The other surviving hall house, the Old Bakery/Village Stores, is too fragmentary to be certain, but was probably of the same type. The hall, which was the communal living area of the house, would have had a very smoky atmosphere. The smoke from the fire drifted up and found its way out through the roof covering and the triangular gablets at either end of the roof which were left open for this purpose. Over the years the smoke from the hearth stained the roof timbers with soot, and sooted timbers are still visible in the roofs of these houses.

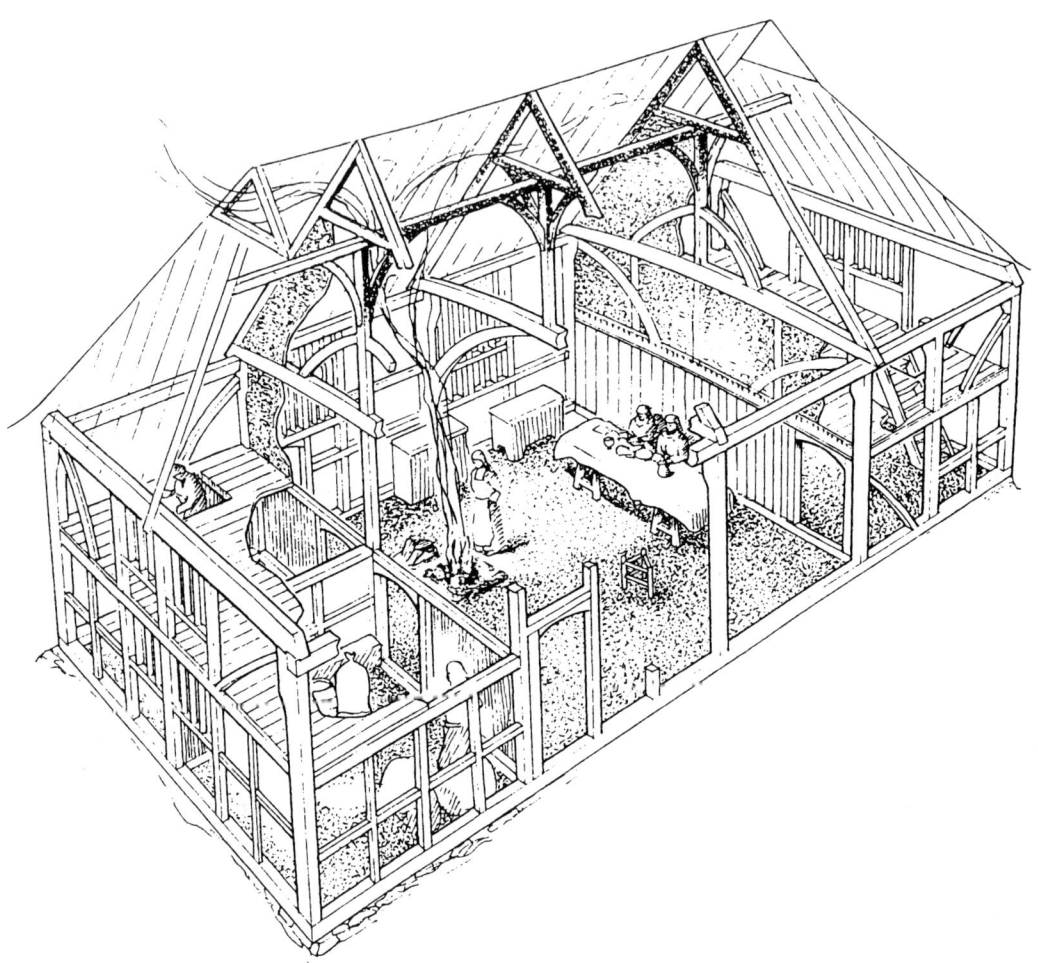

Fig. 5. *A typical hall house with a two-bay open hall; the high end is to the right and to the left is the service end with two ground-floor rooms*

From around 1550 new houses were built with a smoke bay rather than an open hall. The smoke bay was a narrow bay some three to four feet wide which was open from floor to rafters as the hall had been, but the smoke was now confined within a small area (Fig. 6). The smoke was further restricted as it was usual for one side of the bay to be partitioned off to form an entrance lobby which sometimes also contained access to the first floor. There are three houses of this type in the village. Chewton and Slinfold House have an end smoke bay, while in Churchyard Cottages the smoke bay is central.

Fig. 6. *From left to right: a smoke bay, an external chimney, and a chimney within a narrow bay*

Open hall houses were often modernised by inserting a smoke bay within the hall and flooring over the rest of the hall to form a new upper chamber. At Collyers, with its long hall, a smoke bay was constructed more or less centrally, allowing a new chamber to be formed on either side.

Brickmaking had increased throughout Sussex in the 16th and early 17th centuries and bricks, which had been expensive and the sole preserve of the rich, were now available to those of much more modest means, and by the second quarter of the 17th century most new houses in this area were built with a brick chimney. The stack could be place centrally within a specially designed narrow bay, as at Chapel Cottage, or it could be to one end. The end stack was very often external to the framed building, but could be contained within a narrow bay, as with Old House. Occasionally the stack was placed to the side of one of the bays; this arrangement can be seen at White Briars. The typical Sussex stack above the roof line was taller and more substantial than those of many parts of the country and it was capped with several oversailing courses. A good example may be seen on the rear range of the Old Bakery, although the top few courses are modern replacements.

By the end of the 17th century the older houses had been updated by the addition of brick stacks. A chimney was built at the end of the open hall in the Kings Head and a new chamber created over the rest of the hall. Chewton and Churchyard Cottages had stacks inserted within the old smoke bays, while at Slinfold House the stack was built to the rear of the house, allowing the former smoke bay to be incorporated into the living area.

There was then a period of stagnation and no more building took place until the late 18th century. By the time new dwellings were constructed the style of building had completely changed. No longer was timber-framing used, the houses were brick-built and they now had a symmetrical façade with a central hall and rooms to each side. There were no more narrow ranges just one room deep, the buildings were now more or less square with four ground-floor rooms. The brickwork was Flemish bond, with alternating headers and stretchers, which lent itself to the attractive chequerboard pattern to be seen on several houses in the centre of the village.

Horsham stone had previously been predominantly a roofing material, although it was also used as flooring, and timber-framed buildings had a few courses placed under the sill beams to help preserve the timbers from the damp. From the late 18th century it began to be used for mass walling. Stone is used for the northern end wall of the new front range of the Old Bakery and by the mid-1830s complete buildings were being constructed of Horsham stone. The new church of 1861 had Horsham stone walls with Bath stone dressings. Sale particulars of Strood (Farlington School) in 1886 claimed that the stone had come from their quarries at Nowhurst, while the booklet listing the benefactors of the new church stated that the stone had been given by the Shelleys of Field Place.

New materials began to appear. The new houses around 1800 had tile roofs, but then slate came into fashion, brought in by canal to Newbridge. For the first time a building material which was not local was used, the start of a trend which has caused the disappearance of local building styles. The first dwelling to use this new roofing was Windalls in 1828/9. Slate required a lower pitch and it is interesting to notice the difference in the roof line of Taylors, built c. 1833, and Holdens which was erected in 1841, the former a steeply pitched tile roof and the latter a much shallower roof of slate.

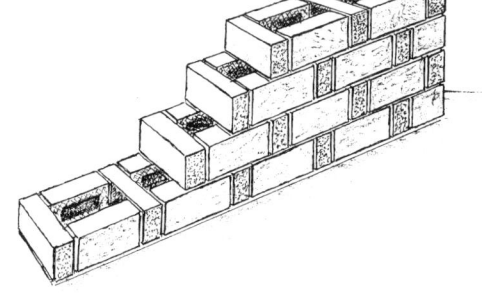

Plate 10. *Rat trap bond, Forge House*

Fig. 7. *Rat trap bond. Notice the cavity which gives the bond its name*

One interesting type of brickwork used around 1840 to 50 in the Street is rat trap bond. Here the bricks are set on edge, with alternate headers and stretchers arranged in such a way that a square space is formed at intervals, the *rat trap* (Fig. 7). It is in effect an early type of cavity wall, but that was incidental. The reason for using this bond is that the wall could be constructed more quickly using less bricks. A very attractive example of rat trap is Forge House, where alternate red stretchers and blue headers have been used. Another use of rat trap was the wall between Holdens and the Kings Head car park, which has been rebuilt only recently. But the builders of many rat trap cottages were only concerned with saving money and ignored the aesthetics. It was thought better to use an ordinary bond behind chimney stacks, so that often there is an untidy section of bricks laid normally stretching up the middle of a wall otherwise constructed of rat trap. Also it is impossible to use rat trap for gables. An example of both these features is the end wall of Pratts Cottages beside Stane Street on the way to Billingshurst.

By the 1880s houses were being intentionally built with cavity walls and to enable the cavity to be formed the walls had to be constructed of stretcher bond. There are several examples of this in the Street, Church House and Regency House being two of them.

Most roofs from the 1880s onwards were tiled, although Regency House, built 1880, and York Cottage of the early 1890s used slate. One of the reasons for the decline in popularity of slate as a roof covering may have been the closure of the Wey and Arun Canal in 1871.

The 20th century houses have been built in a variety of styles and materials, vividly demonstrating that there is now no longer a local building tradition. Modern styles have become universal throughout the country.

Key to Plans of Houses:

■   Principal post

┄┄┄┄   Bridging Beam (beam supporting joists for a ceiling)

   Hearth

The influence of Manors on the Development of the Village

The development of the village has been very much influenced by the manors which held land near the church, the particular shape of the landholdings and the differing responses of the various manors to building on the waste. Although the importance of the manors decreased in later centuries, the pattern of the manorial holdings continued to affect the growth of the village. The old pattern is still clearly visible on 19th century maps and it is only in the last hundred years that some of the old boundaries have been moved or lost. Even as late as 1949 much of the original pattern could be discerned on an aerial photograph. Since the manorial holdings have played such a significant rôle in the shaping of the village, it seems logical to describe the buildings of the Street in groups according to their manor.

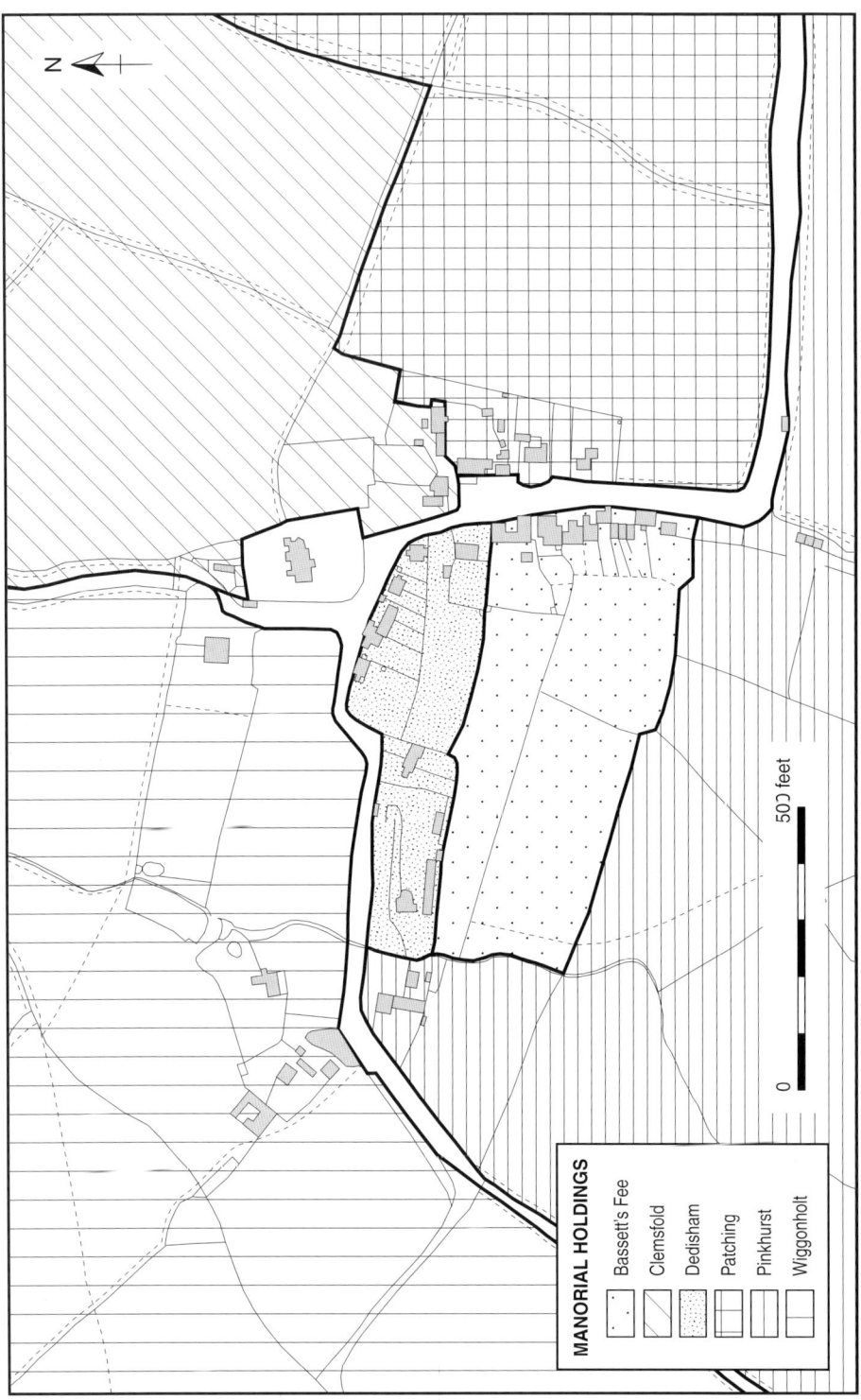

Map 7. *Manorial Holdings in the centre of Slinfold*

HOUSES ON DEDISHAM & PINKHURST LAND

Most of the land belonging to the manor of Dedisham ran in a broad swathe to the west of Stane Street from the Haven Road up to the county boundary in Rudgwick. It added small areas to its holdings over the centuries and one of these was the narrow strip of the common land opposite the church which was enclosed some time after the church was built. This strip was divided between the two medieval properties of Collyers and Stanford House. The farm of Hall Land, belonging to the manor of Pinkhurst, also enclosed an area of the common to the west of the stream, which was added to the already existing farm. This farm had a house somewhere on its land around 1400, but this later became redundant as Hall Land was being farmed with other holdings.

The open space in front of the church was enclosed by the late 16th century and Chewton was the first building to be erected on it. The Lord of the Manor of Dedisham did not discourage houses being built on the manorial waste and many examples of such dwellings occur in Rudgwick parish. Other manors, such as Pinkhurst, were actively opposed to such development.

1 & 2 COLLYERS AND COLLYERS (22)

The original holding known as Collyers was a long, narrow plot to the south of the Street, running from the stream which is now in the garden of Hall Land, and abutting the strip belonging to Stanford House on the east (Map 3). This was enclosed from common land near the church and was held of the manor of Dedisham.

The dwelling for this holding was built at the eastern end of the plot. Within 1 & 2 Collyers is an open hall house dating from 1425 or earlier, which was probably the first house on the site. This house consisted of a large, two-bay open hall, with a small floored end to the east which had an internal jetty (X on the plan). The first-floor room, or solar, projected some eighteen inches into the hall. This increased the size of the solar without making the hall any smaller and it also meant that the owner, when at the high table, was seated under a canopy. The ground floor of this end was divided into two small rooms. The framing of this building has various early features, such as straight up-braces in the walls of the floored end; and the down-braces in the side walls of the open hall which go from the eaves-plate to the mid-rail, rather than springing from the principal post as is normal. This latter feature is unusual and is presumed to be early.

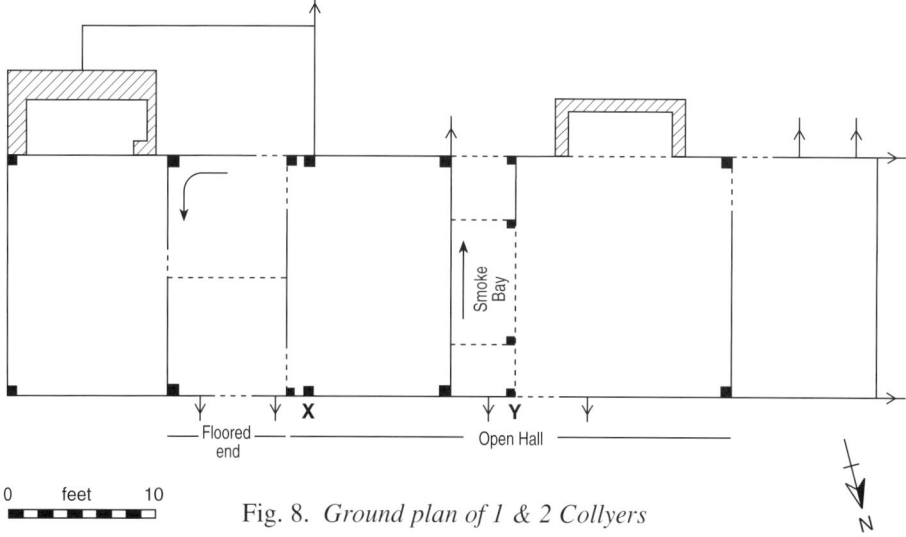

Fig. 8. *Ground plan of 1 & 2 Collyers*

Medieval houses with a two-bay hall and just one floored end are not unusual in Slinfold. What is unusual about Collyers is the size of the hall, with an overall length of 30 feet. The occupant of the holding would have needed to carry on a trade or craft to support himself, and it is likely that the hall was being used both as living accommodation and as a workshop.

The first documentary reference to Collyers is in 1547 when Elizabeth Mose was the tenant. It passed to the Holmans through marriage and was then sold to the Perrins, but it is not clear whether these people were living there or were sub-letting the property. By this time the house no longer had an open hall. A smoke bay had been constructed by inserting a partition in the former open truss and building a new partition some four feet to the west (Y on the plan). This new narrow bay was open from floor to rafters, and the pair of rafters which were cut to make a smoke-hole in the roof are still visible. There would have been a louvre above to give protection from the weather. The new hearth served the western end of the original hall and its bresummer can still be seen in the wall today with later infill below it. The old hall to either side of the smoke bay was floored at this time to give an additional chamber above each part. On the ground floor it would seem that each end of the smoke bay was partitioned off. The main entrance would have been into a lobby at the northern end and the outline of an earlier door can be seen in the later brick-work here.

The conversion from open hall to smoke bay would have occurred around 1580 to 1600 and almost certainly the building was still one dwelling at this stage. Unfortunately the many later alterations have obscured evidence for a door beside the smoke bay through into the other end of the original hall.

In 1600 Reginald Gilbert bought the property. He clearly did not occupy Collyers as he was the village blacksmith and was living and working in premises later replaced by Holdens. The inventories of two of the later owners, John Ede and Edward Lewer, indicate that they were farmers, who would have considered the owning and letting of Collyers to be an investment. By 1649, when Mistress Blount built a new seat in the church for some of the Dedisham tenants, Richard Davye was the owner (see p.49).

In 1651, for the first time, the names of the occupants are given: Richard Sweeting and John Belchamber. Earlier in the 17th century the dwelling had been extended and divided into two cottages. A new bay was added to the eastern end of the building with a chimney stack to the rear. The eastern cottage thus had three rooms on the ground floor, the new bay with its large cooking hearth functioning as the kitchen, and three chambers above. The western cottage was smaller, although there is some doubt as to how far the building did extend. A new bay was added to the west, but the end wall is probably a rebuild of around 1700 as there are no full-height posts here. This cottage continued to be heated by the smoke bay until well into the 18th century, when a stack was added behind the former open hall. The smoke bay was then altered to contain the stairs.

At the time of his death in 1676 Peter Fish owned Collyers and had lived there for eight years or more. His will was dictated from his death bed in the presence of Mr. More, John Fish his brother and Richard Gardiner, the mercer of the Old Bakery/Village Stores. From the will, and the inventory of all his goods and chattels, it is clear that Peter was a weaver who lived and worked in one cottage and let the other. He is typical of the occupants of Collyers over the centuries; a craftsman who supplemented his income by growing wheat upon his plot of ground, fattening pigs and keeping a few poultry; fruit came from the orchard and there was a little barn for storage. An additional income was derived from the letting of the other half of the dwelling. Peter's son inherited all his father's weaving and working tools, and Collyers was left to Peter's wife, Sarah, on condition that she paid rent to their two daughters when they reached the age of 21. Less that a year later Sarah married William Furlonger; a widow with property was a good catch. Sarah died in 1697 and the *William Furlonger, weaver of Wisborough Green* whose death is recorded in the Slinfold parish registers for 1709 is almost certainly the William of Collyers.

The next occupant about whom anything is known is George Crapwell who was at Collyers from c. 1736 until his death sometime before 1756. He was born and bred in Slinfold, one of a large family several of whom died young, including one brother who died of smallpox at the age of 22. George and his wife, Margaret, had just one child, a daughter Sarah who married Samuel Briggs.

Samuel Briggs was a tanner by trade. The tanyard occupied the area to the west of Collyers running up to the stream dividing its plot from Hall Land farm. The stream provided the water which was necessary to the tanning process and the other raw materials, hides and oak bark, were readily available locally. The first mention of the tanyard is in 1754, but it is likely that it was in operation earlier. Possibly father-in-law, George Crapwell, was also a tanner.

There is then a confusion of Williams. Samuel and Sarah sold Collyers to a William Briggs in 1756. However, Samuel's own son William who is known to have been a tanner, was not born until 1758. The William who bought Collyers was obviously a relative and almost certainly a tanner. Samuel himself was later living in Stanford House and may have gone there straight from Collyers.

During the second half of the 18th century the western cottage, which was where the Briggs lived, was doubled in size by building a brick addition to the west. This extension had two rooms on each floor, with a small external chimney at the end. The new build has no ridge-piece at the apex of the roof, which suggests that it dates to around 1750 rather than later. The stack behind the old cottage which replaced the smoke bay is probably part of the same upgrading of the property. These improvements are proof that the tannery was a thriving concern, and if they do indeed date to 1750, this would suggest that the tannery had already been in operation for some time. There is, in fact, mention of a tanner, Thomas Weale, in the parish register for 1707.

Plate 11. *Collyers Cottages, c. 1903, before the building of the large extension behind the right-hand cottage. The children are Violet, Florence, Connie (seated in the cart) & Robert Dawe who lived at Chewton. The cart has 'Robert Dawes' inscribed on the back.*

Although it is known from documents that William Briggs was at Collyers from 1756 onwards, it is not clear when William the relative was replaced by William son of Samuel. William the son married Mary Stanford in 1775 and they had six children, one of whom died in infancy. Mary died in 1786 when their youngest child was only two.

Under William the tanyard continued to do well. From the 1750s the tanyard had leased George's Field to the west of the stream, which was part of Hall Land farm in the manor of Pinkhurst, and clearly the tanning operations spilled over into this field from Collyers plot. The profits from the tannery enabled William to buy the northern part of this field in 1792 and over the next few years to build what is now Hall Land. This new house was completed by 1796 when the Land Tax for Collyers is suddenly increased, and when the list of pewholders in the parish registers refers to Collyers as Old Tanyard House. William moved into this new house, while his eldest son, another William, continued to inhabit Collyers and to run the tanyard.

William, junior, married Ann Stanford and they had just one daughter, Mary, who died at the age of 18. William and Ann were at Collyers for the rest of their lives and were clearly considered to be people of status as they were referred to as Mr. William and Mrs. Ann. The tanyard was still in operation in the 1840s, when William was being assisted by his nephew, William Casson, who was lodging at Hall Land. But by 1851 William had retired and the tanyard had closed. His brother's son had other business interests and, for what ever reason, his nephew William did not take on the business. The tanyard was probably no longer economically viable. The Briggs were shrewd entrepreneurs and would not have closed the operation if it were still a worth-while enterprise.

The Tithe Map of 1839 shows several outbuildings connected with the tannery. One barn-like building was still there in a rather derelict state until 1989 when it was taken down. A former resident of Slinfold remembered his brother working there as a gardener. He cleaned out the tanning pit and turned it into a pond stocked with goldfish. Another resident remembers as a child seeing numbers of cow horns stuck into the side of the stream; he thought they were to hold up the banks.

After the 17th century there is no further record of who was occupying the eastern cottage of Collyers until 1839 when Richard Gravatt, an elderly carpenter, was living there with his wife, Phyllis. On the death of William Briggs and his wife in the mid-1850s, the western dwelling was divided into two, the original timber-framed part being one cottage and the brick-built extension becoming a separate dwelling. Thereafter the three *Tanyard Cottages* as they were called, were occupied by various farm workers and general labourers. John Jeal was in No. 1 for many years and in the 1870s his teenage son, Jack, was working as a ratcatcher.

In 1910 William the younger's great-niece, Mrs. Elizabeth Newman, had the brick cottage greatly extended as a dwelling for her old age. Mrs. Newman owned both Hall Land and the three Collyers cottages. She had spent much of her widowhood at Hall Land before moving away from the area, but she clearly felt the need to return to her family roots. Her enlarged house is now simply known as Collyers, while the other two cottages are Nos. 1 & 2 Collyers. Mrs. Newman only dwelt in the house for a few years before she died in 1919. In her will she left all three Collyers Cottages to Harold Child of Ashlands, and he sold to Frederick Elliott in 1921.

Despite the considerable effect the tanyard must have had on village life when it was in operation due to the unpleasant odour associated with it, the industry itself has left very little mark on the village. Hall Land, and the brick-built addition to the timber-framed Collyers cottages with its subsequent Edwardian extension, are, however, a lasting memorial to the money generated by this profitable business.

Houses on Dedisham & Pinkhurst Land

HALL LAND (19)

As already mentioned above, Hall Land was built by William Briggs senior, with profits from the tanyard, on a plot to the west of the stream marking the boundary between Collyers and Hall Land farm. The plot was the northern part of George's Field, and was purchased in 1792. The whole field had been leased by the Briggs in connection with the tanyard operations for some 40 years prior to this. The new house was completed by 1796 and was thereafter known as *Tanyard House*. Its name was changed to *Hall Land House* in the 1870s. The main house is a square brick building under a tile roof. This roof appears to be hipped from all sides, which results from it being built round a central well. The front façade is symmetrical with a central porch. All the sash windows have been altered from the original small-paned type to Victorian sashes with four large panes. The lower wing to the rear looks as if it might be older than the front range. The part nearest the house is, however, almost certainly a contemporary service wing which has been later extended and there are modern additions in the angle of the wing and the main house.

Plate 12. *Hall Land House, c. 1920*

William senior, moved into the new dwelling, but continued to own Collyers where his son William lived. The two properties were held of different manors, Collyers of Dedisham and Hall Land of Pinkhurst. Manors had by this time ceased to have much influence, although William would have been very well aware of the manors to which his properties belonged and that he owed rent to two different manorial courts.

William the elder began to diversify into farming when he acquired Park Farm in 1804, although it was his second son, John, who went into farming in a big way. John must have had a flair for business and clearly had a London connection, as his only child was born in London in 1803, when he was 25. It was to John rather than to his eldest son, William, that William senior left all his property on his death in 1828. John then set about increasing his landholding. He bought Hall Land farm in 1837 on the death of Thomas Knight of Old House Farm, who had been the previous owner. Hall Land and Park Farm were the only two farms John owned, but he was also managing Gaskins, Ranfold, Hill, Rowfold, Windalls and Nowhurst and he farmed the largest acreage in the parish. In addition to the farms, he acquired the freehold of Churchyard Cottages. In his later life he felt able to call himself a 'gentleman'.

It is not known what John's business connection with London was, but it would seem that he was living up there part of the time. His wife Mary died in London in 1835 and was brought back to Slinfold for burial. Charles Knight, the Horsham grocer, reported that it was a very grand funeral for Slinfold, with a hearse and coach. People wore cloaks and silk hat bands and the cortège was followed by 24 men in *black round frocks*.

After this John appears to have spent most of his time at Hall Land and his widowed sister, Mary Casson, came to act as his housekeeper. Mary's son, William, lived with them and worked as a tanner journeyman for his uncle, William Briggs. John died in 1859 at the age of 80, and a stained glass window to his memory was placed in the chancel of the new church.

John and Mary's son, also John, kept the Slinfold properties and clearly spent part of the time at Hall Land, but he is always described as 'of London'. Like his father, he too called himself a 'gentleman' but on occasions he was referred to as a 'butcher'; he is likely to have been a cattle dealer rather than an ordinary butcher. It would appear that John the younger had overseas contacts as his daughter, Elizabeth, married Frederick Newman, a civil engineer who worked in Montevideo, and his son, another John, died in Montevideo at the age of 31.

With the death of young John there was no one to take over the family business when his father, John the younger, died in 1876. His estates passed to his widow and then to his daughter, Elizabeth Newman, who was by then a widow herself. Elizabeth stayed at Hall Land until the early 1900s, when she moved first to Hove and then to St. Leonards-on-Sea, before returning to Slinfold (see above, p.42). Hall Land was let to Charles England.

When the house was inspected for the Lloyd George's Domesday of 1910 it contained a dining room, drawing room, store room, smoke room, servants hall, kitchen, scullery, larder, two staircases, two WCs, six bedrooms, a bathroom and a cistern room, and the inspector noted that it was *an inconvenient house*. Outside there was a three-stall stable, coach house, harness room, coals, shed and large barn. Because Collyers and Hall Land had been in one ownership for so long, the original property boundary of the brook became unimportant and most of the plot that had formerly been part of Collyers was incorporated into the garden of Hall Land.

Elizabeth Newman was the last of her family and the estate was sold off on her death in 1919. Collyers was left to Harold Child, Churchyard Cottages were sold to the Parish, and Hall Land was sold to Colonel Yorke. He lived there for several years with his son and two daughters, his wife unfortunately having passed away. Thus began several fairly lengthy periods of owner/occupation by different families until 1966, when the present owners moved into Hall Land as their home in retirement. One notable resident was Lord Cornwallis who lived there with his wife for a time in the 1950s. He was then Lord Lieutenant of Kent and moved away to locate more conveniently in Kent.

With the increasing traffic along the Street it was felt necessary to abandon the old pillared entrance from the road to the front door, especially in view of the blind curve in the road at this point. There had been a well-worn track though the former tanyard linking the two properties of Hall Land and Collyers, and the new entrance further to the west utilised part of this track. The main approach was now to the east side of the house and a new front door was put into this face.

In 1986/7 Hall Land lost a substantial part of its garden to a development of new houses. The history of the area was recalled in the apt choice of Tannery Close as the name given to this new road in the village.

HIGH TREES (21)

High Trees was designed and built by Geoffrey M. Harris in the late 1960s for his own occupation. It was one of a pair (Conkers being the other) built on land which had belonged to Hall Land, but which had earlier been part of the Collyers plot. A similar house by the same architect was built in Fittleworth a few years later and received acclaim by appearing in the 1976 Daily Mail Publication *Bungalow Plans*.

The second occupants of High Trees were Mr. and Mrs. Alan Leslie. Barbara Leslie was an architect who used her skills to alter and improve the original design. In 1984 it was purchased by the present owners, Mr. and Mrs. David Bourn, who have made further improvements, so that internally the house is now nothing like the original.

It is a deceptively large and spacious home with a wealth of Colombian Pine beams throughout. In classic 1960s style it has many plain painted brick walls both inside and on the exterior.

THE RECTORY (formerly CONKERS) (20)

Also built by Geoffrey Harris, Conkers was originally designed to be occupied by a disabled person and light switches, sockets, etc. were all at a suitable height.

In 1987 Conkers became The Rectory. The upkeep of the old Rectory (now Ironwood House) had become too much for the majority of clergy to manage. Paul Knight agreed to serve as our Rector provided a more appropriate property could be found for him and his family, and Conkers was at the time on the market and was suitably located near the Church.

The house did not, however, have sufficient accommodation to meet the requirements of a Rectory. In 1989/90 the building therefore underwent drastic alteration and it now bears no resemblance to the original house. It is said that the only room not to have been changed during this refurbishment was the downstairs cloakroom!

There was in the garden of the property a barn-like building which had originally been used in connection with the tanyard. Older residents in the village, however, refer to this as the *theatre barn*. In the early 1900s it had a stage in it and was lit by lamps run on gas-oil like the street lamps of the time. Plays and concerts were held in here and it seems to have been a great success. By 1989, however, the building had become rather dilapidated and it was taken down to be reused elsewhere.

STANFORD HOUSE (29)

Stanford House stands at the eastern end of a long, narrow plot which abuts Collyers to the west (Map 3). Like Collyers, this holding of about one acre was enclosed from common land to the south of the church, and it too was held of the manor of Dedisham. It would have been occupied by an artisan supporting himself both by a craft and by growing a crop on the plot of land and perhaps keeping an animal or two.

The original cottage on this land would have had no garden in front of it and it would have faced on to the west side of the village green. The site of this building would have been a little further forward than the present house, level with the rear range of the Kings Head. The old name for this holding has been lost, the present name referring to the family who owned the property from the 1780s.

Nothing is known of the early owners and occupiers of the holding, the first recorded owners being the Shelley family in the mid-16th century. This branch of the Shelleys lived at Michelgrove on the Downs north of Ferring and they had extensive landholdings in Sussex, Kent, Essex and Warwickshire. William Shelley, Esq. was implicated in the 1572 Throckmorton Plot to murder Queen Elizabeth and place Mary Queen of Scots on the throne. He was attainted of High Treason and imprisoned in the Tower. Nothing could be proved against him, however, and he was eventually released in 1596. The manorial court records of Dedisham which refer to his attainder have the words *High Treason* written in red, even though they are 18th century copies of the originals.

The attainder meant that William Shelley forfeited to the Queen all the lands which he held, including those in Slinfold, and they later passed to King James I. William had had three farms in Slinfold, Nowhurst, Rowfold and Wild Harrys, as well as *two tenements in Slinfold Street*, which were Stanford House and the Kings Head. All rents from these properties had to be paid to the Crown rather than to the manor.

William's lands were eventually returned to his family in the early 1600s and all the Slinfold properties were purchased in 1606 by Thomas Churcher, Esq, who lived at Hill House and was related to the Shelleys by marriage. He would have looked upon the ownership of properties such as the Kings Head and Stanford House as a form of investment.

George Churcher, gentleman, inherited his cousin Thomas's estate when the latter died in 1616. George promptly went to the manorial court of Dedisham to enquire to whom he should be paying the annual rent of 6d for Stanford House. Did the rent still go to the Crown, or did it go to Dedisham as in the past? The court agreed to look into the matter and, although no answer is recorded, the rent was thereafter always paid to the manor of Dedisham.

After George's death c. 1651 the properties went to his nephew, another Thomas. During Thomas's ownership for the first time the name of the occupier is given. Matthew Turner lived in Stanford House for over 20 years, from before 1678 to 1695 or later. But there are no details of what he did. The occupants of the house for the first 300 years or more are singularly elusive.

Thomas Churcher, gentleman, mortgaged his farms heavily and on his death in 1705 they all, including Hill, had to be sold to pay his legacies. His will directed that any properties not sold should go to one of his sons, John, who thus inherited the Kings Head and Stanford House. John lived in Midhurst, but kept Stanford House until 1784 when he sold it to John Stanford of Theale.

From this point more is known about the occupants of the house. Samuel Briggs was already living there when John Stanford bought the cottage. He was a tanner who had previously been in Collyers before selling it to a relative. Samuel was in Stanford House until 1794, after which there were several short-term occupancies.

John Stanford made his will in 1809 and in it he left to his wife Sarah, for her lifetime, his *newly erected messuage and tenement with gardens and orchards in Slinfold now in the occupation of Edward Child*. The present Stanford House was thus built shortly before 1809. It is brick under a tile roof, the tiles being arranged in alternating bands of plain and fish-scale. The house had three reception rooms and a kitchen/scullery, four bedrooms and two attic rooms, as well as a cellar. One bedroom was later converted to a bathroom and two of the reception rooms were knocked together.

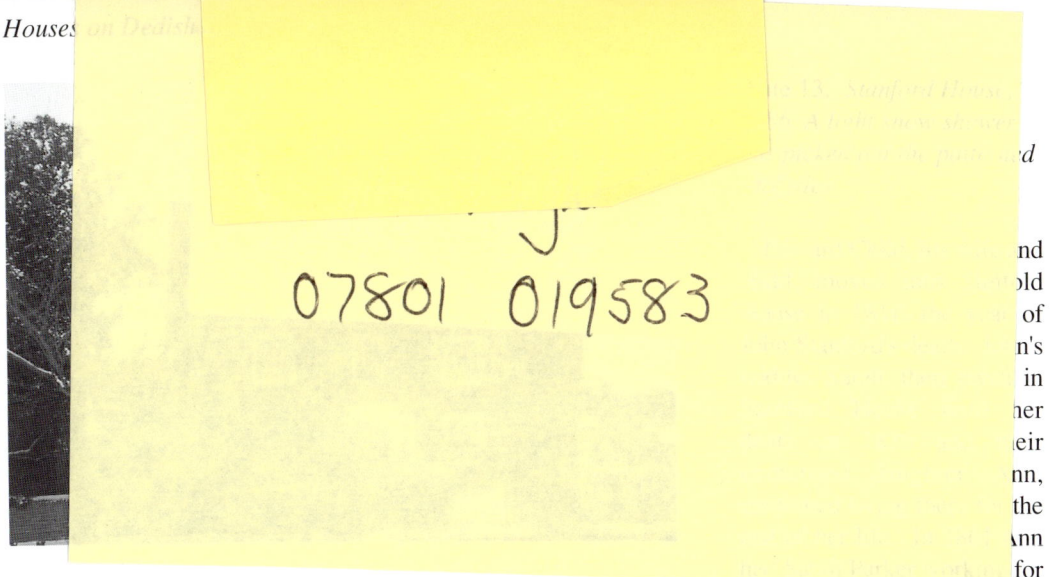

her as a general servant. Also lodging there was her husband, Philip Parker. He was a veteran of the Crimean War who lived to a great age. He had two other wives after Sarah and outlived them all.

The house was put up for auction when Ann Stanford died in 1874. It was bought by Philip Puttock of Lower Broadbridge Farm, who immediately sold to Caroline Puttock and her widowed sister, Susan Holden. Caroline died in 1884 and Susan in 1904, and the house was bought by Miss Steuart. It was during her occupancy that the property was enfranchised in September 1911. The centuries-old link with the manor of Dedisham was finally severed.

There have been a succession of owners during the 20th century, only the Williams staying for a considerable length of time, and the property has recently changed hands again.

CHEWTON (25)

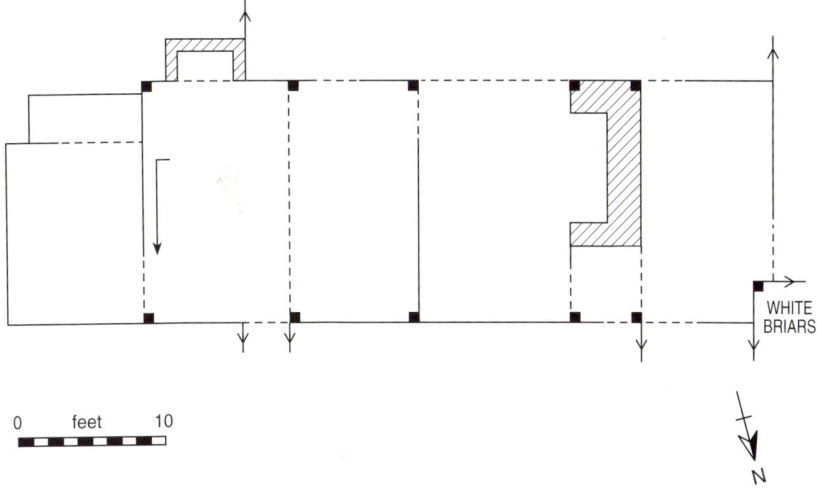

Fig. 9. *Ground plan of Chewton*

The large open space in front of the church and to the north of the plot of land belonging to Stanford House (Map 3) was enclosed by 1576, when the manor court of Dedisham wanted to know by what title John Stringer of Old House Farm held a croft containing one acre. There is no further mention of this property in the records of Dedisham manor, which suggests that when the cottage now known as Chewton was built on the plot a few years later it was let on a long lease, rather than being copyhold.

The new cottage was a four-bay building, the narrow bay at the western end being a smoke bay which was open from floor to rafters, with the smoke from the hearth on the ground drifting up and out of a hole at the apex of the gable. On the ground floor, the northern end of the smoke bay was partitioned off to form an entrance lobby. This lobby opened directly into the main room, the living room/kitchen which was heated by the smoke bay hearth. The central room contained the stairs while in the end bay was a service room. Above, the three chambers were open to the rafters. All the windows had diamond mullions and would have been unglazed. The majority were quite small with just three mullions and these would have had sliding shutters. The windows in the north wall of the kitchen and kitchen chamber were much larger, each having six mullions. The framing of the building, with its curving down-braces, creates a very pleasing effect.

Fig. 10. *Artist's impression of the original smoke bay house, built in the 1580s. Notice the smoke issuing from a hole in the apex of the gable*

By the 1630s the cottage was operating as an alehouse. At this time alehouses were ordinary dwellings which provided drink, food and sometimes lodging. In 1637 the *Weeping Eye alias the Star Inn* was let on a 21 year lease to Robert Strudwick, victualler. When the alehouse was sold in 1646 it was described as

> *The Inne, messuage or dwelling house situated in Slynfold street, commonly called by the name or sign of the Starre alias the weeping Ey, together with the barn, stable, orchard, garden and croft of land containing one acre belonging to the said Inn.*

William Duck and Anne his wife, one of the daughters of Richard Blount late Lord of the manor of Dedisham, sold the property to Richard Gardiner, mercer. Richard, who lived and worked at the Old Bakery/Village Stores, now owned the alehouse, but it was still let to Robert Strudwick. Robert was almost certainly providing lodging as well as food and drink since the alehouse was said to be an inn. The names Weeping Eye and Star are invariably used together when describing the property and there is no hint as to which was the original name of the alehouse. The Star is a fairly common name for an alehouse, but no other examples of the Weeping Eye are known. Village legend says that the alehouse was given the unusual name of *the Weeping Eye* because of its position immediately opposite the church. After a funeral the mourners could go in there to drown their sorrows!

The whole plot enclosed by John Stringer in the late 16th century kept the name of the Weeping Eye alias the Star and later buildings are referred to in deeds as being *part and parcel of the Star Inn otherwise the Weeping Eye*.

There is an interesting entry in the church vestry minutes for 1649 noting that the new seat in the church was built by Mistress Blount of Dedisham for *the alehouse called the Starr in the strete, and for davies cottadge and for the Rowadams*. Davies Cottage is Collyers and Rowadams was part of the property now known as Huntingrove. All the places belonged to the manor of Dedisham and clearly none previously had its own pew.

The 1651 map of the centre of the village (Map 5) shows Chewton, the only building along that stretch of the Street at the time, and it has a flag sticking out from it indicating that it is an alehouse. It is marked as *Naldreds ho*; perhaps one of the extensive Naldrett family had taken over the alehouse from Robert Strudwick.

Around 1680 Chewton's role was taken over by the purpose-built alehouse now known as White Briars and Chewton reverted to being an ordinary domestic dwelling.

Towards the end of the 17th century Chewton was updated by having a brick stack inserted within the smoke bay. This enabled the chamber above to be heated as well. The position of the adjacent property of White Briars probably accounts for the fact that the stack above the roof line leant at a considerable angle to enable the fire to draw. An elderly resident living in the property in the 1970s was concerned that this crooked stack might fall and had it replaced by a straight one; the fire has never drawn well since. The bresummer of the hearth is covered with a large number of ritual protection marks which were thought to prevent witches from coming down the chimney (see Fig. 13).

At the same time as the stack was built a door was inserted between the entrance lobby and the living room. This doorway has decorative door jambs which have ovolo mouldings ending in vase stops. Similar moulded jambs are found at Lower Broadbridge Farm, Dedisham Manor and Pinkhurst Manor (now Ye Old House and Doomsday Cottage), but in all these cases the lintel is also moulded. This, and the fact that all the other moulded doorways are in houses of some quality, suggests that the moulded jambs in Chewton came from another building.

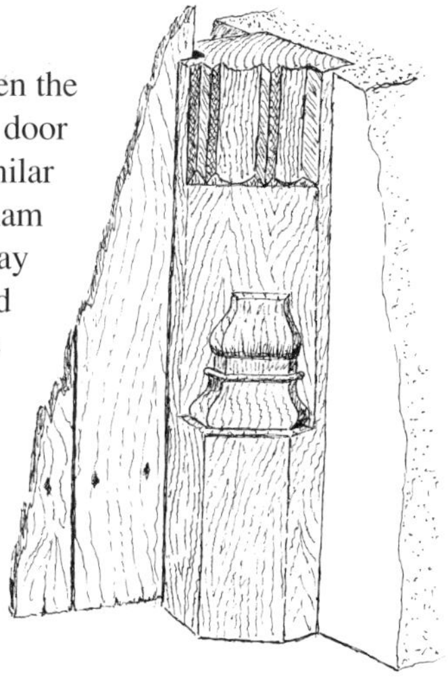

Fig. 11. *Re-used moulded door jamb. The doorway between the entrance lobby and the living room was constructed when the brick stack was built within the smoke bay*

The space beside the chimney and above the entrance lobby was made into a closet, lit by a small window. The space on the other side of the chimney was treated rather differently, however. It has within it an old ladder against the stack, going down from eaves level to below the level of the first floor. The only access to this space is from the loft. (The chambers would have been ceiled about the same time as the stack was inserted.) It may be that this was a bacon loft, but if so there is no evidence of how the smoke would have entered; nor are there any hooks or rails remaining and the ladder itself is not blackened. It seems possible that this area may have been intended as a space in which to hide things.

In the early 18th century an endshot was added to the west of the building, behind the chimney. It clearly post-dates White Briars as the corner post of the latter's stair turret intrudes into the endshot and is weathered.

While the development of the house itself can be traced, nothing is known of its owners and occupants for over a hundred years, from 1651 when it was *Naldreds house* until 1780 when records of the collection of the Land Tax list the names of those who owned it and those who were living there. George Naldrett was owning both Chewton and White Briars from 1780-85. Was there perhaps a connection with the earlier Naldred? One of the Stanford family was then the owner of both for 10 years, after which Chewton belonged to James Knight, the grocer until his death in 1801. The new grocer, Thomas Sturt, then took over the property. In 1818 he acquired White Briars as well and by 1839 Thomas owned 3 & 4 Church View, as well as Saddlers and Peppercorn Cottage. He thus owned the whole of the Weeping Eye plot.

Although the occupiers of Chewton are listed from 1780 to 1839, there is no indication of what they were doing. John Patching, who was in Chewton in 1830 and 31, had earlier lived in White Briars and was probably a relative of Thomas Sturt by marriage.

By this time Chewton would have been two cottages. An extension had been added to the east of the building in the late 18th century. The present front door was inserted to serve the eastern cottage, which was heated by a new stack erected to the rear of the original end bay of the house.

Plate 14. *Chewton before the crooked stack was rebuilt*

These two cottages would have had agricultural labourers or craftsmen living in them. In 1861 George Read and his family was in one of them. He was a carpenter and joiner who used the store and shed in front of the house in connection with his work. He came originally from Penshurst in Kent, while his wife, Elizabeth, was born in St. Pancras parish in London. Their first child was called George after his father, but the next two children were given names not normally found in this area, Evangeline and Lewis. It is surprising how often it is possible to tell that parents are not local by the names of their children. George's sister-in-law Susanna Harmer was with them at the time of the 1861 Census. She was an artificial flower maker and although she is not listed as a visitor, there surely would not have been sufficient demand for artificial flowers in the village.

During the 1860s Chewton and White Briars were owned by the then Rector, Frederick Vincent. Then, from the 1870s, both were owned for many years by the village butcher, firstly James Mitchell, then William Grinsted and finally Walter Herrington.

For around 20 years at the beginning of the 20th century Charles Dawe and his family lived in the western cottage. Charles and his wife had four children, a boy and three girls. The son, Robert, died at the age of four from rat poisoning. The youngest daughter was Connie who for many years ran the Village Stores and Post Office.

In the 1920s the Kinggetts lived in the eastern cottage and Miss Kate Kinggett worked as a dressmaker. She used to make dresses for Emily Grinsted of Amberfield, the wife of William who owned the butcher's shop. Emily's dresses were always the same, ankle length with a lace collar or fichu, and the best dress was always wine red.

From the 19th century the two cottages had been known as 5 & 6 Church View. The property became one again in the late 1930s and it was renamed *Chewton* after a West Country village by a retired schoolmaster, Mr. Corelli Stevens.

WHITE BRIARS (24)

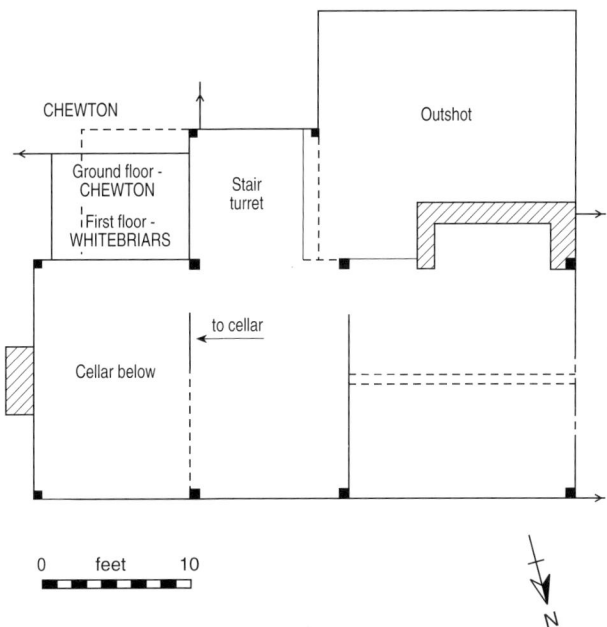

Fig. 12. *Ground plan of White Briars*

After the Restoration of the Monarchy in 1660 alehouses gradually provided better facilities, partly as a result of tighter licensing control. The building of White Briars around 1680 was a part of this move towards improvement; it is a purpose-built alehouse designed to take the place of the earlier alehouse at Chewton and it kept the same name of the Weeping Eye alias the Star. It stands immediately adjacent to Chewton, but further forward, probably on land that was still roadside waste at that time.

Although it does not now appear so, White Briars is a timber-framed building. The framing has brick infill rather than the more usual wattle and daub, and the whole has been rendered at a later date. It is also taller than most timber-framed houses as its roof is of a special form known as dropped-tie construction (Fig. 3). This means that the floor of the attic was some two feet below eaves level, giving attic rooms of good height. The building is of three bays, with a total of nine rooms on three floors. In a stair turret behind the central bay is a fine staircase with moulded balusters, which rises to the attic. This arrangement meant that no space within the main building was lost to the stairs. A brick stack to the rear of the western bay provided a large cooking hearth on the ground floor and a smaller hearth to heat the chamber above. There is evidence of an interesting division of labour when the house was being constructed. The carpenters left a large space in the framing of the back wall for the stack and when the bricklayers had finished building the chimney, they filled in the area between the stack and the frame with rather crude framing.

Fig. 13. *Ritual protection marks thought to prevent witches coming down the chimney. The top two examples are on the bresummer over the hearth of White Briars, while the other two are in Chewton*

The Weeping Eye had no cellar at first; fairly soon, however, one was dug out under the eastern bay. This caused a major upheaval since to minimise the risk of flooding, the cellar was not completely underground. Instead, the floor above it was raised, which in turn meant that the floor of the chamber above also had to be raised and the attic floor moved up to eaves level.

In the first half of the 18th century the alehouse was enlarged by adding an outshot behind the western end of the house which extended as far as the stair turret. This may also have had a cellar beneath it originally.

The ownership and occupation of the Weeping Eye is extremely elusive. It would seem that the Gardiners of the Old Bakery/Village Stores who bought the alehouse at Chewton in 1646, owned the new alehouse until the end of the century when there is an obscure deed mentioning Richard Gardiner, junior, and his wife Margaret.

There is a possibility that the Gardiner family were still connected with the Weeping Eye as occupants into the 18th century as a will and inventory dated 1734 survive for Martha Gardiner, innkeeper and widow. Although the rooms listed in the inventory could be related to the rooms at White Briars, Martha might equally have been running the Kings Head or the Crown (now Park House on Stane Street). But the contents of her cellars make interesting reading. She had forty gallons of home-made wines, 171 gallons of cider, sixteen full casks of beer and thirteen gallons of brandy. The wine, the cider and the beer were all produced on the premises. The brandy, however, raises the intriguing possibility of smuggling. Was the secret space beside Chewton's chimney a place where smuggled brandy was hidden? This is just pure speculation, however, and can never be proved.

Among the outdoor goods listed in Martha's inventory are one set of tenpins, one bowl and one sign. This evokes an interesting picture of people engaging in tenpin bowling in the road on a fine evening. But how annoying that the appraisers of the inventory did not say what was shown on the sign, so that the location of the alehouse could be confirmed!

Sometime prior to 1780 White Briars ceased to be an alehouse and became a private residence. In 1780 George Naldrett was the owner and the house was occupied by Charles Child, father of Edward Child the timber merchant. Charles himself was a carpenter who left Slinfold for Warnham around 1781. For much of the time, White Briars and Chewton were owned by the same person. After George Naldrett, Harry Stanford owned both properties and lived in White Briars. His widow, Mary, continued to occupy White Briars but sold Chewton. After Mary's death in 1816, her son-in-law Thomas Sturt, who had already acquired Chewton, took over White Briars as well. Thomas, the village grocer, let the property to various people, including his son-in-law, John Farhall in the 1830s.

The premises then became a butcher's shop. Around this time the place became known as Church View. The buildings to the east were often also referred to simply as Church View, although officially they were numbered. Peppercorn Cottage and Saddlers were Nos. 1 & 2, the pair of cottages next to Chewton are still known as 3 & 4 Church View, and Chewton itself was 5 & 6.

James Knight was the village butcher in the 1840s and 50s and it is almost certain that he was at Church View with his family. By 1851 there was a young lad, Harry Short, assisting James. There is no doubt that James Mitchell was at Church View in the 1860s and 70s. At first he was only the occupier and the property was owned by the Rector, Frederick Vincent, but from the early 70s James was both owner and occupier.

Plate 15. *Repairs to White Briars in the early 1980s allowed a rare glimpse of the timber-framing, which is normally concealed beneath rendering*

In the 1880s William Grinsted took over the business. For many years William lived in Church View and ran the business himself. He farmed Holmbush Manor Farm and was renowned in the south of England as the finest judge of a carthorse. Around 1900 William retired to Amberfield and the butcher's shop was taken over by Walter Herrington.

Walter bought the premises in the 1920s and continued to run the butchers for many years. His daughter, May, delivered the meat to customers. She carried a huge wicker basket, lined with a white cloth, with all the meat orders inside. One older resident described the butcher thus:

> *Mr. Herrington looked as though he should have been a member of the Diplomatic Corps, extremely distinguished and good looking, and he sliced off a large joint or a small bit of offal for the dog with the same grave courtesy, paying no regard to the considerable number of flies that hovered over the meat.*

There were several outbuildings associated with the butchers, including a piggery and a slaughterhouse. Some of the meat used to come from the cattle reared by Mr. Fladgate of Hill, and once a fortnight Mr. Herrington cycled to Pulborough market to buy animals. This averaged one bullock, eight sheep and four pigs. These would arrive at Slinfold by train and would be put into the field where Little Platt now stands. The animals were slaughtered by Mr. Herrington and blood used to run out into the road; it is said that all the dogs of the village used to go up there. It all sounds rather gruesome to us now, but villagers remember with pleasure the lovely meat and sausages supplied by the butcher.

The butchers finally closed in March 1952, when old Mr. Herrington felt unable to cope with the stricter refrigeration requirements which had been introduced. Thereafter the premises reverted to a private dwelling.

PEPPERCORN COTTAGE & SADDLERS (28)

In the later part of the 18th century, around a hundred years after White Briars was built, another property was erected on the Weeping Eye plot, at its eastern end adjacent to Stanford House. Peppercorn Cottage and Saddlers appear to be a semi-detached pair of cottages and indeed that is what they now are. However, the two parts are not mirror images and were used for different purposes. The building is divided unequally, the northern part (now Saddlers) being the larger. It had a large external stack and two rooms on each floor, plus an attic, and was always a dwelling.

The southern end (now Peppercorn Cottage) had just one room on each floor, with a cellar below, and it was originally unheated. By 1839 it was being used as a store and it would seem that this was its purpose from the beginning.

As with several other Georgian houses in the village, the brickwork of the front façade is a chequered pattern of red stretchers and blue headers, with an attractive dentil course under the eaves. The tile roof is half-hipped with windows below the hip to light the attic. Both cottages have been extended in stages to the rear, mostly over the past 40 years. Originally there were no porches, entry being directly in the front rooms. The window above the porches is a recent insertion, the casement being reused from the rear of the building.

Plate 16. *Peppercorn Cottage, on the left, and Saddlers. The modern extension behind the chimney of Saddlers replaces the shed in which the village bier was kept*

There is no record of who erected this building and nothing is known about it until the Tithe Map of 1839, at which time Thomas Sturt owned the whole of the Weeping Eye plot. He was using Peppercorn Cottage as a *storehouse*, presumably in connection with his grocery business, and he let Saddlers to Elizabeth Freeman. Elizabeth was an old lady who was described in 1841 as a schoolmistress. She must have been running a dame school from her house as the village school had yet to be built. She lived with her son, William, who was a carpenter and a twelve-year old servant, Mary Gravatt. She died at the age of 82 in 1848.

William Strudwick then moved into Saddlers with his wife, Sarah, and his 16 year old nephew, James Mills. Both William and James were agricultural labourers, and later William became parish clerk as well. By 1861 James had married and had a one-year old son, and they were all living in the house with their uncle and aunt. Whether James and his family moved elsewhere for a while or whether they were visiting friends or relatives on the night of the 1871 Census is not clear, but William and Sarah and a niece were in Saddlers on their own then. From the mid-1870s James and his wife, Charlotte, and their family took over the cottage, and they continued there until James died in the early 1900s and Charlotte a few years later.

After Thomas Sturt's death in 1855 the ownership of the Weeping Eye plot was divided. Chewton and White Briars were in one ownership, while the rest of the plot passed to Thomas Sturt's daughter, Mrs. Ann Farhall, and then to her son, Edward. John Freeman became the owner around 1880 and until his death at the end of 1925 he owned Peppercorn Cottage, Saddlers, Regency House and 3 & 4 Church View.

Peppercorn Cottage continued to be used as a store connected with the Village Stores, first of all by Charles Weakford and then by John Capon West. From 1898 to c. 1915 West's Stores only had the ground floor and the room above was used by William Albery, the harness maker. Albery's saddlery business was founded in 1780 in Pulborough by William's great grandfather. It transferred to Horsham in 1795, the main shop being at 49 West Street. William Albery succeeded to the family business in 1885 at the age of 21, with his mother and seven sisters to support. He used to walk out to Slinfold from Horsham once a week to work in the room over the store. Albery was well-known in the district as a calligrapher, musician, supporter of Horsham Museum and a chronicler of Horsham's history. For a time around 1970 the connection with the harness maker was commemorated when the present Peppercorn Cottage was known as *Alberys*. An older resident remembers that the store below was sometime used to keep people's furniture between moves.

There was a brick and tile shed against the external stack of Saddlers which, from 1901 to 1929 or later, was let to the churchwardens as a place to keep the village bier when it was not in use. At that time coffins were never carried, they were pushed on the bier. The bell was tolled at 12 o'clock on the day after a death, and then on the day of the funeral everyone in the village closed their curtains as the funeral was going by. If it was someone special there were flowers all over the cage over the bier. The Bier Room, as it was called, has been replaced by a kitchen for Saddlers.

Plate 17. *The decorated bier outside The Barracks*

In 1926, after John Freeman's death, all his properties were put up for sale and were bought by Henrietta Riddles of Farnham. Peppercorn Cottage was converted from a store to a dwelling which was heated by a chimney erected behind the south-west corner of the premises. Miss Riddles sold the properties in the early 1960s, after which they were owner-occupied.

3 & 4 CHURCH VIEW (26)

These semi-detached cottages were erected around 1800 as a response to the rising population of the time. They are brick-built, of red bricks only, under a shallow tiled roof which has interesting finials above the hips. The front façade, of Flemish bond, has horizontal sliding 'Yorkshire' sashes and matching gabled porches which are almost certainly a later addition. The cottages were constructed as a mirror-image pair with one central chimney stack and simple lath and plaster internal partitions. They were described as *very small* by the inspector for the Lloyd George's Domesday who saw them in 1914, at which time they each had two bedrooms above and a living room and scullery downstairs. Each had a timber and tile extension to the side, which in 1926 was functioning as a wash-house. They have been considerably but sympathetically extended in recent years.

As with Peppercorn Cottage and Saddlers, nothing is known about 3 & 4 Church View until 1839, when Thomas Sturt owned the whole of the Weeping Eye plot. The ownership similarly descended to Thomas's daughter, Mrs. Ann Farhall, then to Edward Farhall, John Freeman and Henrietta Riddles.

The cottages were occupied by farm workers or craftsmen. In the 1840s and 50s Richard Jayes the shoemaker was in No. 3. He had previously been in 2 Churchyard Cottages and he continued to work from an outbuilding near the churchyard even after he moved. He retired to Horsham after his wife's death in 1856 and sold the outbuilding to Charles Child. He lived with his daughter, a seamstress, in Horsham and died in 1862 at the ripe old age of 90.

Plate 18. *3 & 4 Church View in the 1960s*

No. 4 was occupied from 1870 to 1895 by a carpenter with the interesting name of Lorenzo Holland, but there is no hint as to how he came by this name.

Mrs. Blunden and her husband moved into No. 3 in 1927 and lived there for very many years. Her son, Ted, as a young lad tried to rescue Mr. Picton from the fire in 3 Churchyard Cottages in 1937. Mrs. Blunden was still there in 1967 when the cottages were put up for auction after Miss Riddles' death, at which time No. 4 was occupied by Miss Dorothy Cluer.

REGENCY HOUSE (27)

John Freeman acquired the eastern end of the Weeping Eye plot in 1878. By 1880 he had built Regency House as a tailor's shop and dwelling house for himself and members of his family. It occupies a triangular plot squeezed in between Saddlers and 3 Church View and, since it is taller than the buildings either side, it is rather dominating.

The building is L-shaped with a wide frontage and a narrower wing projecting to the rear. It is brick-built, the red bricks being laid in stretcher bond indicating the existence of cavity walls. The roof is slate-covered, with a rather shallow pitch, and the gables have simply decorated barge boards. It has three chimney stacks, one at each end of the main range and one at the end of the rear wing. The house contained three bedrooms and on the ground floor a kitchen, scullery and shop. The shop was double-fronted with the windows projecting forward either side of the doorway.

John Freeman was 25 when he built the tailors shop. He was born and grew up in the southern part of Cherry Tree Cottage, where he lived with his parents, William and Phoebe, and brothers Richard and William, both of whom became agricultural labourers. John, however, was apprenticed to a tailor, presumably one living locally since he continued to live at home.

Once the new shop was built, John moved in there with his elder brother, Richard, and the brother's wife and child. Richard and his family moved away and by 1891 John's elderly parents had come to live with him. They both died around the turn of the century. John continued to live there, looked after by his housekeeper, Mrs. Pipper. He advertised as a tailor in Kelly's Directory until the year of his death in 1925. An older resident remembers the tailor's shop well, but said the tailor was very old and she could never remember him doing any work. The premises were then bought by Miss Henrietta Riddles along with the surrounding properties.

Plate 19. *Topping out of the Village Hall extension, 1982.
Left to right: Andy Hillman, Terry O'Toole, Revd. David Chaning-Pearce,
John Mead and Dick Killner.
The photograph shows Regency House when its original shop windows were
in the process of being changed for the present bow windows*

The shop was let to Mr. and Mrs. Elliott who opened it up as a tobacconists and sweet shop. Afterwards W.H. Pescod took over and carried on with the tobacco and sweets. One person's childhood memory of the shop is as follows:

> *When we came out of school we went up to see Mr. Pescod. When you opened the door there was a bell on the top that went ding-ding, and we saw big jars of humbugs and toffees, a real oldy-worldy shop, and he used to come out and look at us and ask if we had any money. We would give him a penny and if that wasn't enough for humbugs and toffees, we would have a penny gobstopper.*

During the wartime people used to bring their accumulators for their radios to Mr. Pescod and he would arrange for them to be charged.

The Marleys came to the shop in the late 1940s and they sold groceries as well as sweets. Thomas Marley lived there with his wife and two daughters, who went to Slinfold School. He bought the freehold of the premises in 1960. He was a keen photographer and interested in local history. He used to give slide shows in the Village Hall of the material he had collected, and in 1975 he wrote a short history of the village. The shop closed after Thomas's death in 1979, and after almost 100 years the shop became a private dwelling.

In the early 1980s the people living in the house ran a local business called Regency Kitchens. They gave the house its present name of Regency House and tried to make the building fit the name. They removed the old shop windows (although the outer framework of these was retained), and installed pseudo bow windows. They also added mock shutters to the upstairs windows, and the large paned windows were later replaced with double-glazed units with imitation glazing bars.

Houses on Dedisham & Pinkhurst Land

LITTLE PLATT (23)

Little Platt is the final addition to the Weeping Eye plot. It stands on land which formerly belonged to White Briars and was used for keeping cattle waiting to be slaughtered. The slaughterhouse was at the eastern end of the plot. This is a modern house built in the 1950s, but using traditional designs and materials which blend in well with the older houses on this central village site.

Fig. 14. *Undated drawing of the rear of White Briars and its outbuildings, viewed from the plot of ground on which Little Platt now stands*

HOUSES ON BASSETT'S FEE LAND

Bassett's Fee was a Billingshurst Manor which held small amounts of land in other parishes. In Slinfold it had Nibletts and Pensfold Farm. Nibletts was enclosed from the common land after the building of the church and is situated to the south of the Dedisham enclosure. The farmhouse for the holding later became the Kings Head and the land fronting on to The Street south of the Inn was gradually built up from the late 16th century onwards.

THE KINGS HEAD (THE SLINFOLD INN) (30)

The Kings Head was originally a farmhouse with a small holding of land on the west side of the village street, known as Nibletts (Map 3). The farmhouse is one of the oldest buildings in the parish, dating to the beginning of the 15th century, and was a three-bay timber-framed house with one end bay floored to give an upper chamber. The remaining two-bay hall would have been open from floor to rafters and smoke from the hearth on the ground drifted up and out of the roof, leaving a thick layer of soot upon the roof timbers. The early farmhouse is incorporated in the rear range of the present building and the blackened timbers can still be seen.

Plate 20. *Soot-blackened crown post over the centre of the open hall*

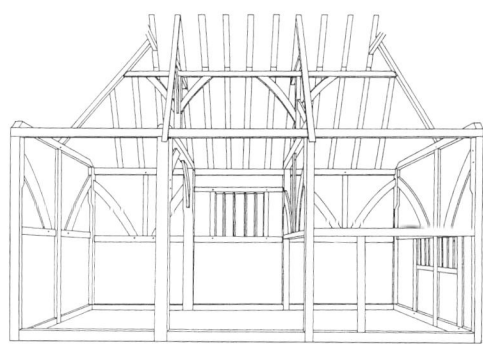

Fig. 15. *Framing of the farmhouse. The floored end is to the right and the two bays to its left form the open hall*

Since the holding of Nibletts was not very large, the owner had to diversify in order to support himself. The farmhouse was being used as an alehouse by the 17th century and possibly earlier, and a further source of income was generated by selling plots of land along the Street frontage. Again this development took place from the late 16th century onwards.

The earliest reference to Nibletts is in 1513 when it belonged to Bridget Hussey of Lower Broadbridge Farm. In the middle years of that century the holding, along with property on the adjoining land held by the Dedisham Manor (now known as Stanford House), was owned by the Shelley family. When William Shelley was attainted of High Treason in 1572 his lands were all forfeited to the Queen and these later passed to King James I who eventually returned them to the family in the early 1600s. In 1606 the Slinfold properties were sold to Thomas Churcher of Hill House and members of his family owned Nibletts until the 1760s, even though they had by this time left the village. The manorial court records refer to *heretofore Seamors*, suggesting that a person of that name was either owner or tenant at some time between the Husseys and the Churchers.

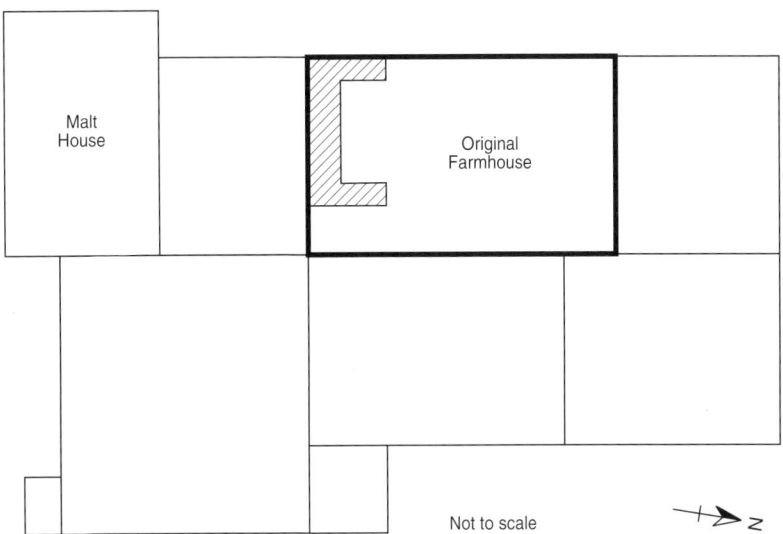

Fig. 16. *The original farmhouse (bold outline) is in the centre of the rear range and is now almost surrounded by later extensions*

The building has a long history as an inn. The manorial records refer to it as the *Red Lyon* in 1687 when it was occupied by a tenant, William Gatton, but on a map made in 1651 (Map 5) the farmhouse was labelled Francis House and was shown with a flag, indicating that it was already an inn. Prior to this, in the 1630s, the manorial court records for Bassett's Fee show instances of one John Penfold, victualler, being fined for selling drink in illegal measures *not sealed and of less than the standard of the King*. As Bassett's Fee had only one other property in Slinfold which was very unlikely to have been an alehouse, it seems reasonably certain that John Penfold must have been at Nibletts. There is further evidence in the inventory of his property made at the time of his death in 1647 which records chattels, land and livestock all of which are appropriate both to an inn and to the Nibletts holding in particular. John Penfold's will was proved by his wife Dorothy who appears to have been formerly called Francis. This is very likely the reason why the property is labelled as *Francis House* on the 1651 map.

During the long ownership of the Churcher family the inn was to change its name again. In a lease document of 1750 it was called *The Kings Head* and this was to remain the name for the next 250 years, until it became *The Slinfold Inn* in 1999.

By 1780 Charles Holden was the owner and occupier of the Kings Head. He was a blacksmith but not the first to combine this trade with that of innkeeper, as twenty years earlier Nibletts had been leased to John Poltick who was also a blacksmith. Bassett's Fee manorial records show that there was a smith's shop, as well as two dwellings, on part of the Nibletts land where the present day Holdens now stands. It would have been convenient for travellers to find accommodation at the inn and attention for their horses at the smithy next door. Charles Holden and his family must have been very prosperous as in addition to being blacksmiths and innkeepers, they were farming both the Nibletts smallholding and considerable other acreage in the parish. In 1851 the widow of Charles's son is recorded as farming 84 acres in all. Charles Holden senior owned not only the Nibletts property but all the land and buildings on the other side of the Street, now known as Cherry Tree Cottage and Slinfold House. It is hardly surprising that he felt able to describe himself as *gentleman* in legal documents.

The Kings Head Inn remained in the possession of the Holden family for more than 70 years. The son of Charles Holden, also Charles, inherited the property and his wife, Sarah, continued to run the inn long after her husband's death in 1836. The Census of 1841 records that Sarah Holden was the innkeeper and was living there with six daughters and one son, ranging in age from 25 to 7 years, and ten years later she is described as *victualler and wine merchant, and farmer*. In 1855 Kelly's Directory lists the Kings Head as a commercial inn and Sarah Holden as the postmistress as well as innkeeper. In recent years a local builder found an old wooden postbox while he was building the new door. The word **POST** can still be seen painted on one of the bricks beside the porch.

By 1859 Sarah Holden had moved into Rose Cottage, built on the site of the old smithy, and had presumably left the innkeeping to a tenant, as she was then 67. In 1865 the Kings Head was sold to a Horsham brewer, Henry Michell, for £1000 plus £100 for fixtures. Henry Michell's long period of ownership gave the inn continued stability and after his death in 1910, and a period of tenure by his executors, the inn was sold to the Rock Brewery Company who were still recorded in the Poor Rate Records as the owners in 1925. In 1941 a National Farm Survey, made in connection with war-time food production, recorded the owners as the United Brewery of Horsham.

Throughout all the years of different ownership there were often tenants in the inn and some of these continued in their tenancy even when ownership changed. George Grinstead and his wife ran the inn for Henry Michell for a few years but by 1867 Charles Reader was shown as occupying *house and garden*. In the 1871 Census there is the first mention of the *Kings Head Cottage* lived in by a young carpenter, William Stanford, and his family. This was presumably a part of the premises which Henry Michell had rented out separately from the inn. When the Rev. G.P. Crawfurd was recording his memories of Slinfold in the 1880s he mentioned William Stanford *who lived in an annex to the inn*.

Plate 21. *The Kings Head in 1907*

Charles Reader died a relatively young man and his wife Mary is recorded as the occupier in 1876 and as the innkeeper in the 1881 Census. Once again the Kings Head was being run by a widow, this time for nearly 20 years. In 1891 Mary Reader's household consisted of her two younger daughters, in their teens, her son Charles who was 27 and a tailor, two domestic servants and a general labourer, John Jeal. Four years later Henry Michell transferred the lease of the inn to George Wickham and there is evidence that Mary Reader occupied the Kings Head Cottage for the next few years.

George Wickham appears to have held tenure of the inn until the death of Henry Michell in 1910 when the Executors installed Barney Spence as the publican, and he remained there until around 1928. A postcard of 1910 depicted the Kings Head and described the publican, Barney Spence, as providing *Good catering for Parties, Luncheons and Teas*.

H.F. Meads was the innkeeper from 1929 until 1933, when E. Gray appears in Kelly's Directory. He was Major Edward Gray, and well remembered by older residents who were interviewed in 1987. The wartime National Farm Survey gave Mrs. G.G. Portsmouth as the innkeeper and she was followed by Mrs. Child, and after by Ted Thorpe. They are all still remembered by older Slinfold residents. By the 1960s the Kings Head had become a Whitbreads pub. For the past 12 years Nigel Evans has been the publican.

The inn premises are described in some detail in the valuations made in 1910. It was recorded as brick-built and tiled and containing Bar, Bar Parlour, Tap Room, Sitting Room, Kitchen, Scullery, Cellar, Dining Room, some 5-6 bedrooms, lumber room, 4 other small rooms, and a W.C. There were outbuildings which included quite extensive stabling, coachhouse and harness room, and an earth closet. There was no electricity, and no water supply to the farm buildings. The valuation makes no mention of the Kings Head Cottage which had presumably been re-integrated into the main house.

Although the Nibletts farmhouse was an alehouse from the 17th century onwards the occupiers also farmed the smallholding and this kind of dual occupation was very common. As late as 1851 Sarah Holden had been described as a farmer as well as an innkeeper and was farming far more than just the Nibletts land.

Any alehouse or inn would usually be one of the centres of village life, certainly for the men of the community. In 1866 members of the Slinfold Benefit Society, established in 1850, were holding their meetings in the Kings Head. The Rev. Mr. Crawfurd wrote *in the old days it was the club-house of the village* and went on to describe the splendid cricket banquet which took place annually at the inn in his day (the 1880s). The Post Office was run from the inn until about 1855 when it was transferred to the grocers and drapers shop run by Charles Weakford across the road.

Plate 22. *The Kings Head from the garden in 1989. The original farmhouse extends from the chimney to just beyond the climbing bush. The malthouse is to the extreme right*

In the early years of the 20th century all the stabling and harness room were rented out, at one time to a Major Fitzgerald who ran a riding-school, and at another time to a Captain Dance who kept several horses. During the 1920s a motor engineer, A.G. Stemp, ran the Kings Head Garage in the back section of one of the barns, and a sign-writer, Sid Torrington had his workshop in the front. The sign-writer was there for many years, certainly into the 1960s, and was still visiting the village to write cricket club signs in 1987. Another barn was used at one time by Charles Wadey, brother of the blacksmith, to carry out light motor repairs. Most of the outbuildings beside the inn were pulled down in the late 1970s to allow the creation of a car park. At one time the last Southdown bus used to park overnight behind the Kings Head, because the driver lived in Slinfold, ready for the first return to Horsham in the morning.

In the years before the second world war a succession of visiting cricket teams, notably the medical students from St. Thomas' Hospital, were remembered for their high spirits at the Kings Head, where they climbed on to the roof one year and dragged out wagons under repair in the Garage on another occasion. During the war soldiers who were camped in Clapgate Lane had their guard room in the Kings Head dining room and there are still memories of them tramping across from the inn to the outbuilding at Slinfold House where they had their canteen.

HOLDENS (31)

Holdens is an attractive Victorian house built on Nibletts land to the south of the Kings Head, on a site which had been occupied by a blacksmith's forge and two dwellings for over two hundred years. The Bassett's Fee manorial records of 1607 describe two properties on the site, one *a freehold messuage, smith's shop and garden* and the other *a leasehold house, backside and a little piece of ground.* The earliest record of a blacksmith tenant is of Reginald Gilbert in 1603. Four years later Gilbert had died and John Snelling was the blacksmith owner until his death in 1610. Snelling left a lasting mark on the property when he granted a lease on part of his property to tenants, and succeeding tenants, for 2000 years, at an annual rent of 1d.

During the 17th and 18th centuries many different owners and tenants occupied the two dwellings and the smithy. Whether the John Snelling who was in residence as blacksmith towards the end of the century was a descendant of the earlier smith of that name is not clear In 1616 the leasehold of cottage and garden was granted to William Cowper, a tailor from Rudgwick. He did not retain the leasehold long but passed it on to James Potter, another Rudgwick tailor, who paid a fee of £15 and the annual rent of 1d decreed by John Snelling.

In the 18th century a few family names appeared for quite lengthy periods as owners or tenants of the cottages and smithy. In the early years the blacksmith was George Farley but by 1744 the records show that the property was owned by Henry Penfold, a Yeoman of Slinfold, and his tenant was the blacksmith William Poltick, living there with his wife and family. The Parish Registers record that three sons of William and Elizabeth Poltick were christened in Slinfold, the first in 1732, so it seems probable that William Poltick was resident in the smithy well before 1744. The eldest son of William and Elizabeth, John, is known to have been the blacksmith in 1760, but living in the Kings Head next door as the innkeeper.. A William Poltick was also recorded as occupying one part of the property in 1772, possibly the second son of William and Elizabeth, who had married Ann Wood in 1763. Even though other blacksmiths came to work, and often live, at the smithy the Polticks were still marrying in Slinfold and having their children christened there until the beginning of the 19th century.

In 1771 Hannah Poltick, who could have been the widow of the blacksmith John Poltick, married Charles Holden and this marriage introduces another family who had a long association with the smithy property and with the Kings Head Inn next door. Charles Holden was certainly the blacksmith in 1770 and ten years later is recorded as the owner and occupier of Nibletts, i.e. of the Kings Head. Holden family papers indicate that a James Holden was a blacksmith in the 1790s and that David Holden was apprenticed to his Uncle James in 1805. The manorial records show Charles Holden as owner of the smithy property from 1804 until 1827. These latter references could be to Charles, the son of Charles and Hannah Holden, who inherited his father's property and dual profession in 1828. The younger Charles was to die in 1836 and his wife continued at the inn for over twenty more years. The Tithe Map of 1839 shows David Holden as the occupier of smithy and cottage, and the Executors of Charles Holden as the owners.

Before the Holdens became owners of the freehold property around 1804, it had been owned by members of the Knight family, relations of James Knight of the Village Shop. His niece, Sarah Bowyer, held it from 1786, first with her husband and then as a widow.

One of the tenants during their ownership was James Wensley, who lived there with his wife and family from 1790 to 1794. He was a Cornishman who had taken up residence in Billingshurst in 1781, where for some eight years he had earned a Government salary of £50 a year as an Exciseman. In respect of this sizeable salary he was rated in that parish, which entitled him to legal settlement there. For some reason he gave up his lucrative post and moved to Slinfold. By the winter of 1794 he was about to become a charge on the poor rates of the parish of Slinfold, something the parish was anxious to avoid. At that time he had eight children living with him, the youngest being only 10 months; his wife, however, was no longer with the family. The Slinfold churchwardens obtained an official order for the removal of James and his children to Billingshurst, *his last place of lawful settlement*. A few years later James was to be found in the Billingshurst workhouse, earning a little money by teaching there, and being given parish help to clothe a daughter and bury a son. The story of James Wensley is an interesting illustration of a man who had been doing well for himself, but who then went downhill in life until reaching rock-bottom in the workhouse. It raises intriguing questions. Why did he leave his well-paid post in Billingshurst? Had he committed some grave misdemeanour, or was he unhappy carrying out a universally unpopular job? What had happened to his wife by 1794? She had clearly been there a few months earlier when the youngest daughter was born, but there is no record of her death in the registers of Slinfold or any of the surrounding parishes. Her absence undoubtedly added to James' difficulties.

Meanwhile a third family name, Hull, became part of the history of the leasehold cottage and garden adjoining the smithy property and this family were eventually to have an important connection with the Holdens. In 1771 William Hull, shopkeeper, married Mary Peters who had been recorded as the leasehold owner from 1780 to 1797. By the following year William Hull appears in the Land Tax Records as both owner and occupier.

William and Mary Hull had two sons, William and Michael. The elder died in 1835 and by the time his father died two years later, Michael Hull, living in Wisborough Green and working as a tailor, had inherited both the leasehold and freehold property. Charles Holden had died in 1836 and had devised the freehold property to Michael Hull whom he described as his *son*. Michael held control over the entire site when his rights under the Holden will were established in 1841. He also owned the neighbouring property, now known as Little Hammers.

Around 1840 the blacksmith David Holden decided to move his smithy across the road. This marked the end of the two properties, freehold and leasehold, as described in the manorial records of 1603. The old smithy and dwellings were demolished and the Census of

1841 describes the site as *house building*. The ownership of the site at this time is unclear. Although Michael Hull had inherited it in 1836, Sarah Holden, the widow of his benefactor, was paying quitrent on the property in 1840 and by 1851 the Census records that Edward Holden and his wife were living in the new house, which was finished by 1843.

Plate 23. *Rose Cottage (now Holdens) around 1880. The ladies are believed to be members of the Holden family*

The house was built of brick under a tile roof, of simple design. By 1924 a sale inventory described it as having dining room, drawing room, study, kitchen and larder on the ground floor, above a large cellar. Three bedrooms, bathroom and lavatory, on the first floor, and a large attic, completed the house. The original combination of leasehold and freehold still existed and the 2000 year lease, established by John Snelling, is detailed in the sale brochure as a *small portion of property is Leasehold .... at a rental of One Penny per annum.* The ancient lease remained part of the property until sometime in the 1960s when the owners took legal action to end it.

Sarah Holden had continued as innkeeper and postmistress for twenty-five years after her husband's death but in 1861 she finally retired and went to live in the house next door. The Census for that year shows her there with several members of her family, including young grandchildren, and two servants. Ten years later she was still in the house, with two spinster daughters, Elsie and Maria, and during their ownership the house was named Rose Cottage. Elsie and Maria Holden both inherited Rose Cottage, in their turn, and the Holden ownership lasted until it was sold to Clifford Money, probably in 1905.

Clifford Money and wife gave the house a strange new name, Kei-a-Gomeena, but no explanation of this name has survived. Mr. Money had fought in the Boer War and it is possible that there might have been a South African connection. He was remembered in later years as having been an eccentric figure who cycled everywhere in his broad Boer War uniform hat. Clifford Money was associated with the production of rather special photographic postcards of local villages and events, a series called Rural England (see Pls. 8, 9 & 58). The actual photographer is believed to have been another Slinfold personality, William Waller, and Money was presumably the business side of the production of the attractive cards. Soon after his wife's death in 1922 Clifford Money moved to Horsham and a family named Milner Hay lived in the house for some time.

In the 1950s Commander Anthony Courtney MP and his wife, Elizabeth, lived in the house, which had now become Holdens. After the death of his wife early in the 1960s, Anthony Courtney sold it to her brother William Stokes. Holdens remained in the possession of the Stokes family for the next 30 years or so, until Mrs. Wendy Stokes moved elsewhere in the village only few years ago.

LITTLE HAMMERS (32)

Little Hammers is one of the older houses in the village and one of the few to retain its exposed timber-framing and Horsham stone roof. It was built in the late 1500s on part of the Nibletts holding of the Manor of Bassett's Fee and incorporated a number of re-used timbers from an open-hall house of c. 1400. The earliest part of the 16th century building is the main range of two bays and this was originally a low building having a height of only 10ft.6ins. to the eaves. It may not have been floored and appears not to have had any heating, which suggests that in the first years it was probably used as an outhouse or workshop of some kind. By the mid-17th century it had been converted to a dwelling by the addition of an external chimney stack to the south. Later the building was squared off by enclosing the space beside the chimney and in the early 18th century the cottage was enlarged by the addition of a crosswing to the north. At the same time the front of the roof over the main range was raised by 2ft.8ins.

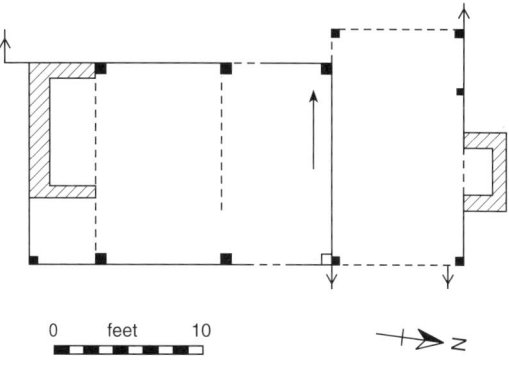

Fig. 17. *Ground plan of Little Hammers*

The first recorded owner of the property was Frances Penfold who left it to her grandson, John Chelsome of Rudgwick, sometime prior to 1711, by which date the cottage had passed to Sam and Mary Greenfield (née Chelsome). The property remained in the ownership of this family for some years as Edward Chelsome, brother of John Chelsome and Mary Greenfield, is recorded as the owner in 1725. Included in the property was a hogstye and small parcel of land which in 1711 was occupied by George Farley, who was the blacksmith at the smithy next door. John Chelsome, and after him the Greenfields, in fact owned the smithy, too. Various tenants lived in the cottage during the Chelsome-Greenfield ownership, including a cordwainer, John Groombridge, a Francis Stringer of Horsham and George Hersey, a gardener.

All the lease documents of this period refer not only to the hogstye and small piece of land but also to the right to draw water from the well at the smithy, as the property had no well of its own.

The access to this well became a bone of contention when the neighbouring properties had different owners, resulting in a legal agreement being drawn up in 1744. The smithy property was now owned by Henry and Joan Penfold and the cottage next door belonged to George Otway, a tailor of Horsted Keynes. The Penfolds erected a fence between the two gardens so that the tenant of Otway's cottage could not get through to the well. It was recorded that Otway had pulled down some five or six feet of this fence because he believed he had a right of access to the well. The legal agreement laid down that Otway should pay half the cost of digging the well deeper and should in future pay half the maintenance charges, including bucket, chain and rope. Further, Otway had to set up a stile or door in the fence at his expense and keep it repaired. For their part, the Penfolds agreed to allow free access to the well *with no other trespass on to their garden, provided Otway pays these charges within three months.*

In 1757 George Otway sold the property to James Gatford of Slinfold, a wheelwright, who did not live there himself but had John Newman and John Freeman as successive tenants. By 1772 James Gatford had died and the new owners (probably his heirs) were selling the cottage, hogstye and access to the well, to James Knight of the Village Shop. It is interesting to note that in the same year that George Otway had sold the cottage to James Gatford he had himself bought the Smithy next door.

Investing capital in property, however small, which could be rented out was an important aspect of yeoman economy and it is interesting to note how many houses in Slinfold were owned at this time by people who did not belong to the village. This small property had belonged to people from Rudgwick, Horsham, Cuckfield, and Horsted Keynes. From 1785 to 1804 it was owned by William Stanford of Broadbridge Farm, Broadbridge Heath. He sold it to William Hull, described as a Slinfold shopkeeper, who was still in possession at the time of his death in 1837. His son Michael Hull, a tailor in Wisborough Green, is of some importance in the intermingling history of all these adjacent buildings, as Charles Holden, blacksmith and innkeeper, bequeathed the smithy property to him in 1840, while he inherited the adjacent leasehold property from his father. Michael Hull inherited Little Hammers from his father, too, but he sold this to Thomas Child in 1841 and it remained in the ownership of the Child family for over 100 years.

When William Hull bought the cottage in 1804 it was occupied by Philip Constable, and the Land Tax Records show Michael Constable as living there from 1809 to 1831. The 1841 Census lists the occupiers as Michael Constable and his wife, Elizabeth, and John Patching, a carpenter. Michael was a casual agricultural labourer who had worked for the farmer Philip Holland and the Holland Account Book for the period from 1805 to 1814 shows the great variety of heavy agricultural labour which Constable carried out and the wages which he earned for each task (see p.18). These were the prosperous years for farmers and their labourers, but in the agricultural depression after 1815 someone like Michael Constable might not have fared so well. The 1851 Census shows him still living in this property, aged 75 and described as a pauper and ex-agricultural labourer. In the same Census five other agricultural labourers were shown as living, or lodging in the premises.

From 1841 and probably earlier the cottage was being let to two families. This was at the time when houses were being split into two or more dwellings to accommodate the rise in population and several Slinfold houses suffered this sub-division. During this time it was named Forge View, because the smithy was by this time opposite on the other side of The Street. From the 1860s until the 1920s the Poor Rates Records give two tenants in the premises, one in the north half and one in the south, and the same names remain on the list for some years. From 1867 to 1876 James Grinstead was living in the south part and Frank Wadey, junior, who worked at the forge, was in the same half from 1892 until 1910. Successive members of the Clark family occupied the north half from 1876 until the 1920s.

Plate 24. *Forge View in the mid-1920s. Fred (on right) and Arthur Dinnage*

Plate 25. *Little Hammers after renovation. The ends of some of the rafters from the lower roof can be seen*

By the mid 1920s Forge View was occupied by the family of Frederick Dinnage and the family of Michael Clark, and with the aid of photographs and living memory the story of the cottage can become more detailed. A photograph of this period shows it to be have been weather boarded beneath a Horsham stone roof. A low wall, topped with iron railings, marked the boundary with the footpath and road, and two boys stand either side of the gate. They were Fred Dinnage who would become a wheelwright, and member of the Slinfold Fire Brigade, and who was killed in service as an airman during the 1939-45 war, and his brother Arthur. Arthur worked for most of his life as the delivery man for the Slinfold Stores and is well remembered with affection by many present-day Slinfold residents. Michael Clark worked in Mr. Child's timber yard beside the railway station and his grandaughter, May Hodgson, remembers: *They* (the two families) *shared the same front door and staircase before parting left and right, two bedrooms to each half, but had separate back doors and long gardens. My grandfather had a pigsty at the end of his, and salted down his own pork in large earthenware crocks.*

For about 15 years in the 1930s and 40s Forge View was lived in by Miss Alice Farley to whom it was leased by the last Child owner, the widow of Harold Child who was Thomas Child's grandson. When Mrs. Child died in 1950 and the cottage was in the hands of her executors, it stood empty for some years until it was sold to Mrs. Winifred Pratt in 1958.

By this time Forge View was once again one dwelling and the weather boarding had been removed to expose the timber framing. In 1965 the cottage was sold to Miss Pamela Foulkes, who moved into Slinfold from Horsham, and she renamed it Little Hammers.

Little Hammers shows an interesting sequence of development, from an outbuilding of the late 1500s, built with timbers from a much earlier open hall house, to a sought-after residence in the late 20th century.

CHAPEL COTTAGE (33)

The earliest part of Chapel Cottage was built during the second half of the 17th century on land belonging to the Nibletts holding. It was a three-bay house with the narrow central bay containing the chimney stack; the main entrance opened into the eastern end of this central bay and in the entrance lobby there would have been three doors giving access to the rooms on either side and to the staircase which was beside the chimney. On the first floor there were doorways to each of two chambers and the staircase continued up to two rooms in the attic. The overall size of this three-bay house may not have been large by modern standards but the total of six rooms was more than would have been found in many dwellings of the period. Each of the ground-floor rooms was heated by a hearth, the one in the northern bay being the larger because this was in the kitchen and it was used for cooking. There would certainly have been a bread oven within this area, too. The two chambers on the first floor were also heated. It was a plain but solidly built house with fashionable brick infill to the timber-framing and a roof of Horsham stone.

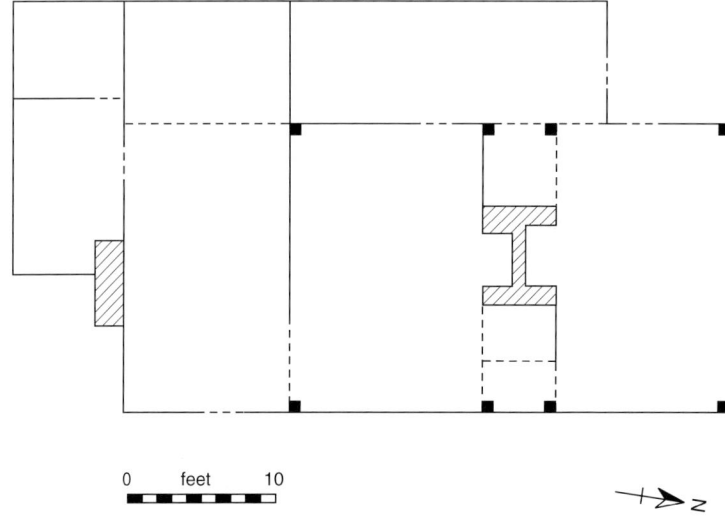

Fig. 18. *Ground plan of Chapel Cottage*

This timber-framed house was the first built on a fairly sizeable plot which included the land on which the chapel and Taylors were later built. The whole of this plot was called *Taylors*, although it is not known whether this referred to the name of the first inhabitant or his occupation.

There are no records of owners or occupants until the 1730s, when James Gatford was living there. He was a wheelwright and, although it cannot be proved, he was probably operating from a workshop on the site of the later wheelwrights, which has since been replaced by the Chapel. In 1736 he took on a young apprentice named James Older. In 1754 James Gatford bought the adjacent Little Hammers as an investment.

By the mid-1770s the Patching family of wheelwrights had taken over the premises from James Gatford. John Patching was followed by his eldest son William who was there in 1775. William had married Mary Butcher in 1774, dying only ten years later at the age of 57. His widow and her family remained in the house until her death in 1829. There are baptismal records for two sons and three daughters of William and Mary, two of whom died young, and at the time of her death the property was to be divided between George Patching *only son and heir* and one grandson and two grandaughters who were the children of William and Mary's daughters who had predeceased her. The younger daughter, Sarah, had married Thomas Sturt the grocer.

At some time towards the end of the 18th century or the beginning of the 19th century the house had been enlarged with a brick extension at the southern end and a single-storey extension at the rear. The rear extension is probably contemporary with the southern addition and both would have been added when the house was divided into three cottages. When the southern extension was built, the building was updated by rendering the whole front façade and inserting new windows.

William and Mary's son and grandchildren jointly sold their property to William Williamson in 1830 when it was described as *All that messuage or tenement garden and detached woodhouse and also the wheelwrights shop and the buildings and garden thereto belonging situate on the south side of such messuage etc first described and being in the parish of Slinfold and were called by the name of Taylors ....*

By this time Chapel Cottage, as it became known later, had been divided into three dwellings and the Tithe Map of 1839 shows all three in the ownership of Williamson and occupied by William Whittington, James Mills, and James Knight. In the 1841 Census one cottage is being lived in by Henry Parkhurst, a wheelwright, and his family and also by James Ireland, described as a wheelwright apprentice.

The cottages remained in the possession of the Williamson family for the next 85 years, passing to William's sons, David and William, when he died in 1866, and to his grandsons, Frederick and Albert in the will of their father, William Williamson the younger, twenty years later. Under the will of the elder William his daughter Esther was to receive rents from the property and she is shown as the owner until 1905 in the Poor Rates Records. David Williamson was still the surviving trustee of the will of William Williamson, the elder, and in 1908 he and other Williamsons (presumably of the next generation) sold the cottages to his son, David the younger. David Williamson the Elder was a J.P. of Guildford and the younger members of the family involved in the sale were severally referred to as an upholsterer, an auctioneer, a civil engineer, and a gentleman. None of them was living in Slinfold, and the new owner, David, was a journalist from Bromley.

The Poor Rates Records indicate that for a period in the late 1890s and the early 1900s the cottages were called Beehive Cottages. By 1910, when David Williamson the younger was shown as the owner they had apparently lost this name and were not given another until the records of 1925 which refer to 1, 2, and 3 Taylors Cottages.

During the years of Williamson tenure the three cottages were lived in by tenants who often stayed there with their families for years. After Henry Parkhurst in 1841 no wheelwright appeared in the records until a Mr. Brown in 1861. George Farley, an agricultural labourer, and his family were in one cottage from 1851 to 1876; Matthew Freeman, a bricklayer, was in another from 1867 to 1900; Thomas Redman was there from 1892 to 1905; John Knight, another agricultural labourer, was in one cottage in the early 1900s, and when George Holland and his brother Luke (one a farm labourer and the other a stone quarryman) were there in 1891 they had a 14 year old grocer's errand boy, Maurice Stemp, lodging with them.

All these are surnames which crop up many times in the history of Slinfold. In a small village community there would always have been inter-marrying, with the same families appearing in different houses through the years. In the case of the Kings Head, the smithy and all the other small dwellings on the Nibletts land, it is often difficult to disentangle the families who were either owners or tenants. There are no indications whether Henry Penfold who owned the smithy property in the 1740s was a descendant of Frances Penfold who owned the Little Hammers cottage prior to 1711, or indeed whether either of them was connected to John Penfold, innkeeper in the 1630s. Could the Maurice Stemp, aged 14, who lodged in one cottage in 1891 have been eventually connected to the A.G. Stemp who ran a garage at the Kings Head in the 1920s?

Plate 26. *Chapel Cottage in 1986*

In 1918 David Williamson sold the cottages to a Miss Helen Pickering of Hove and she had sold each of them, separately, by 1925. By 1930 all three cottages had been bought by Mrs. Maud Coombs of Fulham and remained in her ownership until 1940. They were still described as three cottages when they were eventually sold to Eric Trotman in 1958 who converted them into a very attractive house. Mr. Trotman's widow, Barbara, still lives in Chapel Cottage.

Interviews with older residents in the late 1980s produced memories of Chapel Cottages in the 1920s, and especially of Miss Edwards who lived in the middle cottage. Miss Edwards sold sweets and postcards to the village children but was especially remembered because she looked after homeless girls: *waifs and strays came from some religious thing*. She was said to have three or four at one time, in this very tiny cottage, and two of them were recalled as Irene and Dolly Lewin. One of the Lewin girls married a man called Steer: *They used to run the Chapel, Christian Endeavour and things like that in the Chapel*.

SLINFOLD CHAPEL (34)

The land on which the chapel stands is part of that section of the Nibletts holding, of the manor of Bassett's Fee, referred to as Taylors in the 18th century. Documents relating to the sale of Chapel Cottage in 1827 refer not only to the cottage but also to *the wheelwrights shop situate on the south side of the tenement, which tenement, wheelwrights shop, garden and premises were part and parcel of .... Taylors formerly in the occupation of James Gatford, afterwards John Patching and since Mary Patching*. This suggests that the wheelwrights were operating from a separate outbuilding adjacent to Chapel Cottage from at least the mid-18th century, when James Gatford was living in the cottage and working as a wheelwright. He was succeeded by various members of the Patching family, whose story is told in the previous section on Chapel Cottage. Mary Patching continued to hold Chapel Cottage and the adjoining wheelwrights shop until she died in 1829.

The Tithe Map of 1839 shows William Williamson as the owner of Chapel Cottages (the original cottage had been divided into three dwellings), and Thomas Sturt and William Williamson as the joint owners of the wheelwrights. Thomas Sturt, whose first wife was Sarah, daughter of William and Mary Patching, ran the village stores and acquired a considerable amount of property in Slinfold.

In 1841 Henry Parkhurst, wheelwright, and his family were occupying the premises with James Ireland, a wheelwright apprentice, and Caleb Holden, carpenter. Ten years later the Census did not record an entry for the wheelwrights but the 1859 Kelly's Directory listed Henry Parkhurst as blacksmith and by 1861 he was known to be a master blacksmith and wheelwright and living in Forge Cottage across the road.

The first references to any kind of chapel in Slinfold were to Hayes Chapel in 1812. This early place of worship for *Independents* (who were later to become the Congregationalists) was sited in a wing of Hayes House (now Slinfold Manor) by the owner, John Croucher, at about the same time the first chapel for Horsham Independents was being built. The Hayes Chapel functioned until his death in 1827, when the worshippers apparently transferred to the Chapel in Billingshurst, which had also been built by John Croucher.

The Sussex Census of Churches in 1851 has no record of a chapel in Slinfold, although in later records of the Sussex Congregational Union there is reference to a chapel in Slinfold which was said to have been founded in 1850 and rebuilt in 1878. This conflicts with the Congregational Year Book which first refers to Slinfold in 1869 as having been *formed in 1858.*

Certainly there was some kind of chapel in Slinfold by 1868 as in that year the Sussex Home Mission asked the Horsham Congregational Church to make provision for regular preaching in Slinfold.

The Year Book recorded the Slinfold Chapel as an out-station of the Horsham church from 1869 to 1873, and every year from 1875 to 1959 as either an out-station or branch church of Horsham. There is no indication of why there is no record for 1874-75.

Plate 27. *Datestone of the new Chapel. The only other building in the Village with a datestone is the Village Hall. The Church has a dated foundation stone*

By 1878 the new chapel in Slinfold had been built, largely through the instigation and financing of Mr. Thomas Vickress, a staunch supporter of the Congregational Church, who lived at Hill House. When the Women's Institute made a Slinfold Scrap Book, as part of a national initiative in 1948, they recorded that the Chapel of 1878 was built on the site of an old one *the date of erection of which is not known but it was a smaller building and the back of it was a wheelwright shop which was divided from the Chapel by a wooden partition.*

Plate 28. *The present Chapel, built by Thomas Ayling*

In 1948 the compilers of the Scrap Book had interviewed Mr. Frank Wadey, wheelwright and smith, who had been organist at the Chapel for 62 years. He would have been 11 years old at the time of the rebuilding and presumably the description of the old chapel was based on his memories. In 1934 Frank Wadey had been presented with a testimonial by Congregationalists on the completion of 50 years as organist at Slinfold Chapel. The presentation was reported in the West Sussex County Times & Standard and the following week the newspaper published an interview with Mr. Wadey. It dealt largely with his experiences as blacksmith, but his organ playing was also mentioned and the article stated: *The Congregational Chapel at Slinfold .... was originally held in what had been a wheelwright's shop.*

The new forge had been built across the road at the beginning of the 1840s and Henry Parkhurst, as already mentioned, was known to be working there by 1861. If the first Slinfold Chapel was founded in 1858, as the Congregational Year Book says, then perhaps it was in a disused and converted wheelwright's shop, rather than in just part of it (see Pl. 29).

During the early years of the 20th century a Rev. W. Talbot conducted a number of revivals and missions in Horsham and the village chapels. Of Slinfold it was reported: *People had attended in growing numbers and the Chapel was well filled. Although there were no definite cases of conversion, there were signs of spiritual interest that gave promise of future harvest.* A few months later, however, the reports from Slinfold were not so rosy. Attendance had fallen off disastrously (an evening service had been attended by only one person) and the reason given was the arrival in Slinfold of a certain Mr. C., a faith healer, who had apparently been holding break-away meetings in his house. Chapel members were exhorted to be strong in their allegiance to the chapel and to ignore the doings of the new arrival. Shortly afterwards an evangelist, Mr. F. Cranham, was appointed to work in the village chapels, especially in Barns Green and Slinfold, and in December 1906 the village congregations were speaking warmly of his services.

Three pastors were recorded in the Year Book as working in Slinfold Chapel in the period from 1907 to 1917: Mr. Cranham, Mr. George Millar, and Mr. J.Couchman and, it added, *otherwise supplied from Horsham.*

During his newspaper interview in 1934, Frank Wadey, had regretted that the Slinfold Chapel was not as well attended as it once was. He said that a congregation of 20 was the maximum then but that 40 years earlier services had been attended by 60 to 80 people, there had been a choir of 25 and a successful Sunday School. Mr. Wadey blamed the First World War for much of this decline but later interviews with elderly Slinfold residents remembered the Sunday School and many other chapel activities in the 1920s, referring to the Christian Endeavour meetings and the Church Army. There were memories of the Church Army coming round with a caravan and holding services in the chapel.

The Lloyd George's Domesday included a report in 1914 of the Chapel which was a brick and tile building in good condition, described as *Chapel, Vestry, only services of religious nature*.

In more recent years the Congregational Church became part of the United Reformed Church. The Slinfold Chapel, as a branch of the Horsham United Reformed Church, has regular services taken by visiting ministers.

TAYLORS (35)

In the accounts of both Chapel Cottage and the Chapel reference has been made to the part of the Nibletts holding on which they were built and which was generally known as *Taylors*. When George Patching, the son of William Patching, and his relatives sold his parents' property after the death of his mother, Mary, in 1829 the manorial records referred to the messuage which was divided into three tenements (Chapel Cottage) and to a *newly erected Messuage nearly adjoining*. This new building was the house now known as Taylors and its first owner was Thomas Sturt, who at the same time had bought part ownership of the wheelwrights shop next door.

The Tithe Map of 1839 gives Thomas Sturt as the owner of the house and of the orchard beside it. The following year, in 1840, there is a record that Thomas Sturt had enclosed part of the manorial waste in front of his messuage and that he had to pay 2d a year for it, and by 1847 he had enclosed another piece of land alongside his house for which he had to pay a further 2d a year. These enclosures are part of the early 19th century trend to enclose manorial waste to create gardens in front of properties.

The house, which must have been built about 1832, was a simple double-fronted brick building, with tiled roof, very much in the style of the period when Georgian simplicity had not been affected by the later Victorian embellishments.

The Census in 1841 showed George Whittington and his family as occupying the house and they were still there ten years later. George was an agricultural labourer who was presumably working on one of Thomas Sturt's farms. In 1861 James Grinstead and his family were living in Taylors and this was the beginning of a long family association with this house. During the first few years James Grinstead was a tenant and the property was owned by Mrs. Farhall. Mrs. Farhall was Anne, the daughter of Thomas Sturt by his second wife, who had married John Farhall.

James Grinstead became the owner of the house and land in 1867, having taken out a mortgage with the Horsham Permanent Benefit Building Society. James Grinstead was a farmer of some 110 acres, including the land immediately behind and adjacent to the property. His eldest son, Alfred, a master carpenter, and Alfred's wife Mary were also at Taylors. James had moved away by 1871, but Alfred and his wife, afterwards his widow, continued at Taylors until 1920.

Alfred Grinstead, the master carpenter, became a master builder and carried on a very successful business from Taylors. On the adjoining land which had earlier been an orchard was a carpenter's workshop (Pl. 30) and in the 1870s Alfred had two young journeymen carpenters, both relatives, living with him. On occasions he worked with Thomas Ayling, the master bricklayer who lived across the way in Chapel View, their respective businesses being complementary. It is interesting that Thomas Ayling styled himself a builder rather than a bricklayer only after Alfred's death.

Plate 29. *Taylors before the building of the new Chapel.*
The nearest of the two outbuildings to the right of the picture is now a part of Taylors, while the further one is most likely the earlier Chapel

Alfred Grinstead was a very well-known member of the Slinfold community in his day. He was a keen cricketer and the Rev. G.P. Crawford in his article *Slinfold Fifty Years Ago*, written in 1932, painted a delightful picture of him .....*Alfred Grinstead, the builder and carpenter, upright honest man, a mighty smiter at the wicket, but too bulky to run his own runs* .... Perhaps that bulk was in part responsible for an early death because by 1891 when Alfred would have been only 57, his widow Mary was running the building business. Mary Grinstead continued to run it for many years and was still living in the house in 1915 when she was 79 years old. At some point during the Grinstead ownership the house became called *Hyrstlea* and remained thus until it was re-named *Taylors* in the late 1940s.

Hyrstlea was on the market, apparently being sold by the children of Mary Grinstead, in 1920, and again in 1925, and brochures for both these sales still exist. The house was then described as having four bedrooms, two reception rooms, kitchen, pantry and coal cellar, with outside wood store and W.C. Both sales notices included an adjoining plot of land which contained a carpenter's shop and other outbuildings.

In 1947 Hyrstlea, soon to be re-named, was sold to Mr. Edwin Wood and he lived there with his wife and family until his death in 1963. His widow, Mrs. Janet Wood, stayed on until 1972 and many present Slinfold residents remember the elderly Mrs. Wood, largely because she kept goats in the outbuildings! Taylors was bought in 1972 by Miss Vivian Hamilton (later Mrs. Lauder) who still lives in the house.

CANDLEFORD (36)

The land upon which Candleford stands was enclosed by 1789, when it was described as a *garden*, and the manorial boundary between Pinkhurst and Bassett's Fee went across the middle of it (Map 7). Fifty years later the garden had been planted as an orchard. During the time James Grinstead was at Taylors, outbuildings were erected on this land and in the field behind (see p.82). Most were connected with farming, but one large building on the Candleford plot was used by James son, Alfred, as a carpenter's shop. This carpenter's shop and the plot of land continued as part of Taylors until the mid-20th century.

In the Lloyd George's Domesday of 1914 four outbuildings are detailed as *a timber and tile shed, timber and tile stable, brick and tile workshop, timber and tile lean/to*. The sales brochures for the property in both 1920 and 1925 describe a carpenter's shop, with loft over, a paint shop, cow stalls and cart shed.

Plate 30. *The carpenter's shop belonging to Alfred Grinstead. This photo is contemporary with Plate 29*

For a period during the 1930s the outbuildings became a small factory making chip baskets for soft fruit. It was owned and run by a Mr. Alfred Cox who lived in the house, which was now Hyrstlea, and gave employment to some of the village girls when they first left school. There are still older residents who remember working there for about £1 a week (see p.24). There are also memories of the later period, in the 50s and 60s when these same outbuildings housed Mrs. Wood's goats. Photographs of the outbuildings taken in the 1930s suggest that the earlier carpenter's shop had undergone considerable rebuilding. The outbuildings were largely rebuilt in the late 1970s and early 80s, when the conversion to a dwelling took place. The present Candleford is a much lower building than the original workshop shown in Plate 30.

MORE HOUSES ON PINKHURST LAND

The manor of Pinkhurst had land in Slinfold and Billingshurst. It held farms on both sides of Hayes Lane, Wild Harry's to the east and Hall Land to the west, so the whole of the lane was considered to be manorial waste. Pinkhurst was a manor which discouraged settlement on the waste, unlike Dedisham, and no cottages were built on the roadside of Hayes Lane until the 18th and 19th centuries, by which time manorial control had become very weak. In fact when Stone Cottages were built, the parish considered it owned the land.

YORK COTTAGE (39)

York Cottage was built in the early 1890s as a home for Charles Weakford on his retirement from the Village Stores. The post office, however, moved with Charles to his new house and for a few years was run by his daughter, Ada, from the right-hand front room. The small extension on the side of the house to the right of this room was an entrance lobby so that customers did not need to use the front door of the house. By 1905 the house was owned by Harry Garton, though members of the Weakford family continued to live there until around 1915. Then for some years Miss Tebbit ran a private school from the left-hand front room. This was for younger children of better-off families before they were sent away to boarding school.

Plate 31. *The Post Office at York Cottage, 1903. The Notice beside the door reads 'Pony Trap for Hire'*

The house is brick, which is now painted, under a slate roof. The small slate roof over the two ground-floor bay windows continues across to form a porch over the front door.

The property continued in the hands of the Garton family until the death of Harry Garton in 1946, when it was put up for auction. It was said to be in a poor state of decorative repair and in need of modernisation.

One of the more recent residents was a flamboyant designer called Harald Mahrenholz. He only used the house as a weekend cottage, but he was a familiar sight in the village walking his dalmatian.

STONE COTTAGES (38)

In 1832 it was decided that the two existing parish cottages near the churchyard were so dilapidated that it would be preferable to pull them down and rebuild them in a more convenient place. Money was collected by subscription for this purpose and a piece of land along Lyons Road was given by Mr. Joseph Pocklington of Hill. A terrace of four almshouses was erected here in 1834/5. These were at first known as Red Cottages but became known popularly as the Barracks.

Plate 32. *Stone Cottages c. 1930*

It was realised in 1835 that the subscriptions collected exceeded the cost of the Barracks and the committee in charge therefore agreed to build two more cottages on the waste land belonging to the parish at the corner of Hayes Lane. In fact a terrace of three almshouses was put up here. Unlike the Barracks which were brick, these were built of Horsham stone, hence their name of Stone Cottages. Each had two small rooms up and two down, and their front doors opened straight on to the roadway. The plot of land was long and narrow, typical of roadside waste, and the cottages were set at one end, while at the far end of the garden was a communal earth closet.

On the waste ground at the Street end of the cottages was the parish pump, with a notice warning parishioners that the water was not for the use of cattle! The scene round the pump must have been busy in the past as people gathered for a chat while drawing water.

The cottages were for deserving parishioners and one of these was described by the Rev. G.P. Crawfurd in his reminiscences of his time as curate of the parish around 1880:

> There was Tom Holland at the bottom corner of Hayes Lane, the most Christlike bearer of suffering that I have ever known. He was a helpless cripple with scarcely an organ working in his body as it should do and I believe he had been such from his birth. He had not lain down at night for years. He sat in a chair at the window; and went at night to such sleep as he ever got with his head resting against the side of his chair or the window frame. But I have never known a more joyous man. Somebody pulled his attenuated frame to church on Sunday afternoons in a deal box, mounted on four wheels; and then after church it was the sport of the boys to get hold of the rope, which served as a handle to the box, and pull him down to his home as hard as they could go, the boys shouting and Tom roaring with laughter. Now-a-days (1932) I suppose the cortège would be had up for driving to the danger of the public; but we all enjoyed the fun and no harm ever came to Tom or anyone else from it.

For some time in the early years of this century the cottages were occupied by Moses Hampshire, Mrs. Lilleywhite and Luke Holland. Luke, who lived at No. 1, was a bewhiskered gentleman known as *Old Luke* who is reputed to have spoken the 'ancient tongue of Sussex'. Moses, at No. 3, was affectionately known as *Moke*.

More houses on Pinkhurst Land

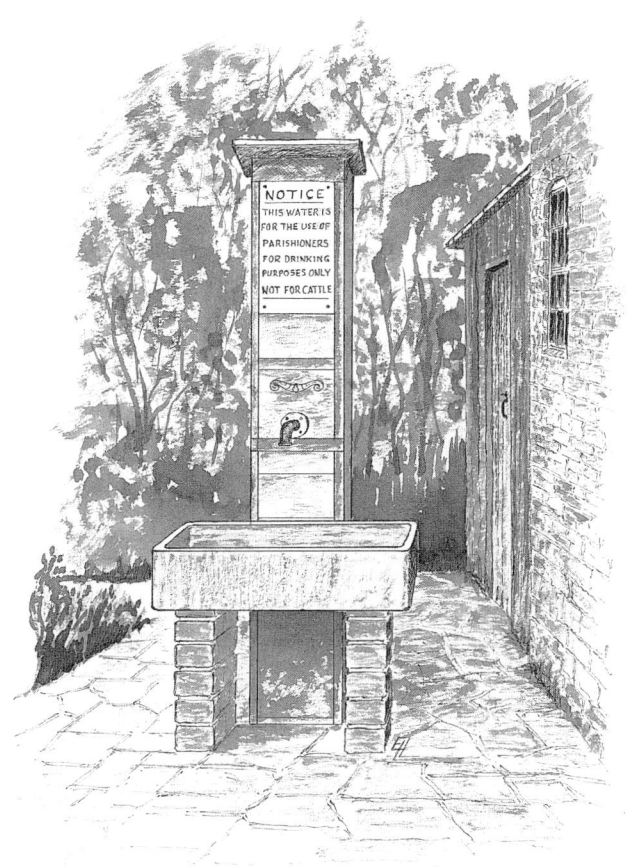

Fig. 19. *The Parish Pump used to stand on waste ground beside Stone Cottages*

The three cottages were later converted to two larger dwellings, and in 1989 the property was completely renovated and modernised. The front doors were moved so that residents no longer stepped straight out into the path of the ever increasing traffic coming round the corner. Stone Cottages still belong to the parish, serving the purpose for which they were built over 160 years ago.

PADORA-NIBLETTS (37)

In the 1860s James Grinstead of Taylors was farming a 13 acre area called Nibletts, as part of a total acreage of 110a. The original seven-acre holding of Nibletts belonged to the manor of Bassett's Fee, but since the second half of the 18th century, the owner of Nibletts had also farmed six acres belonging to Hall Land Farm. At first this combined holding was referred to as *Nibletts and part of Hall Land*, but from 1792 the whole was called *Nibletts*. This explains why the present bungalow has the name Nibletts when strictly it is on land which was part of Hall Land.

Earlier field boundaries had been altered and by 1876 there was one large field behind Nibletts and the houses along the Street as far as Holdens. Access to this field was by a track between Taylors and various outbuildings to the south. The outbuildings nearest the road included a carpenter's shop, while behind were farm buildings. The plot of land occupied by the carpenter's shop, now the site of Candleford, remained a part of Taylors for many years. The farm buildings, which have increased in number over the years, became separated from Taylors once James Grinstead ceased farming.

The land and buildings were used by George Grinstead and then William Grinstead. The relationship between the various Grinsteads is not clear and possibly William is actually William Grinsted, the butcher of White Briars.

When Mrs. Nora Ruse took over the land and buildings in 1927, she had a bungalow built for her own occupation. This was very simply constructed, having a timber frame lined with asbestos and covered with pebble dash. By the time of the National Farm Survey in 1941 Mrs. Ruse was managing a dairy farm totalling 133 acres, which included Rowfold and part of Gaskins. By this time the access track beside Taylors had long since fallen into disuse and Taylors had extended its garden southwards. This meant that a granary belonging to Nibletts was actually within Taylors land; it was subject to covenant between Mrs. Ruse and the owner of Taylors in 1940 which was confirmed in 1947.

In 1950 Mr. and Mrs. Davis bought the bungalow and ten acres of land. Mr. Davis was a farmer nearing retirement and he kept a few cattle on the land. When he did retire he could not bear to be without animals so he replaced the cattle with donkeys and ponies. Their daughter, Dot, married a builder, Pat Pavey, and they built themselves the neighbouring bungalow which they called Padora (now Woodlands). Pat set up his own business in 1963, using the outbuildings belonging to Nibletts as a builders yard. The Paveys moved into Nibletts in 1985, after the death of Mr. Davis. Before doing so, however, they completely renovated the bungalow, removing the asbestos and giving the building a brick skin and new windows, and remodelling the interior. For business reasons they brought the name of their previous dwelling with them, giving the modernised bungalow its present name of Padora-Nibletts.

HOUSES ON PATCHING LAND

Rowfold Farm was the only holding in Slinfold which belonged to the Archbishop of Canterbury's manor of Patching on the South Downs. Interestingly, Patching also had just one holding in the parish of Billingshurst, also called Rowfold. The Billingshurst property has the elliptical shape typical of a medieval deer park and the name *Rowfold* means 'deer enclosure'; almost certainly this was a pre-Conquest hunting park belonging to the Archbishop. While it cannot be proved, it is likely that Rowfold in Slinfold was also connected with the management of deer.

THE OLD BAKERY AND THE OLD VILLAGE STORES (11)

Throughout its long history this property has been one and was only divided into two dwellings as recently as 1979. It has been considerably extended and enlarged over the centuries, and much of the front range has the very attractive late 18th century brickwork of red stretchers and blue headers.

Embedded in the northern end of the timber-framed range to the rear of the building is the remains of a medieval open hall house. It has been much altered but it appears to have been quite small, with a two-bay open hall to the north. There would have been a floored bay to the south, but all trace of this has been lost. This was the original farmhouse for Rowfold Farm. Rowfold was a holding of some 50 to 60 acres stretching northwards to the Arun, but from the 17th century onwards it had been farmed as part of a larger estate which, by the early 18th century, comprised Hill, Windalls, Rowfold and Nowhurst. The estate was run from Hill House and Rowfold Farmhouse was no longer required for its original purpose. Redundant farmhouses were often used to house farm labourers, but the prime position of Rowfold in the centre of the village and fronting on to the village green prompted its use as a shop.

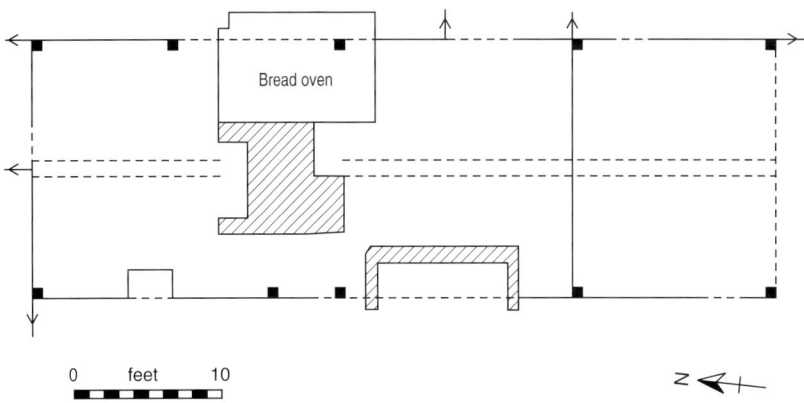

Fig. 20. *Ground plan of timber-framed rear range of the Old Bakery/Village Stores*

By the mid-17th century Richard Gardiner, who was a mercer, was using the premises both as a workshop and as a retail outlet. He is described as a mercer in a deed of 1646 and the map of 1651 (Map 5) shows a building in the right position as *Gardners house*. Richard had married Ann Potter in 1628 and they had seven children. Ann outlived her husband and the inventory taken on her death in 1689 suggests that she was living in one chamber of the house which had passed to her eldest son, another Richard, who was referred to as a shopkeeper in the parish registers of 1695. In that chamber Ann had *a feather bed and steddle, one blanket, one coverlet, two bolsters, one pillow, and bedhangings.* She also had *one box, one trunk and a little box of drawers, one wicker chair, one small silver spoon, one little box, three small pieces of pewter and a little brass pot.* All these, apart from the pieces of pewter, were left to various grandchildren in her will, her grandson Richard, eldest son of Ann's son Richard, receiving the most valuable item, which was the bed with all its furnishings.

The Gardiners took in poor girls of the village as apprentices *to learn the art of housewifery,* or in other words to work as domestic servants. Two of these were Mary Clarke who was apprenticed in 1669 and Elizabeth Robeson in 1697.

While the Gardiners were at the Old Bakery/Village Stores the property was modernised and extended. A chimney stack was built towards the southern end of the hall, the roof of the old building to the north was raised and the original south end of the house was replaced by two new bays. At this time the room to the north of the chimney was the parlour, the room to the south became the kitchen with the large cooking hearth, and the southern room, which is now within the Old Village Stores, was doubtless used by Richard Gardiner as the mercer's workshop.

There was a break in the property's use as a mercers in the earlier part of the 18th century. At one point it was used as a workhouse for lodging the poor of the parish, and later it was occupied by a cordwainer, John Knight.

In 1743 the premises were sold to Walter Knight and for the first time the property was officially separated from Rowfold Farm. Walter was variously described as a mercer, tailor or shopkeeper. He was working in Slinfold by 1737, but whether he was leasing the Old Bakery/Village Stores before he bought it is not clear. In 1738 he took in a village lad, John Farley, to learn the trade of tailor. (For more details of the mercer's trade, see p.10)

Walter died in 1748 and in his will he directed that his widow, Judith, should continue the business *so long as she shall be capable.* He also directed that his son Stephen should be trained to take over the business. In fact, it was not Stephen but another son, James, who carried on after his mother's death in 1787.

James ran the business until he died in 1801. There is no record of what his shop was selling, but by this time it must have expanded from a mercers and tailors into a general store. The very large bread oven which had been inserted beside the chimney, cutting into the original kitchen hearth and considerably reducing its size, suggests that bread was being baked commercially. The shop must have been a thriving concern. His mother, Judith, had two other houses apart from the shop. These she left to James and she was able to bequeath the equivalent in money, £300, to another son John. James himself was referred to as *Mr. James Knight of the Shop House* in 1796. And it was during his time that the northern part of the front range was built, greatly increasing the accommodation available. The large hearth at the rear of the room to the right of the front door indicates that for a time at least this must have been used as the kitchen in place of the earlier one in the old part of the building, while the cupboards and drawers beside this hearth suggest that the room functioned as the shop at one stage.

James Knight had no direct descendants and his niece sold the shop to Edward Child in 1801. This was the first property in the parish that Edward acquired. He let the premises to Thomas Sturt who was about to marry Sarah, the daughter of William Patching the wheelwright who lived at Chapel Cottage. The Old Bakery/Village Stores was an ideal place for him to establish a family home combined with a profitable business. Thomas and his wife had two daughters, but sadly Sarah died after just four years of marriage. Two years later Thomas married Mary Stanford and he and his new wife had a further eight children. They were all given just one Christian name, apart from the youngest who, in 1826, was christened Harry Stanford, following the new fashion of using the mother's surname as a second name. His mother, Mary, died when he was only seven.

By 1830 both Thomas's daughters by his first wife had married. Harriet became the wife of Frederick Churchman, a farmer who lived at Naldretts House in Rudgwick, while Mary married Charles Knight, who grew up at Old House Farm. Charles was a grocer with premises in West Street, Horsham. For a number of years from 1830 onwards he kept a diary, which he wrote every Sunday evening. From this it is clear that he and Mary and their two small girls often came to visit relatives in Slinfold, Itchingfield, Rudgwick and Loxwood, and there are frequent references to *dining with Mr. Sturt*. Normally they walked everywhere, but on occasions Thomas Sturt lent them his pony chaise. One memorable incident happened after Charles and various friends and relatives had gone to *New Inn, Cradles* in Warnham. Charles reported that:

> *Returning home Frederick Churchman's pony ran away. Started from Cradles of a full gallop, cleared Roman Gate being open, and kept on to Buck Green Gate, which being shut he ran against it with such force bursted it open, broke both shafts of the gig and threw them all out, but none of them seriously hurt.*

As well as running the shop, Thomas Sturt engaged in farming and by 1839 he was managing a total of 182 acres and employing nine labourers. He had Waterland, Lyons Farm and Bakers & Icemongers in Slinfold, and Southlands, near Buckmans Corner, in Rudgwick. In 1845 he was described as a farmer and grocer, and insurance agent for County Fire & Provident Life.

Although Thomas did not own the premises he lived and worked in, he gradually acquired other properties in the village and by 1839 he owned White Briars, Chewton, 3 & 4 Church View, Saddlers & Peppercorn Cottage; he thus owned the whole of the plot enclosed by John Stringer in 1576. He was also the owner of Taylors, which he probably had built with a view to his eventual retirement there.

Thomas must have been responsible for the building of one of the southward extensions of the front range. The section immediately to the south of the late 18th century front range has very similar chequerboard brickwork and would have been built in the early 19th century. It was purpose-built as a shop, having a central doorway with large windows to either side. In the inventory taken of the shop fittings after Thomas's death in 1855 one window was described as the *Grocery Window* and the other as the *Drapery Window*. Within there was a grocery counter and a drapery counter, together with various shelving, nests of drawers, rails etc. The *Lower Shop* had shelves and two deal counters with drawers and must have been to the rear within the timber-framed range, but there is no indication of what was being sold in this part. The inventory also mentions a *Flour Room* with shelving, which may have been located upstairs as it was in later years.

Thomas Sturt's youngest son, Harry Stanford, was working as a grocer in his father's shop in 1851, but he did not take over the business when Thomas died four years later. The shop was let to Charles Weakford, who continued the grocery and drapery business. By 1859 the post office was also in the shop; previously Sarah Holden of the Kings Head had been the postmistress.

At the time of the 1861 Census Charles, his wife and two small children were residing in the Old Bakery/Village Stores, together with one male and two female servants. Also, in the *Grocers Shop House* was Henry Cane with his wife and baby son. He was a builder from Brighton, presumably the son of Thomas Cane of Brighton, the builder to whom the contract to erect the new church had been given. Henry was clearly staying in Slinfold to oversee the building work.

Plate 33. *The Village Shop in 1860 before the southern extension had been built. Notice also that the addition to the right of Slinfold House was not there at this time*

Although Charles Weakford was not a farmer like Thomas Sturt, he not only expanded the shop's trade but also enlarged the building by the addition of a further southwards extension, which in later years housed the post office. By 1871 he had a grocer's assistant and an apprentice living and working in the premises. Ten years later his own children were old enough to be employed. His eldest son, also Charles, was the grocer's assistant, while the next son, Walter, is described as a *merchant's clerk*. He is later referred to as a *Civil servant, H.M. Inland Revenue*. Is there a connection between his son's job and the fact that Charles Weakford collected the Land Tax from parishioners?

By 1891 the son, Charles, had married and had a young family and they had moved across the road to live in the Kings Head Cottage. Charles was still working as his father's assistant, along with two other young men who lived in. But when Charles, senior, retired to the newly built York Cottage a year or two later his son did not take over, just as Thomas Sturt's son had not carried on the business. The post office moved with Charles Weakford to York Cottage and for a few years was run by his daughter, Ada.

The shop was then let to John Capon West and the entry in Kelly's Directory for 1895 shows the range of goods he was offering for sale:

> J. Capon West & Co., *grocers, provision merchants, draper, bakers, corn, coal & coke merchants, ironmongers and china & glass dealers*.

The post office was back in the Stores by 1904, increasing Mr. West's wide-ranging trade.

Already in Thomas Sturt's time there were some outbuildings beside and behind the premises. These were altered and added to over the years and by the end of the century the brick building to the south had appeared. This was connected to the rest of the premises by a covered way with large double doors at the front. In the yard behind was a tall building. This is believed to be a Ministry of Building and Public Works design of around 1900 for a post office stable block. It is constructed of nine-inch solid brickwork with wrought iron reinforcing at intervals, and the whole sits on massive foundations. Within were a stall and a loose-box with a harness room between and above was a hay loft with a projecting hoist at the gable end facing the yard. The sketch plan of the property made in 1910 for the 'Lloyd George's Domesday' shows a coach house nearby.

In 1910 the main building contained the post office, shop, sitting room, drawing room, nine bedrooms including bathroom, kitchen, scullery and bakehouse. When the premises were sold in 1979 the accommodation was much the same, except that part of the first floor had been turned into a self-contained flat, and the bakehouse was no longer being used for that purpose.

Mr. West was a well-respected man who was much involved in village affairs. His shop supplied all the needs that could not be met from people's own kitchen gardens. He fattened turkeys on land near Lyons Farmhouse and at Christmas they could be seen hanging outside the shop together with rabbits.

Plate 34. *Slinfold Stores & Post Office in 1931*

Around 1920 Connie Dawe started work at the shop. She grew up at Chewton, and attended the village school where she went on to become a pupil teacher. She went away to train as a teacher, but after helping in the shop in the holidays she was invited to take a permanent job there. She very quickly became Mr. West's right hand in the business and she became as one of the family. When Mr. West died in 1926 Connie was able to be of great assistance to Mrs. West. Mrs. West moved away to be near her sister when war broke out and Connie took sole charge. The business was left to her by Mrs. West and later, she was able to acquire the premises too.

Connie Dawe became an important figure in the community and her sensitivity in delivering bad news personally during the war years was much appreciated. Ill health forced her to retire in 1958 and she then moved to Horsham and married an old friend.

Lois White worked in the post office at the shop for many years. She started in 1939, and she remembers that the shop then sold a wide range of products including groceries, confectionery and tobacco, haberdashery, medicines, and oil and paraffin. Newspapers were delivered, except on Sunday as Miss Dawe did not agree with Sunday working. The general stores were entered through the double doors and stretched through into the back range of the building, which was at a lower level down two steps. To the south was the post office which had a separate entrance, and behind was the sorting office. The front part of the outbuilding which now houses the shop was a first aid room during the war. To the rear was a store room and beyond that a cycle shed used both by the shop assistants and the postmen. The present computer offices were still stabling with a garage adjacent.

Plate 35. *Connie Dawe on her retirement in 1958*

In the 1940s and 50s service, for both the customers and the shop, was instant. It did not matter how many times a person rang for something in a day, Arthur Dinnage would appear promptly with it, at first on a bike and later in a van. Nearly everything the shop itself needed was supplied by a Dorking firm called Kinghams. The salesman was George Perkins, who lived locally but worked from Dorking. If an item was not available for a customer in the shop in the morning, Connie Dawe would phone George and he would deliver it to the shop on his way home.

After Miss Dawe retired in 1958 the shop had eight different owners in the next 20 years. The first, Mr. Hampson, was a retired Stoke City footballer who only lasted six months. Mr. Lee then had the shop from 1959 to 1961, returning again in 1965 for another six years.

The final purchaser, Mr. Waller, arrived, altered the interior and traded for a while on a dwindling stock of goods before closing the shop and selling the property as two private dwellings in 1979. One part became the Old Bakery and the shop side was sold separately after all the shop fittings and remaining stock had been removed. The village was without a post office for a time while Lois White was gaining permission to run it from her home, 4 Lyons Road.

The old shop became part of the living accommodation for the southern dwelling, although the shop windows and central doorway have been retained. The former post office was used briefly in 1981 as a greengrocers and when this closed after a few months, Bennie Bridgland opened a small food store in this same room. This has been very successful and in 1995 moved into specially adapted premises in the nearby outbuilding. The post office returned to the Village Stores on Lois's retirement in 1987.

The Old Bakery/Village Stores has a long history as a shop. The shop itself has, however, moved within the premises. It was at first within the timber-framed range to the rear, then in the late 18th century build in front. It has then moved progressively southwards until it reached its present, and perhaps final, position.

WINDALLS (13)

The plot of land upon which Windalls stands was bought by Edward Child of Slinfold House in 1828. The land was a part of the field known as Shop Field which belonged to Rowfold Farm.

Edward's only son, Thomas, was about to get married to Caroline Churchman of Maybanks in Ewhurst, just to the north of Rudgwick. The house which Edward built on the plot was intended for the newly married couple and was an up-to-date brick house with a slate roof. It is, in fact, the earliest example of the use of slate in the Street, the slate presumably being shipped by canal. It had no bay windows at first and probably no porch either. The porch is identical with that on Slinfold House and also with the one at Holdens. Since Holdens was not erected until 1841 the porches are all likely to date to around then, and interestingly the occupants of all three houses were related.

The house at first consisted of the front range only. This had a symmetrical façade and contained four rooms downstairs, two on each side of the central hall and stairs. On the first floor were five bedrooms. The right-hand room at the back of the house was the original kitchen, the rear stack providing a large cooking hearth. There is a cellar under the two front rooms, with a metal game larder in it. Within less than ten years the house was extended to accommodate the growing family and the servants required to look after them. A rear wing was added to the south-east which had just one room on each floor.

To the north-east of the main range, but completely detached from it, was a sizeable brick and slate building which is shown on the Tithe Map of 1839 and is probably contemporary with the rear wing. This was later connected to the house by a passage of timber and glass with a slate roof. In the 1940s and 50s this building was being used as a kitchen; there was a fireplace in the long east wall with a coal-fired range for cooking, a sink along the southern wall and a big deal table in the centre. There was doorway leading out of the end wall nearest the shop and, also at this end, a ladder to a storage area above. The rooms listed in Lloyd George's Domesday of 1910 suggest that at that time the outbuilding was also being used as the kitchen. It seems likely that, even if it was not built as a kitchen, it very soon became one in order to increase the accommodation available within the house, and it is therefore an extremely interesting throw-back to the detached kitchens of medieval times. It was demolished in the late 1950s.

The track between Windalls and the Village Stores leading to land behind the shop and Slinfold House at first belonged to Edward Child, but soon became part of Windalls property. To the north of this track there are two outbuildings. One, a granary on brick piers with Horsham stone caps, was there by 1839. The other, immediately opposite the detached kitchen, was built before 1877. The interior is whitewashed and it is known to have functioned as a wash-house in later years. On the other side of the track, against Windalls garden wall, is an old privy and a coach house and stables, all shown on a map of 1877. A loose box was later added.

Although Thomas and Caroline lived in the house from their marriage in 1829, the house did not become Thomas's until his father's death in 1850. Thomas and his wife had six children, three boys and three girls. Unfortunately the two younger sons, Edward and John, died young. Charles, the eldest child, took over the timber-merchant side of his father's business and moved the timber yard to Stane Street (see p.17). Jane, the eldest daughter, married Frederick Braby, the founder of a company which ran a number of iron foundries, and two of her brother's sons were later connected with this company. The two younger daughters, Ellen and Kate, never married.

Plate 36. *Windalls in the 1860s before the bay windows were added*

Plate 37. *Windalls some years later with bay windows and decorative ridge tiles*

Thomas Child (Pl. 5) was an entrepreneur who was quick to spot a gap in the market which he could fill, such as the need to bring coal into the area in the 1830s and 40s, and his business dealings made him a wealthy man. His wealth enabled him to keep an establishment of some style. There was a large greenhouse in the garden by around 1860. The house itself was updated in the 1860s by the addition of bay windows. The windows in these bays had 'modern' sashes with just two large panes in each sash, whereas the original windows each had a total of sixteen small panes. The window over the porch was also replaced and even the brick surround was altered to match those of the bay windows. A wooden dentil course was added as decoration under the eaves. At the same time decorative ridge tiles were set along the apex of the roof, as well as on the small roofs capping the bays.

One facet of the upgrading was the calling of the property by a distinctive name. Until the mid-1860s it was referred to in the poor rates and censuses simply as a *house in the Street*. The name Windalls meant the small farm to the east of Clapgate Lane and, more specifically, the original farmhouse of the property. In 1863 Thomas Child bought much of Hill Farm together with Windalls and Rowfold, and he was responsible for the rebuilding of the original Windalls, which was thereafter known as Clapgate Cottages. Thomas must have felt that since he now owned Windalls, he was justified in moving the name to his own house, even though the house had no connection whatever with Windalls Farm.

Thomas and Caroline were both very much involved in village affairs. Their names were always to be found on every list of subscribers supporting a good cause and Thomas was churchwarden for a total of thirteen years. When Thomas died in 1870 at the age of 69, this involvement was reflected in the obituary which appeared in the West Sussex Gazette:

> *In the parish his death will leave a terrible blank. Whether it be riding about the farm with a kind remark and genial smile for everyone, or whether it be in his accustomed place in church twice every Sunday, following devoutly every portion of the service, it will be a long time before Slinfold will realise that Mr. Child is gone to his last rest, never, never to return. .... Although Mr. Child had made a considerable fortune, be it said to his honor, that he never used it except for the good of his fellow creatures, and never once applied a single farthing to purposes of self aggrandisement.*

Caroline continued to carry out her good works although left speechless by a stroke, until she died ten years after her husband at the age of 79. The parish magazine was first issued in 1880, the year of her death, and in a black-edged tribute to her, it stated that the issue of the magazine was mainly attributable to the encouragement and support of Caroline Child.

Caroline's will suggests that Windalls was a comfortable, well-furnished residence. All the oil paintings were left to her son Charles and son-in-law Frederick Braby, all the framed prints and engravings to her daughter Jane Braby and daughter-in-law Ellen Child, and to her daughters Ellen and Kate went all the furniture, linen, plate, books and watercolours.

Plate 38. *Caroline Child in her widowhood*

After their death, the children and grandchildren of Thomas and Caroline gave the village hall in their memory and also in thanks for the two memorial windows placed in the south aisle of the church by their friends and neighbours.

Windalls was now occupied only by the two unmarried daughters, Ellen and Kate, and their servants. By 1881 Harriet Fuller was at Windalls, the first of the Fuller family to work for the Childs in an association that lasted some 80 years.

The photograph album of the Park House branch of the family suggests that the Childs travelled extensively at this time, taking holidays both in this country and abroad. The elder daughter Ellen died while she was in Nice in 1887. Thereafter, Kate was on her own in Windalls, with a cook and a housemaid, but her family lived nearby and she received frequent visitors. In spite of this the house must have seemed over large to her on occasions. In 1910 the rooms were given as the drawing room, dining room, smoking room, servants' hall, two pantries, larder, kitchen, scullery, five bedrooms, bathroom, tank room, and attic. The house also had two lavatories, one upstairs and one downstairs; this was at a time when the majority of houses, even Slinfold House, still had only an earth closet out in the garden.

Kate Child died in 1913, the last Child to be a great benefactor to the village. It was said in her obituary that she was *'the' lady of the parish*. But times were about to change. Village men went off to the Great War and when they came back they no longer wanted the gentry of the village to run their lives for them as in the past, they wanted to make their own decisions (see p.30).

Windalls had been left by Thomas to Charles of Park House, and by the time of Kate's death it had passed to Charles' son Harold as one of the executors of his father's will. For a few years the house was let. Then in 1922, Charles Child, brother of Harold, bought the house from his father's estate. Charles was a land agent. He never married and lived in Windalls for the rest of his life. He was an ardent cricket fan and if the rear wall of the garden is examined closely, it can be seen that the central section was at one time lower, so that Charles could sit in his garden watching the game in progress on the cricket field. Charles was churchwarden for over 20 years and was clearly involved in village life, but there was no longer the same ethos as in the past, and he was not expected to display the same degree of paternalism as his forbears.

Mabel Fuller, who had started work for the Childs in 1908 at the age of 14, was Charles' cook and housekeeper, a position which she held until his death in 1956. She was, by all accounts, a very good cook and a great conversationalist. In 1952 Charles made Mabel a life-tenant of Forge House, and thus for the last few years of his life she was not living in.

In 1957 Windalls was sold and the house's long association with the Child family came to an end. The new owners extended the drawing room southwards, which meant demolishing the chimney at this end of the house. The present owners bought the house in 1979. The house has thus been in the ownership of only three families throughout its 170 years.

THE GARDEN HOUSE (12)

Over the years some of the land behind the Village Stores and to the east of the garden of Slinfold House, all of which initially belonged to Edward Child, had become attached to Windalls. It was on this land that the owner of Windalls, Lady Mackintosh, had a new house constructed for her own use in 1979. It is an attractive house of modern design. It is brick-built under a tile roof, and is part two-storey and part single-storey. All the roofs are capped with an unusual lead ridge with decorative lead finials.

FORGE HOUSE AND THE OLD FORGE (14 & 15)

David Holden was the village blacksmith in Slinfold in the 1830s-40s. He came from a family of blacksmiths, his father having worked in Kirdford and Wisborough Green and his grandfather in Plaistow. Family tradition recounts that David was not strong as a boy and was sent to an uncle James Holden at Slinfold. He was apprenticed to James and eventually succeeded to the business. There is unfortunately no record of James working as a blacksmith, although both James and his wife Phoebe were buried at Slinfold. However, one of James' daughters, Sarah, married Charles Holden the younger, the innkeeper of the Kings Head. Both Charles and his father before him were blacksmiths as well as innkeepers.

Whether David was apprenticed to uncle James or to his cousin by marriage, Charles, by 1839 he was working from the forge on the west side of the Street on the site of the present Holdens. As well as occupying the cottage to which the forge was attached, David also had a house and stables on the other side of the road on a plot of land which he had purchased from Rowfold Farm in 1829. David and his family could well have been occupying both the cottage and the house opposite as he and his wife, Sarah Holden, a distant relative, had 17 children, most of whom survived infancy. One had sadly died in 1837 by taking arsenic that was laid for rats.

Once the original forge and cottage were demolished to make way for Holdens, which was being erected in 1841, David either altered or rebuilt his premises on the east side of the Street to become the forge. The building had chequered brickwork and consisted of a two-storey central section with storage in the upper part, and single-storey wings to either side. The central section contained the forge and anvil, while the horses were taken into the right-hand wing. The left-hand wing was the wheelwrights (Pl. 7).

Plate 39. *The Old Forge with Forge House beyond, 1998. Forge Cottage can just be seen behind the Old Forge*

The plot of land between the forge and Windalls had been bought by Edward Child, also in 1829, but nothing had been built on it by 1839 when it was being used as a garden. It is not clear whether Forge House was built by David on Edward's land or whether it was built after 1850, when David sold out to Thomas Child. On balance it seems probable that it was built in David's time, both from the style of the building and since he and his family would have needed somewhere to live.

Forge House is brick-built under a shallow slate roof. It has sash windows and interestingly the window above the porch is a dummy, put there purely to improve the look of the façade. Although it has two front doors, it was never divided into two dwellings. It is more probable that the left-hand one, which is a stable door, opened into a shop selling goods made in the smithy. The discovery of hooks and shelves in that front room points to this being the most likely scenario. The bay windows are a later alteration and the framework for these is apparently constructed in the same way as a cart wheel. There used to be a small forge in an outbuilding to the rear of the house.

The brickwork is a pleasing arrangement of red stretchers and blue headers, but the bricks are set on edge in a bond known as *rat trap* (p.36). This rat trap bond suggests that the house was built in the 1840s rather than later. Forge House is an attractive building, which is not always the case with rat trap.

Although David Holden sold the forge to Thomas Child in 1850 it would appear that he continued working there for a while as he is listed as living in the Street in 1851. But by 1861 Henry Parkhurst was the master blacksmith and wheelwright living in Forge House. He had earlier been working at the wheelwright's shop where the Chapel now stands.

By the time the 1871 Census was conducted Frank Wadey, master blacksmith, lived in Forge House and carried out his business at the forge. Mr. Wadey was born in Five Oaks and served his apprenticeship with Mr. Etherton, who was in business in West Street, Horsham. Mr. Wadey and his wife, Charlotte, had 13 children; the eldest child, Frank, born in 1867, left school at the age of 13 and went to work for his father. Charles, a younger brother, also joined the family in the business. Frank Wadey, junior, lived for many years in Little Hammers with his family, while working at the forge.

Plate 40. *Frank Wadey, senior, and his children outside Forge House. The children are wearing black armbands and the photo was almost certainly taken after the death of their mother at the age of 50 in 1892*

At the turn of the century two shoeing smiths, a wheelwright, a man and a boy, as well as Mr. Wadey and his son, were kept continuously at work at the forge. The men took a pride in their work; the day started at 6 am and finished at 7 pm. Apart from their work with the horses, they repaired clogs worn by women while working in the dairy or outside the house. In slack periods, such as harvest time when farmers were busy, a wagon or a cart would be made and a buyer was soon found.

The horses were tied to two trees by the road while they were waiting to be shod. The iron hooks to which they were tied can still be seen. The children of the village enjoyed going to watch the horses being shod and the sparks flying on the anvil as the shoes were bent into shape, although they thought the smell of burning hoof was rather horrid.

As demand for shoeing horses declined and less wheelwrighting work was done, the Wadeys branched out into the installation of hot water systems and pumps, and overhauling lawn mowers. They also became cycle agents and repairers.

The forge continued to operate until Frank, junior, died in 1850, and then Charles Child as owner sold the property to his niece, Ruth Morris, while Annie, Frank's widow, sold all the fixtures and fittings and stock to Ruth. The inventory of fixtures and stock shows the wide-ranging nature of the business at this time. As well as the traditional skills of shoeing horses and making wheels, they were able to produce iron gate fittings, mend stoves and tanks, install hot water systems as well as wash basins and taps, make farm and garden tools and ladders, and much more besides. The village must have missed their ability to make and mend almost anything when they were no longer there.

Ruth Morris and her mother, Maria, sister to Charles Child of Windalls, converted the forge into the dwelling now known as the Old Forge. It was unfortunate, but probably unavoidable, that the brickwork had to be rendered.

When the forge ceased operating and Forge House became vacant, Charles Child let his cook, Mabel Fuller, live there and, under his will, she became a life tenant. Mabel's brother, Harold, was also there. Harold had worked for Harold Child at the timber-yard from the age of 17. He was good with horses and used to drive a timber-carriage through Horsham on occasions; the carriage could pull out to 24 feet from wheel to wheel, with a 50 foot tree on it. There was one corner in the middle of Horsham where he was always worried that the tree might go right through Freeman Hardy & Willis' window. On his 21st birthday Mr. Harold sent him to buy four horses for the yard. When he asked how much he should pay, he was told he could spend up to £1000. In fact he spent 407 guineas and he never forgot that day. When asked years later how the horses turned out, he replied *Them horses turned out all right*.

Mabel and Harold finally moved into an old people's home in Horsham in 1979. Peter Child, Charles' great-nephew, sold the house, the last piece of property in Slinfold owned by the Childs and the end of a chapter.

FORGE COTTAGE (16)

In the 1850s Thomas Child erected a new dwelling behind the forge to house his farm bailiff. This building is surprisingly tall for its depth. It is brick-built under a slate roof, and entirely covered by tile-hanging. It had just two rooms downstairs, with a central entrance lobby and stairs, and two bedrooms above. Later a small outbuilding attached to the northern end of the cottage was incorporated into the house and there are modern extensions to the rear.

James Mills was the Childs' bailiff in the 1860s and 70s, and by 1881 Kester Garman was living here with his wife. Kester had earlier been an agricultural labourer working for Thomas Child and living in Clapgate Cottages. He clearly showed promise and continued as bailiff until around 1900.

Forge Cottage had no connection with the forge until about 1915 when Charles Wadey lived there. Around this time it became known as *Lower Forge*. Frederick Johnson moved there in 1919 when he married. He was connected with the Wadeys as his relative, John Johnson, was Frank Wadey senior's brother-in-law and had been apprenticed to him. Frederick's son, Johnnie, was born in the house and lived there until his marriage at the age of 26. He remembers that they had to fetch their water from the pump in the Wadey's back kitchen.

In 1957 Ruth Morris, who was by then living in the Old Forge, bought Forge Cottage from the estate of Charles Child.

CHAPEL VIEW (17)

Chapel View was erected in 1878 by Thomas Ayling who had come to the village a few years earlier and dwelt at first in Chewton. He was a master bricklayer who, in 1881, employed four men and one boy. The house he constructed for himself is very similar in appearance to two others in the village which were built by him, Church House and South Lodge. Chapel View is, however, larger both in width and depth and therefore provides more accommodation than the others, having four rooms on each floor rather than three. It also has a chimney stack at either end of the building, whereas the others each have a central chimney.

There was another builder in the village at this time, Alfred Grinstead of Taylors. Thomas Ayling continued to refer to himself as a bricklayer rather than a builder until the 1890s, when Alfred had died and the business was being run by his widow. Thereafter, it was always *Aylings the builders*. However, the two businesses must have been complementary as Alfred was a carpenter rather than a bricklayer like Thomas.

Plate 41. *Chapel View with Thomas Ayling and his wife, Emily, on either side of the gate. The sign reads 'Thomas Ayling, Builder, Contractor, Carpenter, Painter, Paperhanger, Undertaker & Carman'*

Thomas's son, Walter took over in the 1920s and he was followed in due course by his son, Frederick. The business has gradually wound down in recent years.

Chapel View is on part of Shop Field belonging to Rowfold Farm, and when Thomas put up his house this was owned by Charles Child of Park House. The property was bought from the Childs in the 1950s.

As might be expected there were numerous outbuildings connected with the business in the grounds of Chapel View, some of which still survive. These have been changed and rebuilt over the years as the need arose, and at one time some of them were let out to other tenants. For a long time the Aylings also had the use of the adjacent field on which Birchwood now stands, and this was often referred to as *Aylings Field*.

BIRCHWOOD (18)

A new house was erected on *Aylings Field* in 1959. Designed by C. Wycliffe Noble, it has single-storeyed and monopitch two-storeyed parts, forming an L-shape. The garage is connected to the building by a loggia. It is constructed of old red bricks and weatherboarding. Nairn & Pevsner, in their *Buildings of England - Sussex, 1965* describe it as *a paradigm of how to fit a completely modern house into a pretty old village. .... It is now two years old (1961): in terms of mellowness it might well be two hundred.* Not all villagers have agreed with Nairn & Pevsner. The house was originally named Brickwood, presumably a reference to the materials of which it is built.

HOUSES ON CLEMSFOLD LAND

Clemsfold was formerly a part of Drungewick Manor which became a small independent manor in its own right. It held a block of 300 acres of land including Brookhurst and Smithaw as well as Clemsfold farm itself. It also had a separate area of some 13 acres near the centre of the village. This would have been enclosed from common land some time before the building of the church and became the farm known as Windalls. The original farmhouse for Windalls was on the site of Clapgate Cottage, which was rebuilt as farm labourers' cottages in the 1860s. The present Windalls in The Street has no connection with the farm and is not even on Windalls' land.

1 & 2 CHURCHYARD COTTAGES (5)

These cottages are set in a triangle of ground bounded by the churchyard to the south, Clapgate Lane to the west and a footpath to the east. There are now two cottages, earlier there were three, but the original building was one single dwelling.

Although the cottages are now entered from Clapgate Lane, the east side was originally the front of the house. There has always been a track on either side of the building, the two tracks joining into one just north of the property. When the house was built, the eastern track was clearly the more important and it was still the main one when the extensions were built at what was then the rear of the building. The track to the west became the main one in the late 18th century when the turnpike coming northwards from Billingshurst turned east and entered the village via Clapgate Lane. By the early 19th century the eastern track had been incorporated into gardens for the cottages and the footpath was reinstated only by purchasing a strip of land along the edge of Churchyard Field.

Plate 42. *Churchyard Cottages. The original front of the building now faces back gardens and the footpath beyond.*

The building is a three-bay timber-framed house of the early 1600s. It had a kitchen to the south and a parlour to the north, separated by a narrow bay containing the hearth. The western half of the bay was open from floor to rafters and smoke from the hearth on the ground drifted up and escaped through a hole in the roof, probably with a louvre above to give protection from the weather. The wattle and daub at the back of the hearth was protected by a stone reredos which can still be seen. The hearth served the kitchen, while the parlour was unheated. The front door opened into a lobby at the eastern end of the narrow bay and a door either side gave access to the kitchen and the parlour. Between the entrance lobby and the hearth were the stairs, reached by a door in the kitchen, and doors either side of the first-floor landing led to the two upstairs chambers. These would have been open to the rafters. The side-purlin roof is gabled and was originally healed with Horsham Stone. The smoke bay was very efficient and did not have a brick stack built within it until the mid-18th century.

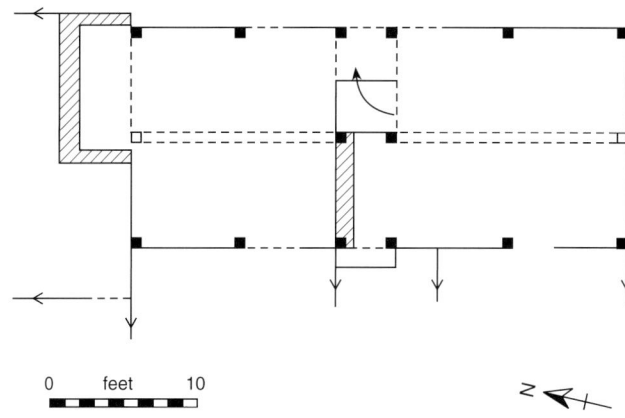

Fig. 21. *Ground plan of timber-framed range now at the rear of the building*

This house was built on a very small piece of wasteland belonging to the manor of Clemsfold, but it was larger and better built than might be expected of a squatter's cottage. The most likely explanation, given its position right next to the earlier north gate into the churchyard and opposite the Rectory, is that this was built to house the curate. Since many of Slinfold's rectors were pluralists or had additional duties as prebends of Chichester Cathedral, much of the running of the parish fell to the curate and this house was ideally situated for his work.

Apart from the probability that the house was at first occupied by the curates of Slinfold, nothing is known about the property until 1707 when it is mentioned in the will of John Freeman. By this time it had been divided into two cottages. This was achieved by blocking the lobby and landing doors leading into the northern room and the chamber above, and inserting new stairs against the wall behind the original stairs. Heating for the northern cottage was provided by building a new chimney within an already existing single-storey extension to the north of the former parlour.

John Freeman let the southern cottage to tenants and lived in the northern cottage with his son John. It would appear that the extension to the west of this northern part had been built by this time as John senior's inventory suggests that he himself was occupying one chamber and one downstairs room, while his son, with his wife and children, must have had the rest of the cottage.

The will and inventory of John Freeman, senior, give an interesting insight into the perceived status of an individual at that time. John not only owned both parts of Churchyard Cottages, leaving the northern half to grandson John and the southern half to grandson James, he also owned Little Bleachmers or Pinkhurst Gate which he left to a third grandson, Richard. (Little Bleachmers, since demolished, stood on the northern corner of Park Street and Stane Street, the site now marked by an apple tree.) Because he owned these properties he felt justified in calling himself a yeoman in his will, although he had no landholding. His inventory calls him a husbandman and it shows that he owned very few possessions, the total value of which was just £4 17s 6d, while the parish registers describe him as a labourer, which was indeed how he earned his living. His inventory includes his husbandry tools, worth 5s.

Grandson James Freeman sold the southern cottage to Judith Knight in 1749. Judith was the widow of Walter Knight of the Village Stores and she would have let the cottage. She did not keep it long, however, but sold in 1754 to John Gardiner, a cordwainer who both lived and worked there. On his death in 1788 the following bequest was made according to his will:

> *My acquainted Edward Harbroe of Rudgwick, Apothecary, hath attended upon and administered medicines unto me and my late wife for which he hath refused to receive any money or other satisfaction. Now I do hereby in consideration of such civilities give and bequeath unto his son Thomas Harbroe the sum of £20.*

John and his wife had no children and he left the cottage to John Piggott Jones, son of his good friend the Rev. John Jones, late Rector of Slinfold, who immediately sold it to Elizabeth, wife of John Garman, a husbandman. John and Elizabeth already had two children and a further eight were born to them while they lived in the cottage; there were 18 years between the oldest and the youngest, and it is unlikely that all ten children were living at home at the same time. The cottage had been extended by this time, the extensions to the west having been built sometime before 1750.

Plate 43: *Churchyard Cottages are now entered from Clapgate Lane. This side was originally the back of the building*

After Elizabeth died in 1825 the property was auctioned at the Kings Head and was bought for £140 by William Briggs, the tanner. His son William inherited it, and he sold it to his brother, John, in 1842.

It is not clear what happened to the northern cottage after the grandson, John Freeman, inherited it as there are no further records until 1780 when Judith Knight owned it. She had earlier owned the other half for a short while. The northern end went to her son, James, of the Village Stores and then from 1803 until 1824 it was owned by James Older. Judith and James Knight and James Older were owners who let the cottage to a succession of tenants; these would have been craftsmen or labourers. The only one whose occupation is known in Richard Jayes, a cordwainer who lived there from 1810 to 1824.

In 1825 John Mills bought the property. He was a tailor who both owned and occupied the premises. He was still working in 1841, by which time his grandson, Henry, was living with him and was employed by him. John had retired by 1851 and Henry, who had by now married and had four small children, ran the business himself. When John died in 1855 he left the property to his grandson, who sold out to John Briggs the following year. Both parts of Churchyard Cottages were now in the same ownership for the first time since the 17th century.

When the property was divided into two cottages, the stack added at the northern end of the building to heat the north cottage was built within an already existing single-storey extension, as mentioned above. Around 1750 this single-storey extension was replaced by a two-storey addition. This extension is wider than the original timber-framed building and its width was probably dictated by the earlier single-storey addition; the stonework in the western ground-floor wall may be the remains of this earlier phase. This addition, together with the single-storey extension beyond it, has sometimes functioned as extra accommodation for 2 Churchyard Cottages and at other times has been used as a completely separate dwelling known as 3 Churchyard Cottages.

One inhabitant of No. 3 in the 1880s was Beccy Farley. She was a chronic invalid and lived with her mother, earning her living as a seamstress. Beccy told the curate, the Rev. G.P. Crawfurd, a rambling tale of a witch who came through the hedge and ran through her garden in the shape of a hare. The curate also recorded another story which possibly concerned the same hare:

> The Squire had then a field adjoining Beccy's cottage, and his keeper, George Andrewes, a believer in the same cult, decided to kill it, and rid the village for ever of this supernatural pest. But he said that from what he had always heard it was of no use to try and shoot a witch with lead shot; it must be silver, and so he broke up some silver coins into small pieces, loaded his gun with them and killed the hare. I have an idea that it was a white one.

Churchyard Cottages continued to be owned by the descendants of the Briggs until the death of Mrs. Elizabeth Newman around 1920. From then until 1970 the property was used as parish cottages for deserving poor inhabitants of Slinfold.

During this time one very tragic event occurred. On 4th December, 1937 No. 3 caught fire and Mr. Hubert Picton was trapped inside and burnt to death. Mr. Picton was a retired official of the Midland Bank and was related by marriage to the Copnalls who had previously lived in Slinfold House. The West Sussex County Times report tells of two strange events which occurred just prior to Mr. Picton's death. He was a regular at the Kings Head and the last thing he did before leaving on the night of his death was to play the Dead March; and during the night his neighbour, Mrs. M. Francis of No. 1, dreamt that a fire broke out and, although she was called to help, she was unable to go. No. 3 was seriously damaged in the fire and considerable rebuilding took place at this time.

Another occupant of No. 3 was Mrs. Laura Hopes and her family, who were there for about five years from 1943. The soldiers camped up the lane towards Hill were very kind to them and would give them rations in return for listening to the Hopes' radio.

While they were parish cottages, repairs and improvements were done as cheaply as possible, and tenants did not always look after their property. The daughter of Mrs. Hayes, the home help to Mrs. Francis of No. 1, recalls helping her mother during school holidays in the early 1960s. The experience made a great impression on her as Mrs. Francis' lifestyle was somewhat eccentric. She only used the downstairs rooms and there were rats upstairs; Mrs. Hayes tried to block up the holes to stop the rats coming down. The old lady and her cat used to share their meals off the same plate! Mrs. Francis had a wig and Mrs. Hayes' daughter used to take it to a hairdresser in Horsham on her way to school and collect it on her way home.

Plate 44. *An old shoe, a broken wooden doll and various bones forming part of a ritual deposit placed behind a brick at the base of the smoke bay in Churchyard Cottages. The deposit was intended to keep witches from coming down the chimney.*

Since 1970 the property has been in private hands and has been sympathetically restored. It is once again just two dwellings as Nos. 2 & 3 have been combined into one. As might be expected with an old house, all kinds of reminders of life in previous ages have been found, both in the garden and within the house, such as old coins, clay pipes, pieces of pottery and glass, and a horse brass. But the most interesting find was a ritual deposit placed behind a brick at the base of the reredos of the original smoke bay hearth. This included a wooden doll, an old shoe and various bones and was put there as a protection against witches coming down the chimney.

Despite being divided into two and having various later alterations and extensions, the original timber-framed smoke bay house is remarkably well preserved.

SLINFOLD HOUSE & CHERRY TREE COTTAGE (10 & 9)

In the late 16th century part of the open space on the east side of the Street to the south of the church was enclosed and the building now encased in Cherry Tree Cottage was erected on it. There is one timber-framed bay of this date surviving behind the southern end of the present brick cottage, but the original form of the building is not clear as the front range has undergone considerable rebuilding.

In the early 17th century a small cottage was built against Cherry Tree Cottage, which was timber-framed and consisted of two bays with an end smoke bay. This provided a living room with a cooking hearth, and a small service room abutting Cherry Tree Cottage. Above, the two chambers would have had no ceilings, but would have been open to the rafters. The cottage was sideways on to the Street, facing the village green, and is the rear range of Slinfold House.

Plate 45. *The low timber-framed range to the rear of Slinfold House and Cherry Tree Cottage. The smoke bay was at the left-hand end. To the right of the chimney, the first window belongs to Slinfold House while the other two light the timber-framed bay of Cherry Tree Cottage*

Both cottages would have housed craftsmen or labourers. In the late 16th and early 17th century a more private lifestyle was becoming the norm among yeomen. Farm labourers who had previously lodged in the farmhouses now had to find their own accommodation, and a piece of waste ground belonging to a manor which did not mind cottages appearing so long as they paid their rent was very welcome. The open space enclosed for Cherry Tree Cottage and Slinfold House was adjacent to land belonging to Windalls Farm and was therefore waste of the manor of Clemsfold. The two semi-detached cottages were always described as being *parcel of Windalls*.

New cottages built at this date were normally held from the manor on a long lease and the first documentary reference to the cottages is in 1642 when the inventory taken on the death of John Stringer notes that he held the lease of the two cottages for the term of ten thousand years *whereof the most part of the sayd tearme is yet to come & unexpired*. Unfortunately, John Stringer probably was not living in either cottage; it is more likely that he owned the leasehold and was letting them to others.

Towards the end of the 17th century Slinfold House was modernised by replacing the smoke bay with a brick stack. The stack was built to the rear of the house, giving a large cooking hearth on the ground floor and a smaller hearth to heat the chamber above. Siting the stack to the rear meant that the space previously occupied by the end smoke bay could be incorporated into the living area.

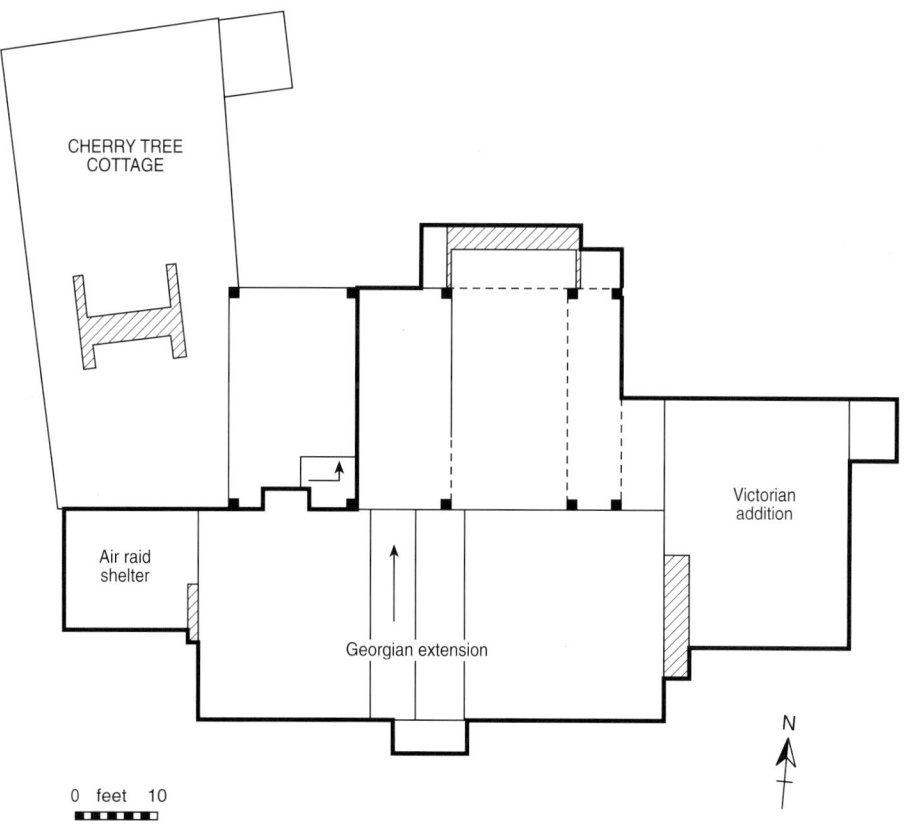

Fig. 22. *Ground plan of Slinfold House (bold outline) and Cherry Tree Cottage*

By 1700 the cottages were owned by members of the Puttock family, relatives of the Puttocks of Dedisham Farm. It is possible that James Puttock and his son John, who were butchers, lived here.

Their heirs mortgaged the property and presumably got into difficulties since, in 1740 the Rector, Dr. Thomas Manningham, took over the property and the mortgage himself. He then left the cottages to David Worsfold the younger in his will. David was descended from the Puttocks; he was a cordwainer living in one of the cottages with his father, another David who was also a cordwainer.

At the time of David the father, there was yet another cordwainer, John Knight, working from the other cottage. John took as apprentice one Thomas Worsfold, son of a David Worsfold who was a farmer in Abinger in Surrey. Thomas must surely have been related to David, father and son, and would have been lodging next door to them. By 1753 John Knight had been replaced by John Mills. He was a tailor who came from the parish of East Meon in Hampshire, and the churchwardens of Slinfold demanded an indemnity bond from that parish stating that if John, his wife and three small children fell on hard times and became a charge on the parish, then East Meon would pay for their relief.

In 1774, after the death of David Worsfold the younger, the property was sold to Charles Holden, who was both innkeeper and blacksmith. He let the cottages and continued to occupy the Kings Head. During the later years of the 18th century he upgraded both cottages. Cherry Tree Cottage was converted into two dwellings. The front range was encased in brick and almost certainly extended northwards to provide enough accommodation for the second cottage. Old timbers do survive within the brickwork but they are totally hidden and give no information about the original form of this range. The 17th century central chimney stack does, however, survive up to eaves level.

The other cottage had a large extension built in front of it, which also extends across the timber-framed bay to the rear of Cherry Tree Cottage. This addition is constructed of a light-weight wooden frame-work known as stud-walling, covered on the interior with lath and plaster and on the outside with a brick skin. The brickwork is a most attractive arrangement of red stretchers and blue headers. It provided two good-sized rooms on each floor with a central hallway and stairs. Because it was built with a cellar under the west side, the level of the ground floor was somewhat raised, which created a problem as the floor level of the original cottage was considerably lower. To overcome this, the cottage floor was raised and, to compensate for the loss of height, the upper floor was also raised.

These alterations carried out by Charles Holden completely changed the character of the pair of cottages. Cherry Tree Cottage, which had been a moderate sized dwelling, now became two small cottages, while Slinfold House changed from a small cottage to a house of some standing.

In 1808 Charles gave the whole premises, together with the $1\frac{1}{2}$ acres of land that went with them, to his daughter Ann and her husband Edward Child. Edward and Ann, and their son Thomas who was about ten years old at the time, moved into Slinfold House in 1811. They, however, called it The Cottage, a name which stayed with the house until the 1930s.

Up to this date it is impossible to know which of the cottages a particular person was inhabiting. The deed of gift from Charles to Edward and Ann states that the premises were occupied by John Mills, John Patching and James Davey, but there is no way of knowing who was where. With the arrival of the Childs in Slinfold House, it becomes easier, but unfortunately there is a gap in the records as far as Cherry Tree Cottage is concerned until the 1839 Tithe Map.

Edward and Ann had live-in servants to look after them, and Edward ran his timber and farming business from the house (see p.16). The house had been built with a flight of stairs up to two small unlit attic rooms and it was here that Edward kept old papers connected with his work. One bundle of hewing and sawing bills from 1804 slipped between the floorboards where they remained until they came to light during repairs in 1981. They provide an interesting insight into the timber business of that era. The Childs converted one of the unlit attic rooms into a usable room by building a gabled extension to the rear of the roof. The little triangular piece visible from the front of the house projecting above the ridge is the roof of this new room.

Edward and Ann stayed in Slinfold House until their deaths in 1850 and 1862 respectively. Ann was 87 when she died, by which time she had been in the house for over 50 years. The Child family continued to own the whole premises until 1937, but after Ann's death no member of the family lived there.

For some years Slinfold House was used as the residence for the curate of the parish and it was probably at this time that the extension to the east of the house was added. This had just one room on each floor, a pantry on the ground floor connected by stairs to the housekeeper's bedroom above. The Rev. Gibbs Payne Crawfurd, in an article written many years later about his time as curate in the village, wrote of a previous curate

> *It was Mr. Andrewes' habit to sit up reading late at night into the early hours of morning ...... and at the other end of the main street lived a Mr. James Grinstead, (in Taylors) who got up so early in the morning hours that the people used to say the village was well guarded by the two men through the night!*

The Rev. Crawfurd moved into the Rectory around 1880 when the Rector took leave of absence due to ill-health. After this a succession of people lived at Slinfold House, including an elderly widow called Phoebe Puttock, who was in the house for several years at the end of the century, and another curate, the Rev. F.W. Clarke, who was there with his family for about 10 years in the early part of the 20th century. In his time the drawing room was to the left and the dining room to the right of the front hall, the stone-floored range at the back contained the kitchen heated by the large rear stack, and a scullery, and the Victorian extension at the side had a pantry on the ground floor connected by the back staircase to the study (formerly the housekeeper's room). There were four bedrooms and one attic room.

Plate 46. *The Cottage c. 1885. The house has hardly altered since, although its name has been changed to Slinfold House*

In the early 1930s E. Bainbridge Copnall was in the house with his wife and family. He was both artist and sculptor and is said to have executed designs for various cinemas, including the Odeon, Leicester Square. A book by C.W.R. Winters entitled *The Queen Mary - Her early years recalled* stated that in the main dining room were fourteen carved panels by Bainbridge Copnall illustrating the history of shipping from the Egyptian era. The author thought that these were the most interesting and satisfying of all the works in the ship, but he felt they were so high up on the walls of this very high room that many passengers would have failed to appreciate them. Horsham Museum has two of his paintings and one, called *Whither*, was displayed at a temporary exhibition on death which was put on at the Museum a few years ago. This painting is not highly regarded and is thus not on permanent display in spite of its apparent Horsham connection with the parish church in the background.

In 1937 Mrs. Kathleen Doll, wife of Dr. Doll, a retired physician, bought the whole property including Cherry Tree Cottages and Church House, which had been built on the land, from Dr. Stanley Child. Thus ended the Childs' connection with the premises which had spanned almost 130 years. The Dolls changed the name of the house from *The Cottage* to *Slinfold House*. They also made a few changes to the house, such as lowering the floor of the timber-framed range and raising the ceiling of the inglenook room. The Horsham Stone floors which were removed were used to create a patio at the back of the house. Some years later Mrs. Doll became concerned about the leaning chimney on the rear stack and had it rebuilt.

The Dolls were well-liked and respected in the village. They had two grown-up sons, the elder of whom, Sir Richard Doll, is an eminent cancer specialist. The younger, Christopher, was a fighter pilot during the war and won the DFC. Cliff White in his book *Horsham, The War Years*, tells of Christopher's habit of coming back over Slinfold in his Hurricane, sweeping over the garden of his parents' house and dipping his wings before returning to the airfield. Friends pointed out that this was not a good idea because his parents worried that he had been shot down on the days when he did not fly. Mrs. Doll organised a Hurricane Fund and raised a considerable amount of money for this. There were many Spitfire funds but this is believed to be the only Hurricane Fund in the country.

Towards the end of Mrs. Doll's life Christopher and his wife took over the house and bought it on her death in 1977. Christopher had worked in television most of his life and his wife, Josephine Doll née Douglas, came to public notice as a compère, with Pete Murray, of the first ITV Pop Music Show *Oh Boy* in about 1958-60. Later she directed at least one Hammer House of Horror movie.

In 1979 the Dolls moved to another house in the village (White Briars) and there followed two short-term occupancies before the present owners moved in 19 years ago.

There are various outbuildings in the garden of Slinfold House which were most likely built by Edward Child. The property was described as *a messuage, garden, orchard, croft or close* in 1763, while by 1871 there is mention of a *stable, coach house and outbuildings*. In 1910 there was a *large store, coach house and stable for one horse, coals etc.* The coach house and stable have been replaced by a modern garage. The outbuilding described as a large store is still there. It is nowadays known as *the barn* although it quite clearly never functioned as one. Over the years it has had many uses. Edward may have used it as a garden and fruit store, or it may have had a use connected with his business interests. In January 1880 the curate, Rev. G.P. Crawfurd, opened a Parish Reading Room in this outbuilding. It was *comfortably furnished and provided with numerous objects of instruction and amusement*. It was intended to provide healthy instruction and rational amusement to the working men of the village. A lending library was also established in the Reading Room. This venture was obviously a great success for later in the year there was a proposal to enlarge the accommodation if sufficient funds could be obtained. The funds were duly raised and the new extension to the outbuilding is clearly visible today. The Reading Room did not have a very long life, however, as both it and the library moved to the Village Hall when this was built in 1881.

Houses on Clemsfold Land

The outbuilding was apparently used for occasional dances in the early 20th century, and a pump was at one point installed in it to pump water from the well into a water tank within the house. In the early 1930s Bainbridge Copnall used it as his studio and the central section of the north-facing roof was replaced by glass. During the Second World War, when Canadian troops were stationed in the village, it became the officers' mess and older residents in the village still refer to it as *the canteen*. It is now used as a venue for occasional meetings of groups connected with the present owners.

Cherry Tree Cottage was earlier known as 1 & 2 The Street, but there is no information available on the inhabitants from 1808 until 1839. By this date the northern cottage was occupied by Richard Jeal and his family. In 1851 Richard, his wife and their seven children, plus a lodger, were in this small cottage. It is difficult for us these days to comprehend how people managed in such cramped circumstances. In the 1880s a cleaver and carpenter, Thomas Redman, and his family were in this cottage and then for many years George Ede. In the late 1920s and throughout the 1930s Alfred George Stemp lived here and ran a cycle repair business, partly from his home and partly in the outbuildings of the Kings Head. In one local directory he described himself as Motor Engineer of the Kings Head Garage. His wife was a postwoman and people who remember her describe her as a great character.

William Freeman and his wife Phoebe lived in the southern cottage with their family from the 1840s. The youngest son, John, became a tailor's apprentice and when he was qualified he moved into purpose-built premises now known as Regency House. By 1891, in their old age, William and Phoebe had joined their son John at his house. Jesse Buckman was in the cottage for a number of years at the turn of the century.

In later years one noteworthy occupant of Cherry Tree Cottage was Miss 'Jane' Horsman who was for many years matron of Horsham Hospital. A ward has been named in her memory in the newer part of the hospital. Miss Horsman combined both cottages into one dwelling after she purchased the property from Mrs. Doll in 1952. For the first time in its history Cherry Tree Cottage was no longer in the same ownership as Slinfold House. These two properties show very clearly how the status of a house can change over the years.

Plate 47. *Cherry Tree Cottage*

THE VILLAGE HALL (7)

The Village Hall was built in 1881 in memory of Thomas and Caroline Child by their children and grandchildren. The Deed of Gift to the Parish of Slinfold was signed by their son and three daughters, by a daughter-in-law, and a son-in-law, and by twelve grandchildren. The brick and tile building stands in the centre of the village, close to the Church, and is inscribed on the front with the monogram TCC and the title VILLAGE HALL AND LIBRARY.

Both building and land were provided by the Child family *to be devoted to the Parish benefit for religious, moral, and social purposes, for ever.* The Deed of Gift laid down that the governance of the hall should be under the direction of the Rector of Slinfold and the Parish Churchwarden *for the time being* and two direct descendants of Thomas and Caroline Child. In the first instance these were to be Charles Child and his sister Kate and provision was made that if they died or were unable to act then their successors were to be elected by a majority vote amongst members of the family living in the parish at the time. Finally, the conditions of the Deed stated that if there were ever fewer than four members of the Child family residing in Slinfold, then one or two trustees should be elected by the ratepayers of the parish.

Thomas Child was the son of Edward Child who had lived in Slinfold House for many years. Thomas and his wife Caroline lived in the house now known as Windalls from 1829 until their deaths in 1870 and 1880 respectively and were both very much involved in village affairs. Thomas had been a most successful and enterprising businessman, generously supporting countless good causes in Slinfold and serving as churchwarden for thirteen years.

In November 1881 the Parish Magazine reported that the new hall had been completed and only awaited its internal furnishing. The Hall Committee were appealing for generous parishioners and friends to provide the necessary items of furniture and these were presumably forthcoming as the hall was formally opened in January 1882 at a parish tea-party given by Lt. Col. and Mrs. St. John. A Village Hall Club had been instituted and 35 residents had signified their intention to join, at a subscription of 2d a week or 2s a quarter.

At the time of the opening, the Parish Magazine was appealing for any volumes of light literature suitable to place in the library and indicated that any of the works of Walter Scott, Charles Kingsley and Charles Dickens would be especially welcome. In February 1882 the new hall was also the venue for the first lecture delivered to an embryo group of people interested in the work of the St. John Ambulance Association.

A number of books, constituting a small village library, had been previously housed in the outbuilding at Slinfold House, but in 1887 a Parish Library was formally founded with a fund set up to celebrate the Golden Jubilee of Queen Victoria. The Committee and subscribers walked in procession from the Jubilee Tree, outside the village hall, through the village to the cricket ground, headed by a Horsham Band.

The ground in front of the hall became a place of celebration for the village and a big group photograph of residents was taken there on the occasion of the Diamond Jubilee. Behind the large crowds of villagers can be seen the hall decorated with bunting, flags, and loyal messages (Pl. 48).

The village hall was obviously a valuable addition to the life of the village and many activities took place there, taking meetings away from the Kings Head which had formerly been the only club-house for Slinfold. The Ministering Children's League, of which Kate Child was the Secretary, met in the hall on Saturday mornings and would certainly never have met in the Kings Head! The children were kept busy making scrapbooks to be sent to local hospitals. The Mothers' Union held monthly meetings there, and the Church Lads Brigade and the Girl Guides all used the hall. Later the Women's Institute held their meetings there and, in present times, the Thursday Club for the over-65s.

At one time the hall was used for the distribution of loaves of bread to the needy, and during the 1939-45 war orange juice and cod liver oil for babies were distributed there.

In the early years of the 20th century the hall became an extension of the village school because it was used for the girls' cookery classes. In 1904 33 students registered for the classes at a fee of 1s for 10 weeks. The Lady Manager of the enterprise was Miss Kate Child and the teacher was a Miss Annie Edser. Four

Plate 48. *Queen Victoria's Diamond Jubilee, 1897.*
'A good muster of parishioners' joined in the celebrations, which included lunch for the men and boys and tea for the ladies and girls!

years later the West Sussex Education Committee was apparently not too happy about the arrangements, largely because although there was a kitchen range in the hall, there was no water. In 1910 the Education authorities were authorising the classes as long as the lavatories at the school were available to all attending the cookery course. At the same time they requested that before another application for approval was made a sink with water supply should be provided. The Slinfold Hall Committee said that this was not possible and after some deliberation in 1911 the Education Board said that they recognized the exceptional circumstances and would not insist on the sink and water, as long as lavatories were available. They approved the classes for 18 girls, and the water was apparently fetched from Church House next door.

During the Second World War the caretaker of the hall was Mrs. Mary Waters, who lived in Church House. Her niece, Sylvia Smith, recalled both her own memories of the hall and her mother's:

> *My mother told me of dances held in the village hall during the First World War. What assignations were made between the Valeta and the Military Two-step? My cousin, Lena Broom, recalls that later, during the Second World War, there were Canadian soldiers stationed in the village. The Village Hall was their recreation centre and they held dances every Saturday evening. Feeling very grown-up, I was chaperoned by my Aunt, Mary Waters, who was the caretaker of the Village Hall.*

Today the Village Hall needs to be extended and improved if it is to meet the ever-increasing needs of the Slinfold community. A great deal of effort has been expended by planners, architect and fund-raisers over the last few years and finally the plans are coming to fruition. Some hundred and twenty years after the construction work carried out through the generosity of a Slinfold family, new building work in the Millennium year will give their old Village Hall a very new look.

Plate 49. *The Village Hall and Church House in the early years of the century before the erection of the War Memorial*

CHURCH HOUSE (8)

Church House is brick-built under a gabled tile roof. The front façade is symmetrical apart from the small bay window to the right of the front porch. The gables above the upstairs windows, the porch and the barge boards all have decorative finials at their apex. The brickwork is stretcher bond, a bond which was introduced to allow the creation of cavity walls. There is a single-storey flat-roofed extension to the rear, but from the front the house still looks as it did when it was erected. It is very similar in appearance to Chapel View, but a little smaller, and there is no doubt that Church House was also built by the Aylings.

Houses on Clemsfold Land

The house was built in the 1880s for occupation by the Rectory gardener. Albert Johnson was the first inhabitant and lived there until the early 1900s. After two fairly short occupancies, Leonard Waters moved there in 1914. These are the memories of Church House by his daughter, Lena Broom, who was born there in 1915 and lived there until 1979:

> *My Parents, Leonard and Mary Waters, came to live in Church House upon their marriage in 1914, my Father being the gardener at the Rectory at that time. I was born in Church House in 1915. When my Mother was alone in the house in 1915, due to the war, Mr. Capon West of the Post Office gave her a bell to ring out of the window at night time in case of emergency.*
>
> *There was no running water or electricity. Water came from a well with a pump outside which was shared by three houses. Lighting was by candles and oil lamps, heating from wood and coal fires (three in all).*
>
> *There were three bedrooms, and downstairs, to the right of the front door was the 'front room' and to the left a living room and large scullery. In the living room there was a kitchen range, and a copper for doing the washing which was fed with fagots. The water was put in with buckets, and taken out with a long-handled bowl (called a handle-dish). Ironing and cooking etc. all took place on a well-scrubbed deal table in the living room. Also in the same room was a brown stone sink for washing up etc. There was no bathroom or toilet. The lavatory was an earth closet outside. There was no garden, only a small piece in the front of the house, the Village Hall being very close.*
>
> *In 1923 at the death of my Grandfather (who had worked for the Child family at Park House), my Grandmother, Mary Holloway, came to live at Church House where she stayed until her death in 1933.*
>
> *I was married in 1941, during the war. My Husband was in the Army and I stayed with my Parents. Both my sons were born in Church House, delivered by Nurse White, the village nurse, and Dr. Jago.*
>
> *My Husband came back from the war in 1945 and my Father died shortly afterwards. We stayed on with my Mother and bought the house in 1956 (from Mrs. Doll). Then began modernisation. A kitchen and bathroom and toilet were added at the back and a conservatory to the side. Frank Killner and his sons did the building with my husband as 'labourer'. We were able to buy a piece of land at the back of the Village Hall to make a garden. Main drainage came about 1953-4, electric light just before the war.*
>
> *My Mother lived with us until she died in 1979. We then sold Church House. I had lived there 64 years.*
>
> *Church House has had several occupants since, and there is now a loft conversion.*

Church House was built on land belonging to the Childs, part of the original property given by Charles Holden to Edward and Ann Child, and it postdates the Village Hall (see Pl. 3). The house was sold with Cherry Tree Cottage and Slinfold House to Dr. & Mrs. Doll in 1937 and Mrs. Doll sold Church House to Frank Broom in 1956.

SOUTH LODGE (4)

This was built in the 1880s and is identical in design to Church House. South Lodge was also built to house a gardener, this time for Hill House. It was called Hill Lodge until the West Lodge on Stane Street was constructed about 1905. A rather unattractive flat-roofed extension was added to the north side of the house, but this has recently been rebuilt in a much more acceptable style.

Plate 50. *South Lodge stands beside the drive up to Hill House which used to be beautifully kept in earlier years*

ST. PETER'S CHURCH (6)

People have been worshipping on the site of the present church for nearly nine hundred years. The old church was built in the 12th century and was small, consisting of just a nave and chancel. It was at first a chapel of ease belonging to Steyning and thus to the Abbey of Fécamp in Normandy, and did not become a parish church until it came into the hands of the Bishop of Chichester in 1231. At that time an agreement was made between the Bishop and the Abbey, whereby all Fécamp's rights to the churches of Slinfold, Nuthurst and Bury were transferred to the Bishop in exchange for the church of Steyning being entirely free from episcopal control.

Over the centuries the church has been constantly altered and updated to meet the changing needs of the worshippers. The nave had no seating to begin with, but it was the focal point of community life and acted as a parish hall; within its walls agreements were negotiated, disputes settled and fund-raising events such as church ales were held. Benches would have been installed in the later middle ages when sermons became popular.

A chantry chapel belonging to the Lord of the Manor of Dedisham was built to the north of the chancel in the late 12th century, and the nave was enlarged by the addition of a north aisle in the 15th century. Around 1530 a tower was erected, built of massive timbers and very similar to the one at Itchingfield. An early 16th century rood loft would have been swept away after the Reformation. In the 17th century a gallery for musicians was added at the west end of the church.

Plate 51. *Painting of the old church from the Grimm drawing of c. 1790*

A major renovation took place in the 1790s when the nave windows were altered, new pews installed and a three-decker pulpit placed against the south wall of the nave. Despite this the church was in a bad state of repair by the mid-19th century when the parish came to consider ways of enlarging the church to fulfil the requirements of the time. A hundred new sittings were needed and a number of plans were put forward to enlarge the church by pulling down the tower and extending the nave westward. After much deliberation it was considered that the best option was to demolish the old church and build afresh. The parishioners gave generously towards the building of the new church, but perhaps the most memorable contribution was made by the Rector of the time, Frederick Vincent, who gave up his carriage and pair and put the savings towards the rebuilding.

A few items were saved from the old church. The Duke of Norfolk, as lord of the manor of Dedisham and therefore life tenant of the Dedisham Chancel, particularly asked for the Lady of Tregoz to be kept. She now lies at the back of the church, and the charming custom of placing a posy of flowers in her hands each Easter still continues. Also from the Dedisham Chancel is the kneeling figure of Katherin Blount, youngest daughter of Richard Blount of Dedisham, who died in 1617. She has been placed high up in the porch. The old parish chest, also in the porch, was made in 1631 at a cost of nine shillings. It has three locks, and the Rector and the two churchwardens each had a key; all three had to be present before the chest could be opened. There are two old brasses, one each side of the altar. One, dated 1533, is in memory of Richard Bradbrydge and his wife and children, who lived at what is now Lower Broadbridge Farm, and the other is to Edward Cowper of Strood (now Farlington School) who died in 1703. The font also came from the old church.

The new church has continued the centuries-old pattern of alteration and updating. The organ was originally at the front of the south aisle, the pulpit has been moved from the other side of the nave and seating has been taken out from the back of the church. The vestry was enlarged to mark Queen Victoria's Diamond Jubilee in 1897, a chancel screen was installed and later removed and a new altar entailed alteration to the sanctuary step and the altar step. Within a few years of the consecration of the new church its tall stone spire was causing problems. These continued until the spire was finally removed in 1970. This pattern of change and alteration will hopefully continue into the future. Without it the church ceases to be a living part of the community and becomes nothing more than a fossilised reminder of the past.

Plate 52. *The Church in 1995*

HOUSES ON WIGGONHOLT LAND

The parent manor of Wiggonholt lay between Pulborough to the north and Parham to the south. It had outlying land in Billingshurst and Slinfold, the Slinfold holding running from Lydwick to the south, as far as Old House Farm in the north.

OLD HOUSE FARM (1)

Old House is set well back from the Street. It lies beside a stream and there is a sizeable garden in front, which was until recently an orchard. Up to the 1950s this was a farm of about 100 acres, but now the farmhouse is completely separate from its land.

The name *Old House* does not appear in many of the earlier records, where the property is called *Blechmeres*. This was a source of confusion when unravelling the history of the farm, since the name *Blechmeres* also refers to what was later Crown Farm and is now Park House on Stane Street. The manorial records for the property on the Street, which survive back to the late 17th century, call the farm *Old House and part of Blechmeres*. Looking at old maps it becomes clear that originally *Blechmeres* was a strip of land running up beside Stane Street, across Park Street, to a point just south of the footpath known to the locals as the Cinder Path. *Old House Farm* was an adjacent strip to the east of Blechmeres. Later Old House incorporated all the Blechmeres land to the north of Park Street into its own holding.

In 1587 the death of John Stringer of Blechmeres was recorded in the parish registers. Some ten years earlier John, *inhabitant next to the church of Slynfold*, had enclosed the area of common land to the south of the church on which Chewton was then erected. Chewton was later an alehouse and indeed, may have been so from the start. Was this perhaps a business venture to supplement John's income from his farm?

From the early 17th century the property was owned by the Cooper family who were letting it to tenants to farm. Old House was leased to Edward Thayre from 1621 and he was still there in 1639 when Richard Naldrett purchased the farm from the Coopers. The previous year Richard had married into the Thayre family.

The present Old House dates from the mid-17th century and was built as a suitable home for Richard and his new wife, Mary. It is an L-shaped building, the main range lying parallel to the road with a wing extending to the north-east. The house incorporates a number of features which are in advance of its time. The ground-floor walls are timber-framed with brick infill, but the first-floor walls are constructed of stud-walling and are the earliest example of this technique known in the area. The light-weight timber frame was never intended to be seen and was from the start covered with tile-hanging on the exterior and lath and plaster on the inside. The internal partitions are also stud-walling and here the timbering has since been exposed in a number of instances.

The main range and the rear wing are contemporary. The front range has a central entrance bay with access to the first floor; to the west is the hall/kitchen heated by a large cooking hearth contained within its own narrow bay, and to the east is the parlour. This is heated by an ingenious triangular stack which also provides a hearth in the wing. Both these hearths are semi-circular, as are the first-floor hearths in the chambers above. The house was built with a cellar under the parlour and also had attic rooms in both main range and wing. The name *Old House* has been around for a long time and must refer to whatever was on the site before the present house was erected. The re-used timbers in the roof of Richard's house almost certainly come from this earlier building.

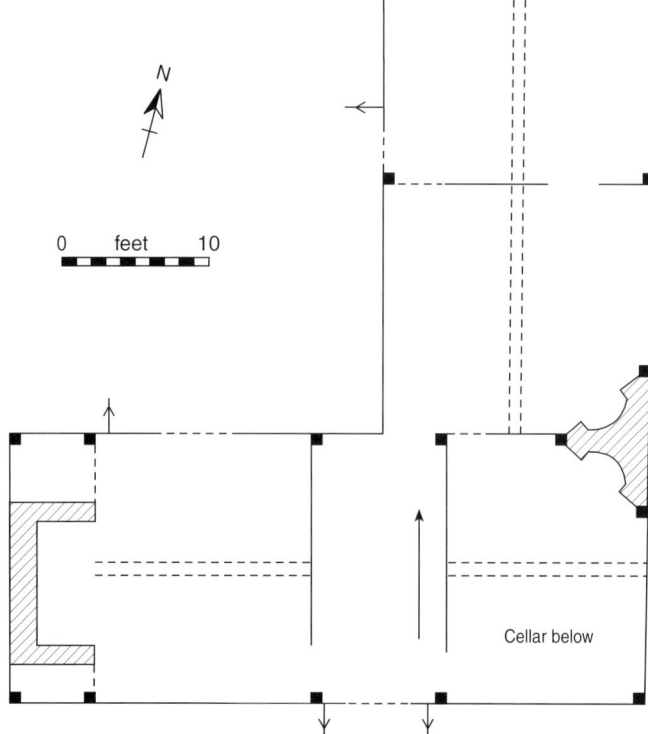

Fig. 23. *Ground plan of Old House Farm*

Old House is larger than might be expected of an ordinary farmhouse and reflects Richard Naldrett's status as a member of one of the wealthier Rudgwick families. It must also have reflected Richard and Mary's hope of a large family, which sadly was not fulfilled. There were live-in servants in the house, one of whom was nine-year old Mary Chelsom who was apprenticed to Richard in 1664 to be taught housewifery.

Richard lived at Old House until his death in 1669. The rooms listed in the Inventory of his goods and chattels correspond very well with those in the house. *His bed Chamber* and the *Maid's Chamber* are on the first floor in the wing, with *two Low Chambers* on the ground floor below them. The *Hall* is the room to the west of the main entrance and the *Parlour* is to the east, while on the first floor above them are the *Chamber over the Hall*, the *Parlour Chamber* and between them the *Stair Chamber*. The *Cellar* is mentioned and the wool and flax would have been stored in the attics. There must have been one or more outbuildings containing the *Bakehouse*, the *Milk house* and the *Brewhouse*. A *Barn* and a *Stable* are also mentioned.

Old House Farm passed to Richard's nephew George Naldrett, of Naldrett House in Rudgwick, and then to his great-nephew, another George. Richard's widow, Mary, continued to live in the house until her death in 1705 at the age of 88, and her interests were looked after by both Georges. A lease of Old House Farm by George Naldrett to Francis Greenfield of Slinfold in 1704, states that Mary is to continue to live in the part of the house she currently occupies and that she is to have half of the fruit from the trees in the orchard.

Mary Naldrett may not have had any children, but her will makes it clear that she had an extended circle of godchildren, relations and friends. She left numerous legacies and she appointed two executors to deal with all these. She asked that she should be buried:-

in Christian burial in the Parish Church of Slynfold as near to my late Husband Richard Naldrett, deceased, as conveniently may be. And I doe hereby Desire my Executors to ley out and Expend the sume of Twenty pounds equally between them for the Entertainement of such friends and relations as shall be pleased to accompany my body to the nave in such decent manner as to them shall seem most requisite and convenient.

Old House Farm continued in the hands of the Naldretts and their heirs, descending through marriage to the St. Johns of Slinfold Lodge. However, Richard Naldrett was the only owner who actually lived in the house. Thereafter it was let to tenants, many of whom are anonymous.

Plate 53. *South and east elevations of Old House Farm. The two ranges are contemporary*

By 1780 Nathaniel Knight was the tenant and he may have already been there for some time. He had been farming Hayes Grange since 1756. Thomas Knight succeeded him at both farms in 1782. Thomas was also farming Hall Land from 1790 and under the will of his uncle, Thomas Holland, he became the owner in 1794. For almost 30 years Thomas farmed all three properties, but in 1822 he ceased to occupy Hayes Grange. After his death in 1826 two of his sons, Thomas and Nathaniel, carried on a combined farming operation. Thomas lived at Old House, while Nathaniel was at Fulfords Farm in Itchingfield, and their father had left them Hall Land Farm as tenants in common.

Another brother, Charles, was a grocer in Horsham's West Street. In his diary, which he wrote every Sunday, he frequently mentions visiting his family at Old House. By 1834 Thomas's health was causing concern and in February 1835 Charles noted: *My Brother Thomas is in a Very poor State of Health & has been for some time*. In January 1836 he reported: *My Brother Thomas is still very Poorly. I fear he is not long for this World*. In April Thomas consulted a Physician in London, but to no avail: *I fear his case is quite hopeless, he keeps Wasting away*.

Thomas finally died in November 1836 at the age of 46, leaving a widow and four young children. Hall Land Farm was sold to John Briggs of Hall Land House the following year, and Thomas's widow, Mary, ran Old House Farm until her death in 1854. Her eldest son, another Thomas, took over the farm assisted by his younger brother, Alfred, and their elder sister, Mary, returned home to act as their housekeeper. In the 1860s Thomas moved away and Alfred, who was now married, lived there with his growing family. He too left Old House in the early 1870s, ending the hundred-year old association of the Knight family with the farm.

They did, however, leave their mark on the place. One of the outbuildings associated with the farm was a cartshed with granary above. The ceiling of the granary was plastered over and the Knights and their friends and visitors had for generations signed their names on the plaster. The cartshed and granary still survive, but sadly, the ceiling became dilapidated and a few years ago it was removed.

Plate 54. *Names of the Knights and their friends on the granary ceiling. 'M K' stands for Michael Knight who later lived at Holmbush*

The farm was then run for some 20 years by Charles Gander and his wife. Around this time Old House had the last working ox in the area. Its chief work was to draw two-ton loads of grain from the old brewery at Horsham, at a speed of about 1½ miles an hour!

Around 1892 Mrs. Mary Boniface took over the farm. The Bonifaces ran a dairy farm and several villagers remember having to call into Old House after school to collect milk. One said their name suited them as they both had ruddy faces and were very genial.

A Mr. Edwards had the farm for a few years round 1930 and then it went to the Hobbs in 1940. Mr. Hobbs was a part-time farmer, being a company director as well. The National Farm Survey of 1941 described the farm as well-managed. One section of the questionnaire asked whether there was a heavy infestation with weeds and if so, what kind of weeds. Whoever filled in the form used the delightful phrase *Fair normal weeds!* George Hobbs, the showjumper, took on the farm after his father and used to practise in a field near the farm buildings. George would have liked to buy Old House Farm, but Major St. John preferred the farm to be let as it always had been.

With the death of Major Edward St. John in 1953 the 300 year old link with the Naldretts came to an end, and the trustees of his will sold the farm to Mr. Buckle of Fladgates, who in turn sold the farmhouse and released plots of land along the Street and Park Street for building. Of the farm buildings, only the cartshed/granary remained with the farmhouse. The stables and cowsheds were converted into the dwelling named **The Old Stables,** and the barn is in the grounds of **Barn Cottage.** Nearby **Fosseys** is the third house in this little group at the western end of the Street. None of these is within the Conservation Area.

It was only recently, after the farmhouse had been separated from its land, that Old House was for the first time extended, when a single-storey room was built in the angle between the two ranges. Most old timber-framed buildings have been added to over the years as the occupants felt the need for an increasing amount of living space. Old House is very unusual in this respect, a result of being built by a member of the minor gentry who erected a dwelling suitable to his status but much larger than was needed by subsequent tenant farmers.

SLINFOLD SCHOOL (2)

In 1845 Edward Brice Bunny and his wife Emma, of Slinfold Lodge, gave a piece of land to the Rector and Churchwardens of Slinfold as a site for *a School for poor persons of and in the Parish of Slinfold and for the Residence of the Schoolmaster.* The site was a small plot of 26 perches (probably about 30 yards square) of land to the west of the church, belonging to Old House Farm and known as the Church Croft. To the south and east it was bordered by the road from Park Street Corner to the village.

The deed of gift stated that the school was to be conducted according to the principles of the National Society for Promoting the Education of the Poor in the Principles of the Established Church and would be under the management and control of the Rector and the Churchwardens. The school would be maintained largely by voluntary subscriptions from the wealthier members of the parish, and over the years a succession of Rectors laboured endlessly to secure these subscriptions. The school's statement of account in 1850 showed a total of £25 18s in subscriptions, several of which were from donors outside the parish like the Duke of Norfolk, although he was not a complete outsider as he was the Lord of the Manor of Dedisham. The largest donation at this time was from the Rector himself.

The school was built in 1849, of Horsham stone from the local quarry at Nowhurst with brick quoins and a slate roof. It was a simple building comprising one large school room, 36 feet long, attached to a two storey house for the schoolmaster with a scullery and living room downstairs and two bedrooms upstairs. The rooms had fireplaces and the schoolroom had a fireplace at each end. The original school was intended to house 100 pupils, although this number increased over the years necessitating various alterations and enlargements to the buildings. During the 1870s an additional classroom was built, the schoolmaster's house, after urgent pressure from the incumbent, was enlarged, outhouses were improved and the schoolyard gravelled. The Rector's wife had given £5 for the erection of a school bell and turret. The front porch was added in 1882 and by the time further additions had been made in 1884 the school could accommodate 140 children, aged from 5 to 14.

A new infant room was added in 1899 and by 1912 new lavatories had been erected at the back of the school on some of the extra land newly leased to the Rector and Churchwardens for 99 years at an annual rent of 5 shillings. This year also saw the arrival of the long awaited new desks which had been promised two years before when a School Inspector had found the old desks in a decrepit state. A plan of proposed alterations to the school at this time showed it with 3 classrooms, (Infants, Lower Juniors, and Upper Juniors), an office, a cloakroom with basins, an internal room designed to hold two lavatories and basins, a staff room, and a separate block of boys' and girls'

Plate 55. *The School in 1906. The porch was removed when a footpath was created along the side of the road*

lavatories. The part of the original building which had been the schoolmaster's house was now included in the school premises and was not shown as a dwelling in the Lloyd George's Domesday Survey in 1915.

For many years the financial position of the school was a source of great concern to its management committee and particularly to all the Rectors in turn. The children were charged a weekly payment and in 1869 there was a graduated system whereby small farmers and tradesmen paid 4d a week for their first child and 3d each for their siblings, and farm labourers paid 2d for their first child and 1d for others. This may have proved unnecessarily divisive or complicated and by the autumn of 1880 the payment was set at 2d for every child in the school. A year later an appeal was made to rate-payers in the parish to contribute a one-off extra payment of 3d in the £ with a future annual rate of 4d, instead of the 3d they had apparently been paying. The appeal failed and in 1882 it was agreed that the school should become a Board School, in accordance with the 1870 Education Act. The praiseworthy efforts of all the Rectors of the period had managed to maintain the school by voluntary subscription for the first 33 years of its life but for the next 20 years it was to be run and maintained by the Education Board. After the 1902 Education Act, however, Slinfold reverted to denominational status and became a *non-provided* Church School. This gave the Managers more control over the choice of teachers (although they were still paid by the Education Authority) and returned the ownership of the land and buildings to the local Trustees. The Rector at this time, the Rev. F.G. Hughes, wrote *As the National Parish School has now reverted to us, we ask for an annual subscription amongst the Parish Charities for the upkeep of the exterior of the Building.* In this appeal letter Mr. Hughes referred to the fact that the Parish would now be able to continue its use of the school playground *which is outside the school area,* and that the present owner of the field around the school (Mr. Brice Bunny, who donated the original site,) had given assurances that there would be no difficulty in extending the school building in the future if this was required.

In the early years no teachers stayed very long in Slinfold. The first school master and his wife were Mr. and Mrs. Penny who were paid 44 guineas a year and allowed to keep half the proceeds of the evening school, which in 1850 amounted to 8s 5d. One year later the census shows Miss

Ann Path, aged 24, as the schoolmistress. Over the next 15 years there were at least three women teachers, Miss Emily Richardson (only 19 years old), Miss Funnel and Miss Osborne. The last named was thanked by the school management committee *for her ability and general conduct in her management of the school especially as H.M. Inspector had just visited and expressed himself much pleased with the progress and satisfactory state of the school.*

Despite Miss Osborne's good record the management committee decided in 1869 that they should engage a schoolmaster and wife, chiefly because the school was being enlarged to take in a class of older boys. An advertisement was placed in the National Society's magazine and resulted in the appointment of Mr. and Mrs. Mortimer. It was Mr. Mortimer who in 1872 threatened to resign if the schoolmaster's house were not enlarged.

A pupil-teacher system had been established by the National Board in 1846 under which suitable candidates, aged 13, were apprenticed to teachers for 4-5 years and received $1\frac{1}{2}$ hours of daily instruction in addition to their teaching duties. They had to pass annual examinations and prepare for the Queen's Scholarship at the end of their apprenticeship. Successful candidates went on to college for two years and if they then passed the final government examination became *certificated* teachers, entitled to a third of their salary from public funds. In Slinfold one of the older boys, Alfred Stanford, was apprenticed as a pupil-teacher in 1871, with wages of £10 p.a. in the first year, gradually increasing to a maximum of £20 at the end of the apprenticeship. Sadly this was not a successful apprenticeship as Mr. Mortimer reported later that he was *unlikely to succeed in the profession of schoolmaster* and his indentures were cancelled.

Mr. and Mrs. Mortimer resigned in 1874 and there is record of temporary teachers, including Richard Burton and Mrs. Elizabeth Cane, during the next four years until William Brown and his wife arrived in the autumn of 1878. Mr. Brown was only 22 years old but he was a *certificated elementary* teacher and received an annual salary of £90. He stayed at Slinfold school for over 42 years, retiring in 1921 but still living in the village in 1932. His wife was Assistant Mistress for 34 years and some years ago there were still older residents who remembered them. Mr. Brown was said to be very strict - used the cane - but a good schoolmaster and apparently much respected by the whole community.

The school day lasted from 9am to 3.45pm, with $1\frac{1}{2}$ hours for lunch. Many children went home for lunch but those who lived further away obviously took food with them as in 1881 the school committee decided to build *a porch in which the children might place their clothes and dinners.* As in most schools of the period the curriculum was based on the three Rs and, as this was a Church school, there was a compulsory period of religious instruction at the beginning of each day taken by the Rector. By 1896 the obligatory subjects were the three Rs, history, geography, domestic economy, needlework for the girls, and drawing for the older boys. Needlework was considered very important as the girls were expected to be capable of making and maintaining their families' clothing once they married. The school management committee had arranged in the 1860s that ladies of the parish should superintend the needlework instruction and an annual sale of items made in the class brought in much needed extra income for the committee.

In the early 1900s girls were also taught dairywork and laundry work, and there were cookery classes in the village hall. By 1905 woodwork lessons were mentioned and by the 1920s the older boys were playing football, usually on the Rectory meadow, and the girls were playing stoolball.

At the school prize days there were prizes for conduct, progress and good attendance. Discipline was strict, corporal punishment being used in the case of lying, playing truant, and swearing. In the early years there were probably four main reasons why children missed school: illness (epidemics of serious childhood diseases like diphtheria, scarlet fever, measles etc.

affected the whole village on occasion); inability of parents to pay the weekly fee; bad weather which made walking long distances in inadequate clothing difficult; and seasonal events. The last cause of non-attendance was always recorded in rural areas like Slinfold as the children of farmers or farm labourers were needed to help in the fields with planting, haymaking and harvesting.

By 1910 medical inspections had started in the school, including head examinations for lice and teeth inspections. In 1912 the report of a medical officer indicated the Slinfold children were on the whole very healthy with only two instances of head lice and two children with defective vision who would have to sit nearer to the blackboard!

The village school always played an important part in the community. The teachers were often very active members of village societies and the school premises leant themselves to all sorts of other functions. Slinfold school was used for flower shows, concerts, the annual dinner of the Slinfold Agricultural Association, the Girls' Friendly Society, and many other events.

Plate 56. *The Loan Exhibition held in the School in January 1892*

In January 1892 the school housed a very special Loan Exhibition. The exhibition of *articles of rarity, beauty, interest and value* contained over a thousand items ranging from valuable works of art (a Correggio, 2 Turner oils, a George Morland and a Kaufman), to curios collected from around the world and small examples of cottagers' crafts and treasured mementoes. The exhibition was opened by Sir Walter Barttelot, the M.P. for North West Sussex, and reported at great length in both the County newspapers and in the parish magazine. The West Sussex Gazette described it as *one of the most interesting and notable that has probably been held in Sussex for many years* and in the Parish magazine several pages listed the exhibits. It was certainly a most eclectic collection, including treasures of Egyptian archaeology, a model of the Taj Mahal in soapstone, an autographed letter from Charles II, hairs from the heads of Henry IV, Isaac Newton and Napoleon, and a great display of oriental porcelain.

The exhibition was insured for £2000 against fire for a premium of £1 and a police constable was present day and night during the whole period. This involved three policemen and cost £3 6s. Some 1470 visitors were recorded during the week and the final profit, of £6 6s 5$^1/_2$d, was invested as the first instalment of a reparation fund for the village hall!

Many present-day residents of Slinfold remember their own years at the village school, some back into the twenties and thirties. There are memories of stoolball, skipping and playing marbles in the playground (with the comment that marbles were only played in springtime, *never after Good Friday*), of the special inspector who came for the scripture examination, of cocoa being provided for elevenses, and toasting bread in front of the big classroom stove at dinnertime. In 1923 the school had its first outing when 82 parents and 40 children went to Bognor by train, setting a precedent for the annual outing to the sea remembered still by many.

IRONWOOD HOUSE (formerly THE RECTORY) (3)

Ironwood House, which was until 1985 the Rectory, lies to the north-west of the church beside Clapgate Lane, on a long, narrow plot of some two and a half acres. A perambulation of the bounds of the manor of Wiggonholt of 1791 places the Rectory within that manor.

A survey of the house and glebe-land taken in 1635 describes the property thus:

> *One dwellinge house containinge three roomes in one floore with lodgings over them, with certaine outletts adioyninge to those romes, together with a brewhouse and bakehouse, one large barne for corne and one less for hey, one orchard and gardine and one other smale peece of pasture.*

No trace remains of this house, with its three ground-floor rooms, three chambers above, and service rooms in an outshot along the back, so it is not possible to tell whether it was an open-hall house which had been modernised or whether it was a more recent build. The brewhouse and bakehouse would have been in a separate building and the 1651 map (Map 5) does show a little building with its own chimney behind the parsonage house. The corn barn and the hay barn would have been for storing produce received as tithes. There was no other glebe-land in the parish apart from the plot on which the Rectory stood. Many parsons elsewhere had much more land with which to support themselves; on the other hand Slinfold Rectory was monetarily a rich benefice.

One of the Rectors to live in this house was Matthew Woodman, grandson of Richard Woodman who suffered martyrdom at Lewes in the reign of Queen Mary. Matthew was educated at Magdalen Hall, Oxford. He was a Presbyterian who was intruded into Slinfold in 1647. While he was at the Rectory he had a large family, the first child being born in 1653 when there is an entry in the parish registers for the baptism of *Kathrin, daughter of Mr. Woodman, minishter*. He was in Slinfold throughout the difficult years of the Protectorate, officiating at church services that many of the parishioners must have found strange and hard to accept. But Matthew Woodman was later described as *a meek man and of moderate principles and his carriage was so inoffensive that he was universally beloved*. The character of the man probably overcame any scruples local people may have felt. He was confirmed in his office at the Restoration in 1660, but was ejected from his living in 1662 as a result of his noncomformity. He spent the rest of his life preaching in Horsham, where he is buried.

Thomas Manningham, DD, whose father was Bishop of Chichester, was at the Rectory from 1711 until his death in 1750. As well as being Rector of Slinfold, he was also Rector of Selsey, treasurer of Chichester Cathedral, prebendary of Westminster and chaplain to the Speaker of the House of Commons. In spite of his various offices, it is clear that Thomas spent much of his time in Slinfold and was concerned for the wellbeing of his parishioners (see p.104). He married Mistress Mary Yates at Warnham in 1713 and several children were born to them during his time here, and he himself was buried in Slinfold. He also acquired several farms in the parish: Lyons, Buckmots (near Five Oaks), Lydwick and Dann. Thomas is said to have studied botany and in pursuance of his interests, he is credited with introducing some rare plants into the parish. The Hairy, or Coral Spurge, was referred to in 1847 by the well-known botanist William Borrer as growing in Slinfold Parsonage, and in his Herbarium it was said to be the only known specimen in the British Isles. Coral Spurge can still be found to this day in the garden and nearby in Clapgate Lane.

When George Bland became Rector in 1834, he found the Rectory in a state of considerable disrepair and asked permission to rebuild it. A surveyor was sent to report on the state of the building and assess whether it would be preferable to repair and extend the old building, or to demolish it and build anew. He began his report by stating that:

> *The Rectory House has been built at different periods, and consequently presents an irregular and unsightly appearance.*

The old timber-framed building described in the survey of 1635 had clearly been updated in the 18th century by giving it a brick façade, and a new wing had been added which the surveyor considered to be *of exceedingly slight and indifferent construction.* This sounds like the stud-wall construction typical of the 18th century, which may look slight but which lasts well enough when looked after. The surveyor concluded that the best course was to pull down the old dwelling and start afresh.

This report shows the difference in attitude towards old buildings prevailing then and now. These days the irregular appearance of the various phases of the old Rectory would be considered to have its own charm, and every effort would have been made to repair and conserve the old building whilst modernising it.

Having decided to build anew no time was wasted. The plans for the new dwelling were put forward in April 1835 and Charles Knight reported in his diary for 24th May that the *Old Parsonage House at Slinfold is now pulled down and a new one is building for the New Vicar Mr. Bland, the Expence of the New House estimated £1500.* The surveyor/builder had quoted a price of £1200 less £200 for materials from the old building. Whatever the true price, it is put into perspective when compared with the £120 plus various donated materials spent on the row of four almshouses (The Barracks), which were erected around the same time.

The new Rectory was a large rectangular brick building under a slate roof. The house was aligned on the same axis as the demolished building, with its front façade facing south. The central front door opened on to a hallway running the length of the building with the stairs to the rear. To the right were the service rooms and to the left were the drawing room, study and dining room facing out over the garden. There was a cellar below and above were six bedrooms. The stables and coach house are probably contemporary with the house.

George Bland was a single gentleman and this new Rectory was more than adequate for his needs. However, when Frederick Vincent became Rector in 1844, he found the accommodation somewhat cramped for his family and numerous servants. The 1851 Census lists a total of 17 people in the house. At some point during his incumbency he almost doubled the size of the Rectory by adding an extension on the garden side of the building. This was in a totally different style to the original build, which has a Georgian appearance. The new wing was taller, with accommodation on three floors, and looked uncompromisingly Victorian with square bays under gabled roofs on the west façade and a further square bay projecting from the southern end. When Frederick Vincent handed the building over to his successor, Robert Sutton, in 1868, it had a total of 13 bedrooms and at least 11 other rooms. Robert Sutton had an even larger household of 19 people!

Plate 57. *The new Rectory built for Mr. Bland in 1835/6 with the later Victorian wing to the left*

In 1910 the accommodation was said to consist of seven bedrooms, one dressing room, bathroom, two servants bedrooms, boxroom, drawing room, dining room, morning room, Parish room, library, servants hall, kitchen, scullery, butlers pantry and conservatory. By this time various small, single-storey extensions had been added to the rear and side of the original service rooms.

Plate 58. *The peace Pageant in August 1919. The Rectory garden was the setting for many entertainments and garden parties over the years*

With the advent of smaller families and fewer live-in servants, the Rectory had become vastly too large by the 1930s. The Victorian wing was pulled down some time during this decade, the exact date being a matter of debate. One old resident claimed that Alan Hughes only consented to become Rector in 1939 on condition that the Rectory was made smaller and modernised. His father, Frederick Hughes, had been Rector for twenty years at the beginning of the century. The cement rendering of the exterior of the building and the new sash windows are presumably part of this modernisation.

Fifty years later, the upkeep of even the smaller residence was too much for any incumbent without private means and, after David Chaning-Pearce left in 1985, there was a long interregnum before it was finally decided to find a more suitable dwelling for the new Rector. The Rectory was put up for auction in 1988 and one of the conditions of sale was that there should be no mention of the word Rectory in the house name. The property is now known as Ironwood House.

APPENDIX

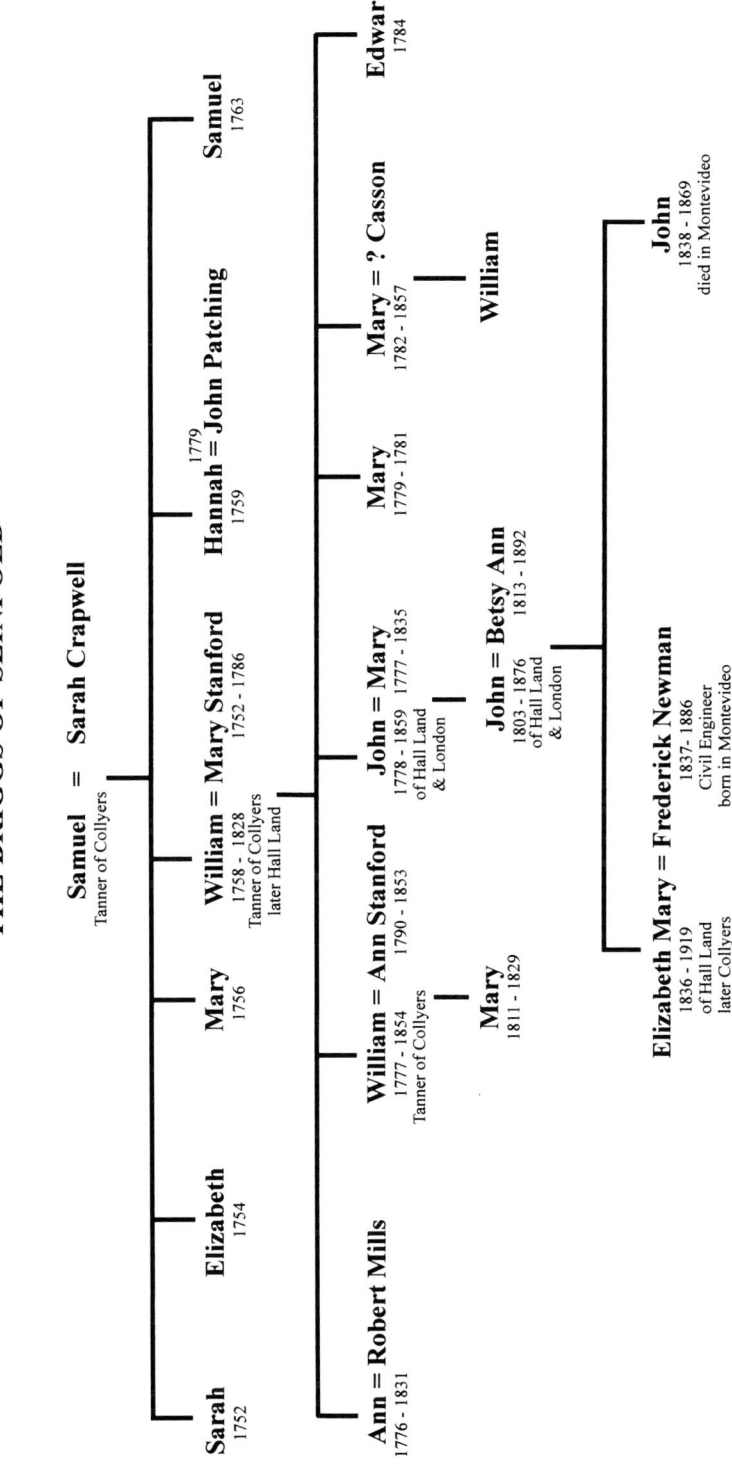

THE CHILDS OF SLINFOLD

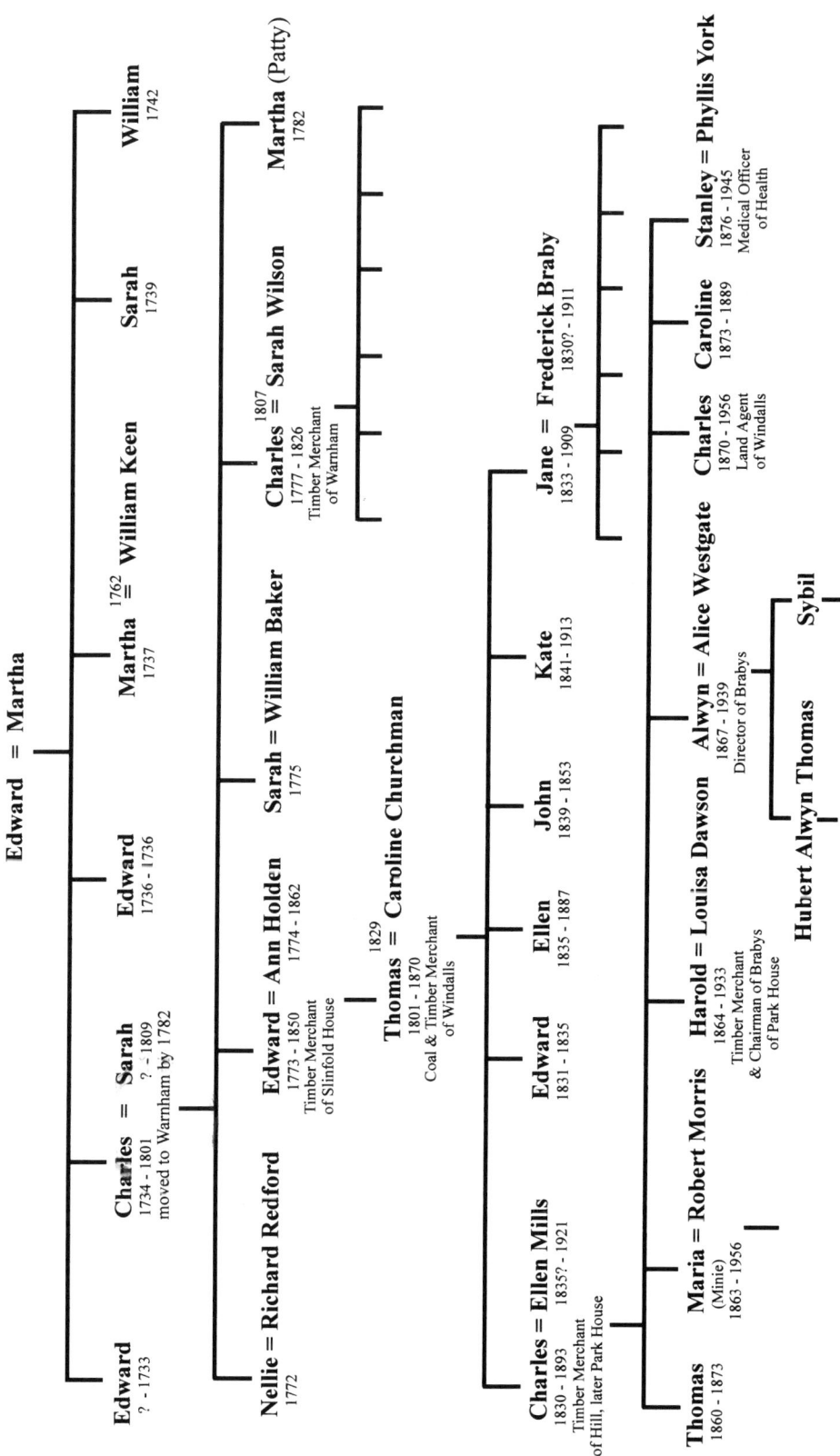

GLOSSARY

Brace Timber running between vertical and horizontal members, stiffening the frame by triangulation.

Down-brace - timber from a vertical member to a lower horizontal member.

Up-brace - timber from a vertical member to a higher horizontal member.

Bresummer The sill of the upper wall above a jetty; also a beam spanning an opening and carrying a wall above it, such as the beam above the hearth of a fireplace.

Census returns A census of the population was taken every ten years starting in 1801. From 1841 the records show the name of each person at the address at which he or she spent the night of the census date.

Dentil course Oversailing courses of brickwork (see below) were frequently used to break the transition from wall to roof. One course was often a course of headers with every other one projecting and this was referred to as the dentil course or dentilations.

Eaves-plate See wall-plate.

Endshot See outshot.

Glebe Land assigned to the incumbent of a parish as part of his benefice.

Inventory A list of personal belongings, goods and chattels, usually with a valuation. Normally drawn up after a person's death for probate purposes.

Jetty The projection of the wall of one storey to overhang the wall of the storey below.

Land Tax A tax imposed on real estate from the end of the 17th century until 1963. Duplicates of the records survive for the years 1780-1832 and are held in the County Record Offices.

Lloyd George's Domesday As a part of Lloyd George's proposed reform of the land tax in 1910, every property in the country was surveyed. The resultant field books and maps give invaluable information.

Messuage A dwelling-house with the ground around it and any outbuildings.

Mid-rail Horizontal timber dividing wall frame into two large panels which are then subdivided by rails, studs and braces. Also known as a Side-girt.

National Farm Survey	Survey undertaken during the early years of the Second World War, both in connection with increasing food production during the war and to provide data for post-war planning.
Outshot	Single-storey area behind a building which is roofed by a continuation of the main roof, but partitioned off from the main space. An outshot at the end of a house is also known as an endshot.
Oversailing	One course of brickwork projecting further than the course below.
Ovolo moulding	A moulding which, in section, is a quarter round.
Poor Rates	Lists of rates collected for the relief of the poor, listing owners and occupiers of properties, together with the rateable value.
Tithe Map	A tithe was a tax of one-tenth of the profits and stock of parishioners, which was formerly levied to support the clergy and the church. The Tithe Commutation Act of 1836 allowed tithes to be commuted to rent charges and commissioners were appointed to negotiate land values in each parish. The survey records of the commissioners and their large-scale maps give details of land use and property ownership.
Vase stop	A bulbous decorative feature normally found on a door frame, shaped like an upturned vase.
Wall-plate	Lateral timber which runs the length of the building at eaves level.
Waste	Land belonging to a manor which was not held by any tenant. Often refers to commons, but also to the land beside a road.

BIBLIOGRAPHY

Abbreviation

SRS - Volumes published by the Sussex Record Society.

Alcock, N.W., Barley, M.W., Dixon, P.W. & Meeson, R.A. (1996) *Recording Timber-Framed Buildings: an illustrated glossary,* Council for British Archaeology, Practical Handbooks in Archaeology No. 5 (revised edition).

Bettey, J.H. (1987) *Church & Parish, A Guide for Local Historians,* Batsford, London.

Brandon, P. (1998) *The South Downs,* Phillimore, Chichester.

Brown, R.J. (1986) *Timber-Framed Buildings of England,* Robert Hale, London.

Chatwin, D. (1996) *Timber-Framed Buildings in the Sussex Weald, the Architectural Heritage of Rudgwick,* Rudgwick Preservation Society, Rudgwick.

Comber, J. (1931) *Sussex Genealogies, Horsham Centre,* Heffer, Cambridge.

Crawfurd, Rev. G.P. (1932) 'Slinfold Fifty Years Ago', *Sussex County Magazine,* Vol. 6, 1932.

Drewett, P., Rudling, D. & Gardiner, M. (1988) *The South-East to AD 1000,* A Regional History of England, Longman, Harlow.

Fletcher, A. (1975) *Sussex, 1600-1660, a County Community in Peace and War,* Longman, London.

Friar, S. (1996) *A Companion to the English Parish Church,* Alan Sutton, Stroud.

Grieves, K. (2000) 'Investigating local war memorial committees: demobilised soldiers, the bereaved and expressions of local pride in Sussex villages, 1918-1921', *The Local Historian,* Volume 30, No. 1.

Hey, D. (1996) *The Oxford Companion to Local & Family History,* BCA, London.

Hillman, G. (1993) 'Wealden Landscape as a Resource for Mesolithic Foragers', *Paper given at the Autumn Conference of the Sussex Archaeological Society.*

Nairn, I. & Pevsner, N. (1965) *The Buildings of England - Sussex,* Penguin Books, Middlesex.

Peckham, W.D. (ed) (1925) *Thirteen Custumals of the Sussex Manors of the Bishop of Chichester,* SRS 31.

Peckham W.D. (ed) (1942/3) *The Chartulary of the High Church of Chichester,* SRS 46.

Thirsk, J. (1997) *Alternative Agriculture - A History,* Oxford University Press.

Tinniswood, A (1995) *Life in the English Country Cottage,* Weidenfeld & Nicholson, London.

Vine, P.A.L. (1965) *London's Lost Route to the Sea,* David & Charles, Newton Abbot.

The W.I. (1948) *The Slinfold Scrap Book,* Slinfold Women's Institute.

INDEX

A
agricultural labourers 11, 18
Albery, William, harness maker 24, 55-6
Alberys 56
Aldingbourne 9
Alfoldean 1
Amberfield 51, 54
Amberley 9
Andrewes, Mr, curate 105
Anscombe, Harry **Pl 8**
Arun Navigation 20-1
Arundel 9
Ashlands 42
Ayling, Thomas, bricklayer and builder 13, 17, 75, 96, **Pl 28, 41**
Ayling, Emily **Pl 41**
Ayling, Frederick 96
Ayling, Walter 96
Aylings the builders 13, 14, 25, 96, 110
Aylings Field 97

B
Baker's Barn 19
Barn Cottage 119
Barn End 21
Barns Green 74
The Barracks 7, 12, 80, 124, **Pl 17**
Barton Cottage, Hayes Lane **Pl 6**
basket factory 21, 24, 77
Bassett's Fee manor 12, 60
Beehive Cottages 71
Belchamber, John 40
bier 56, **Pl 17**
Billingshurst, Rowfold 83
Billingshurst Chapel 73
Birchwood 21, 97, *Map 1*
Bishop, Sir Edward 29
blacksmiths 10, 11, 19, 24, 25
Bland, George, Rector 124
blanket loan club 15
Blann, Miriam 19
Blechmeres 115, *see also* Old House Farm
Blount family 28-9
Blount, Mistress 40, 49, 114
Blount, Richard 114
Blunden, Mrs 57
Blunden, Ted 57
Boniface, Mary, farmer 118
bootmaker 18

Borrer, William, botanist 124
Bourn, David 45
Bowyer, Sarah 65
box-frame construction 32, *Fig 1*
Braby, Frederick 89, 91
Braby, Jane (née Child) 89, 91
Brackley Burn 31
Bradbrydge, Richard 114
brewing 11, 20
bricks 35
　bonds 36, 94, **Pl 10**, *Fig 7*
brickworks, Hayes Lane 21
Bridgland, Bennie 88
Briggs, Ann (née Stanford) 42, 44
Briggs, Elizabeth 15, 44
Briggs, John (1), farmer 15, 16, 17, 43-4, 100
Briggs, John (2) 15, 44, 100
Briggs, John (3) 15, 44, 100, 117
Briggs, Mary 42, 44
Briggs, Samuel, tanner 15, 41, 46
Briggs, Sarah (née Crapwell) 41
Briggs, William (1), tanner 15, 41-2, 43, 100
Briggs, William (2), tanner 15, 41-2, 43, 44, 100
Briggs family 15, 29
　family tree 127
　tanners 9, 11, 15
Broadbridge Farm, Broadbridge Heath 68
Brookhurst 98
Broom, Frank 111
Broom, Lena 110-11
Brown, Mr, wheelwright 71
Brown, William, schoolmaster 23, 121
Browning, Charles, porter 18
Buckle, Mr 118-19
Buckman, Jesse 107
Buckmots Farm 124
buildings
　bricks 35, **Pl 10**, *Fig 7*
　construction 32-7, *Figs 1-7*
　stone 35-6
　timber-framed 32-5, *Figs 1-6*
Bunny, Brice 120
Bunny, Edward Brice 14, 29, 119
Bunny, Edward John 29-30
Bunny, Emma 119
Burton, Richard, teacher 121
Bury Gate 20
bus service 23
butchers 10, 20, 25

C

Calkett 28
Canadian troops stationed 23, 107, 110
canals 20-1
Candleford 12, 21, 24-5, 77-8, 82, *Map 1*
Cane, Elizabeth, teacher 121
Cane, Henry, Brighton builder 85
Cane, Thomas, Brighton builder 85
Canteen 23
Canterbury, Archbishop of 83
carpenters 10, 11, 17
Casson, Mary 44
Casson, William, tanner journeyman 42, 44
Chaning-Pearce, David, Rector 126, **Pl 19**
The Chapel see Slinfold Chapel
Chapel Cottage 70-2, 75, 84
   18th century 70-1
   19th century 12, 71
   20th century 72, **Pl 26**
   construction 33, 35, 70
   divided 7
   ground plan *Fig 18*
   Map 1
   occupants 18, 24, 70-2
   orchard 12
   origins 5, 70
   wheelwright's workshop 11, 19, 70
Chapel View 13, 96-7, 110, *Map 1*, **Pl 41**
Chelsom, Mary 116
Chelsome, Edward 67
Chelsome, John 67
Cherry Tree Cottage 10, 16, 18, 102-7, **Pl 45, 47**
   18th cent 104
   19th cent 17, 107
   divided 7
   ground plan *Fig 22*
   Maps 1, 5
   occupants 29, 57
   origins 5, 102
Chewton 47-51, 96, **Pl 14**
   5 & 6 Church View 51, 53
   16th century 48
   17th century 49, *Fig 11*
   18th century 50
   19th century 50-1
   alehouse 7, 11, 48-9, 52, 115
   construction 33, 34, 35, 53
   ground plan *Fig 9*
   Maps 1, 5
   occupants 17, 24
   origins 5, 48

   ritual protection marks 49, *Fig 13*
Chichester 9
Chichester, Bishop of 3, 9, 28, 113
Child & Henly, Arundel 16
Child family 15, 29, 30
   family tree 128
Child, Ann (née Holden) 16, 104-5, 111
Child, Caroline (née Churchman) 14, 89, 91-2, 107-8, **Pl 38**
Child, Charles (1), carpenter 11, 15-16
Child, Charles (2), timber merchant 16-17, 53, 56, 89, 91-2, **Pl.4**
Child, Charles (3), land agent 92, 95, 96, 108
Child, Dr Stanley 106
Child, Edward (1) 12, 13, 15
Child, Edward (2), timber merchant 15-16, 21, 46-7, 53, 69, 84, 93, 104-6, 108, 111
Child, Edward (3) 89
Child, Ellen 89, 91-2
Child, Ellen (née Mills) 17, 91
Child, Harold 42, 44, 69, 92, 95
Child, John 89
Child, Kate 30, 89, 91-2, 108
Child, Martha 15
Child, Mrs, innkeeper 63
Child, Peter 95
Child, Thomas
   coal merchant 12, 16-17, 21, 89, 91, 93, 104, **Pl 4, 5**
   Forge Cottage built 13, 95
   memorial 14, 92
   obituary 91
   owner of Little Hammers 68
   Village Hall 107-8
chimneys 35, 36, *Fig 6*
Church see St Peter's Church
Church ales 5, 113
Church Croft 14, 119
Church House 110-11, **Pl 3, 6, 49**
   construction 36
   Map 1
   occupants 110
   origins 13, 96, 110
Church school *see* Slinfold School
Church View
   (no 1) 53
   (no 3) 11, 12, 17, 50, 53, 55, 56-7, **Pl 18**, *Map 1*
   (no 4) 12, 17, 50, 53, 55, 56-7, **Pl 18**, *Map 1*
   (no 5 & 6) 51, 53
Churcher, George 29, 46
Churcher, John 46

Index

Churcher, Thomas (1) 46, 61
Churcher, Thomas (2) 46
Churchman, Frederick 85
Churchman, Harriet (née Sturt) 85
Churchyard Cottages
5, 11, 18, 43, 98-102, **Pl 42-4**
   18th century 99
   19th century 100
   20th century 101
   construction 34, 35, 98-9
   ground plan *Fig 21*
   Map 1
   (no 1) 10
   (no 2) 11, 17, 18, 26, 56, 100-1
   (no 3) 19, 100-1
   origins 98-9
   ritual deposit 102, **Pl 44**
Churchyard Field 98
Cinder Path 115
Clapgate Cottage 3, 91, 95, 98
Clapgate Lane 3, 20, 64, 98
Clark family 65
Clark, Michael 69
Clarke, Rev F.W. 105
Clarke, Mary, domestic 84
Clarke, William, platelayer 18
Clemsfold Farm 9, 98
Clemsfold manor 1, 5, 98
Climping 1
clothing club 15
Cluer, Dorothy 57
Clympsfold 1
Colgate 28
Collyers 3, 5, 39-42, 44
   16th century 39-40
   17th century 40
   18th century 41-2
   20th century **Pl 11**
   construction 32, 34, 35, 39-40
   Dedisham manor courts 27
   ground plan *Fig 8*
   Maps 1, 3-5
   (No 1) 42
   (No 2) 42
   occupants 10, 17, 18, 24
   origins 39
   tannery 9, 11, 15, 41-2
   weaver's workshop 11
commons 2, 26, *Map 2*
Comrades Cross 30, **Pl 9**
Congregational Chapel 14, *see also* Slinfold Chapel

Conkers 21, 45
Constable, Elizabeth 68
Constable, Michael, labourer 18-19, 68
Constable, Philip 68
Coombs, Maud 72
Cooper family 115
Copnall, E.Bainbridge, artist 106, 107
Copnall family 101
Coral Spurge 124
cordwainers *see* shoemakers
Cornwallis, Lord 44
The Cottage *see* Slinfold House
Couchman, J., pastor 74
Courtney, Commander Anthony 67
Courtney, Elizabeth 67
Cowfold 1
Cowper, Edward 114
Cowper, Richard 29
Cowper, William, tailor 64
Cox, Alfred 24, 78
Cranham, C., evangelist 74
Crapwell, George 41
Crapwell, Margaret 41
Crawfurd, Rev G.P., Rector 17, 21, 30, 62, 63, 76, 80, 100, 105, 106
crime 19
Croucher, John 73
Crown alehouse 53
Crown Farm 115, *see also* Park House
crown post roof 32, *Fig 2*
Cumming, Mary 31
cycle repairer 24

D

Dan Farm 1, 124
Dance, Captain 63
Davey, Miss 24
Davey, James 104
Davies Cottage 49
Davis, Mr and Mrs 82
Davye, Richard 40
Dawe, Charles 51
Dawe, Connie 51, 87, **Pl 11, 35**
Dawe, Florence **Pl 11**
Dawe, Violet **Pl 11**
Dawes, Robert **Pl 11**
Dedisham Farm 103
Dedisham Manor 2, 3, 5, 28, 29
   court 27
   door jambs 49
   houses on Dedisham land 39-5

deer parks 28, 83
Denne Park, Horsham 1
Diamond Jubilee 108, 114, **Pl 48**
Dinnage, Arthur 88, **Pl 24**
Dinnage, Fred, wheelwright 69, **Pl 24**
Doll, Christopher 106
Doll, Dr 106
Doll, Josephine (née Douglas) 106, 107, 111
Doll, Kathleen 106
Doll, Sir Richard 106
Doomsday Cottage 29, 49
Drungewick Manor 98
Duck, Anne (née Blount) 49
Duck, William 49

E
early settlement of the Weald 1-2
Ede, George 107
Ede, John, farmer 40
Edser, Annie 108
Edwards, Miss 24, 72
Edwards, Mr, farmer 118
electricity 21, 111
Elizabeth, Queen 46, 61
Elliott, Frederick 42, 58
Ellis, John Henry 12
Ellis, Thomas 12
enclosures 3, 26, 75
England, Charles 44
Etherton, Mr, Horsham blacksmith 94
evacuees 24
Evans, Nigel 63

F
Farhall, Ann 55, 56, 75
Farhall, Edward 55, 56
Farhall, John 53, 75
Farley, Alice 69
Farley, Beccy, seamstress 100
Farley, George (1), blacksmith 64, 67
Farley, George (2), agricultural labourer 71
Farley, John 84
Farley, Rebecca, seamstress 19
Farlington School *see* Strood
farming 26
Farthings farm 9, 28
Ferring manor 9, 28
Field Place 36
Fish, John 40
Fish, Peter, weaver 10, 11, 40
Fish, Sarah 40

Fitzgerald, Major, riding master 63
Fladgate, Mr 54
forge 11, 19
Forge Cottage 13, 73, 95-6, **Pl 39**
Forge House 13, 92, 93-5, **Pl 39, 40**
  brickwork 36, 94, 95, Pl 10
  construction 93
  Map 1
  sold to Thomas Child 13, 94
Forge View 68-9, **Pl 24, 25**
Fosseys 21, 119
Foulkes, Pamela 69
Francis, M. 101
Francis House 61
Freeman, Elizabeth, schoolmistress 14, 55
Freeman, James 99
Freeman, John (1) 11, 68, 99
Freeman, John (2) 99
Freeman, John (3) tailor 25, 55-6, 107
  Regency House 13, 18, 24, 55, 57, 107
Freeman, Matthew, bricklayer 71
Freeman, Phoebe 57, 107
Freeman, Richard (1), agricultural labourer 57
Freeman, Richard (2) 99
Freeman, William (1) carpenter 55, 57
Freeman, William (2) agricultural labourer 57, 107
Fuller, Harold 95
Fuller, Harriet 92
Fuller, Mabel 92, 95
Funnel, Miss, schoolmistress 121
Fure 9, 28
Furlonger, Sarah 40-1
Furlonger, William 40-1
furnace 11

G
Gander, Charles, farmer 118
Garden House 21, 92, *Map 1*
gardeners 11, 18
Gardiner, Ann (née Potter) 83-4
Gardiner, John, cordwainer 10, 99
Gardiner, Margaret 53
Gardiner, Martha 53
Gardiner, Richard (1), mercer 40, 49, 53, 83-4, *Map 5*
Gardiner, Richard (2), shopkeeper 83
Gardiner, Richard (3) 83
Garman, Elizabeth 100
Garman, John 100
Garman, Kester, bailiff 95

Index 137

Garton, Harry 79
Gaskins 15, 18, 43, 82
Gatford, James, wheelwright 68, 70, 72
Gatton, William 61
Gatwick 1
George's Field 42, 43
German plane crashes 23
Gilbert, Reginald, blacksmith 5, 40, 64
Gravatt, Mary 55
Gravatt, Phyllis 42
Gravatt, Richard, carpenter 42
Gray, Major Edward, innkeeper 63
Greenfield, Francis 116
Greenfield, Mary (née Chelsome) 67
Greenfield, Sam 67
Grinstead, Alfred, carpenter 17, 75-7, 96, **Pl 30**
Grinstead, Emily 51
Grinstead, George 62, 82
Grinstead, James, farmer 68, 75-7, 81-2, 105
Grinstead, Mary 17, 18, 75
Grinsted, William, butcher 51, 54, 82
Groombridge, John, cordwainer 10, 67

H
Hall Land Farm 3, 41, 42, 43-4, 81, 117
   19th century 26, 43
   Maps 1, 3, 4
   origins 9, 15, 39, 42
Hall Land House 43-4, **Pl 12**
Hampshire, Moses 80
Hampson, Mr 88
Harbroe, Edward, Rudgwick apothecary 100
Harbroe, Thomas 100
Harmer, Susanna 51
Harris, Geoffrey M. 45
Haven Road 39
Hayes, Mrs 101
Hayes Chapel 73
Hayes Farm, survey *Map 5*
Hayes Grange 116
Hayes House 73
   see also Slinfold Manor
Hayes Lane 12, 21, 79, 80
Hayler, John 10
Hearsey, George 11
Herrington, May 54
Herrington, Walter, butcher 25, 51, 54
Hersey, George, gardener 67
High Trees 21, 45, *Map 1*
Hill 2, 12, 15, 29, 43, 54, 83
Hill Farm 91

Hill House 13, 29, 46, 61, 73, 83, **Pl 50**
Hill Lodge *see* South Lodge
Hillman, Andy Pl 19
Hobbs, George, showjumer 118
Hobbs, Mr, farmer 118
Hodgson, May 69
Holden, Ann 16
Holden, Caleb, carpenter 73
Holden, Charles (1), blacksmith and innkeeper 9, 16, 61-2, 64-5, 68, 104-5, 111
Holden, Charles (2) 62, 65, 93
Holden, David, blacksmith 11, 12, 13, 65, 93
Holden, Edward 66
Holden, Elsie 66
Holden, Hannah 65
Holden, James, blacksmith 65, 93
Holden, Maria 66
Holden, Phoebe 93
Holden, Sarah, innkeeper 19, 20, 62, 63, 66, 85, 93
Holden, Susan 47
Holden family 15, 30
Holdens
   17th century 64, *Map 5*
   18th century 64
   19th century 26, 61, 66, 93, **Pl 2, 23**
   20th century 66
   Maps 1, 5
   occupants 25
   origins 5, 11, 13, 14, 36
   porch 89
   slate roof 36
Holland, George, quarryman 18, 71
Holland, Lorenzo, carpenter 17, 57
Holland, Luke 71, 80
Holland, Philip, farmer 18, 68
Holland, Thomas 117
Holland, Tom, cripple 80
Holloway, Mary 111
Holman family 40
Holmbush Manor Farm 18, 54
Holmbush **Pl 54**
Honour of Arundel 29
hoopmakers 18
Hopes, Laura 101
Horsham 9
   49 West Street 55, 117
   United Brewery 62
Horsham & Guildford Direct Railway 17
Horsham Congregational Church 73
Horsham Independents chapel 72

Horsham stone 18, 32, 35-6
Horsham United Reformed Church 75
Horsman, Jane 107
Hounsom, Dorothy **Pl 6**
Hughes, Frederick 126
Hughes, Rev F.G., Rector 120, 126
Hull, Mary (née Peters) 65
Hull, Michael, tailor 65-6, 68
Hull, William (1) shopkeeper 65, 68
Hull, William (2) 65
Humfrey, Stephen 10
Huntingrove 49
Hurricane Fund 106
Hussey, Bridget 60-1
Hyrstlea 24, 76-8, *see also* Taylors

I
invasion fears 9
Ireland, James, wheelwright apprentice 71, 73
Ironwood House 14, 45, 123-4
    construction 124
    demolished 124
    Map 1
Itchingfield
    Fulfords Farm 117
    tile-works 1

J
Jackson, gardener 31
Jago, Dr 111
James I 46
Jayes, Richard, shoemaker 11, 56, 100
Jeal, Jack, ratcatcher 42
Jeal, John, labourer 42, 63
Jeal, Richard 1076
Johnson, Albert 111
Johnson, Frederick 95
Johnson, John 96
Johnson, Johnnie 96
Jones, John Piggott 100
Jones, Rev John 100
Jubilee Tree 108
Jupp, Robert 9

K
Kei-a-Gomeena 25, 67
Killner, Dick **Pl 19**
Killner, Frank 111
Kinggett, Kate, dressmaker 24, 51
Kings Head 26, 46, 60-4
    17th century 11
    19th century 9, 62-3, **Pl 2**
    20th century 63-4, **Pl 1, 21, 22**
    cellars 53
    construction 32, 34, 35, *Figs 15*
    crown post **Pl 20**
    ground plan *Fig 16*
    guard room of Canadian troops 23, 64
    Map 5
    name 61
    origins 60
    owners 61-2
    Post Office 63
    postbox 20, 62
    Red Lyon 61
    roadway 12
    run by Holdens 19, 20, 61-2
Kings Head Cottage 62, 63, 86
Kings Head Garage 24, 64, 107
Knight, Alfred 118
Knight, Charles, Horsham grocer 23, 44, 85, 117, 124
Knight, Elias, hoopmaker 18
Knight, James (1), grocer 50, 65, 68, 84, 100
Knight, James (2), butcher 53, 71
Knight, John (1), cordwainer 10, 84, 104
Knight, John (2), agricultural labourer 71
Knight, Judith 84, 99, 100
Knight, Mary 118
Knight, Mary (née Sturt) 85, 117
Knight, Michael **Pl 54**
Knight, Nathaniel (1) 117
Knight, Nathaniel (2) 117
Knight, Paul 45
Knight, Stephen 84
Knight, Thomas (1) 43, 117
Knight, Thomas (2) 117
Knight, Thomas (3) 117-18
Knight, Walter, mercer and tailor 10, 84, 99

L
Lauder, Vivian 77
Lee, Mr 88
Leslie, Alan 45
Leslie, Barbara 45
Lewer, Edward, farmer 40
Lewin, Dorothy 72
Lewin, Irene 72
Library 14, 108
Lilleywhite, Mrs 80
Little Bleachmers 99
Little Hammers

    5, 65, 67-9, 70, **Pl 2**
    18th century 67-8
    19th century 68
    20th century 69
    construction 67
    forge 11, 19
    ground plan *Fig 17*
    Map 1, 5
    occupants 7, 10, 18, 19, 94
    roadside waste encroached 12
    well 67-8
Little Platt 21, 54, 59, *Fig 14, Map 1*
Lloyd George's Domesday 44, 56, 75, 77, 87, 89, 120
Loan Exhibition at Slinfold school, 122-3, **Pl 56**
Lower Broadbridge Farm 29, 47, 60, 114
    door jambs 49
Lower Forge 13, 95
Lydwicke 2, 31, 115, 124
Lyons Farm 85, 86, 124
Lyons Road 2, 11, 20, 21
    almshouses 80
    (no 4) 25, 88
    Rowfold Lea 25

M
Mackintosh, Lady 92
Mahrenholz, Harald 79
mains water 21, 111
Manningham, Dr Thomas, Rector 104, 124
Manningham, Mary (née Yates) 124
manorial system 2, 27-31, 37
    copyhold tenure 27
    duties of tenants 9, 27
    freehold tenure 27
    holdings in Slinfold *Map 7*
    influence 37
    leasehold tenure 27
    manor courts 27
Marley, Mr, grocer 25, 58
Mary Queen of Scots 46
Mead, John **Pl 19**
Meads, H.F., innkeeper 63
medieval houses 32-3
mercers 10, 19
Michelgrove 46
Michell, Henry, brewer 62, 63
Millar, George, pastor 74
Mills, Charlotte 55
Mills, Ellen 17

Mills, Henry, tailor 18, 100
Mills, James (1), agricultural labourer 55
Mills, James (2) 71, 95
Mills, John, tailor 18, 100, 104
Milner Hay family 67
Mitchell, James, butcher 51, 53
Money, Clifford 25, 66-7, **Pl 8**
More, Mr 40
Morris, Maria (née Child) 95
Morris, Ruth 95, 96
Mortimer, Mr, schoolmaster 121
Mose, Elizabeth 40
multiple occupancy of houses 11, 68
Murray, Pete 106

N
Naldrett family 29, 49
Naldrett, George 54, 116
Naldrett, George (1) 54, 116
Naldrett, George (2) 116
Naldrett, Mary 115-16
Naldrett, Richard 5, 29, 50, 115-16
Newman, Elizabeth (née Briggs) 42, 44, 101
Newman, Frederick 44
Newman, John 68
Nibletts 3, 5, 60-1, 63, 71, 75, 81, 82
    see also Kings Head; Padora-Nibletts
    Map 3
Noble, C. Wycliffe, architect 97
Norfolk, Duke of 114, 119
Normans 2
Nowhurst 12, 15, 36, 43, 46, 83
    quarry 119
Nye, Mr, *Map 5*

O
The Old Bakery/Village Stores 3, 9, 40, 48, 83-8
    see also Rowfold; Slinfold Stores
    17th century 83-4
    18th century 84
    19th century 85-6
    20th century 87-8
    construction 34, 35, 36, 84, 85
    ground plan *Fig 20*
    Maps 1, 5
    mercers shop 10
The Old Forge 11, 93-5, 95, **Pl 7, 39**, *Map 1*
Old House 2, 3, 5, *Maps 3-5*
Old House Farm 2, 48, 85, 115-19, **Pl 53, 54**
    17th century 5, 115-16

    18th century 117
    19th century 43, 117-18
    20th century 21, 26, 118-19
    construction 32, 35, 115
    granary 118, 119, **Pl 4**
    ground plan *Fig 23*
    Map 1
    name 115
    origins 5, 14, 115
    rebuilt 29
    Wiggonholt manor courts 27
Old Parsonage House 124, *see also* Ironwood House
Old Stables 21, 119
Old Tanyard House *see* Collyers
The Old Village Stores 10, 84, *see also* The Old Bakery
Older, James, wheelwright 70, 100
open hall houses 29, 33-5, 39-40, 83, *Fig 5-6*
Osborne, Miss, schoolmistress 121
O'Toole, Terry **Pl 19**
Otway, George, tailor 68

P
Padora 82
Padora-Nibletts 21, 26, 81-2, *Map 1*
parish authority 28
parish chest 114
Parish Library 108
parish pump 21, 80, *Fig 19*
Parish Reading Room 14, 106
parish records, Vestry Minutes 10
Park Farm 15, 43
Park House 17, 53, 111, 115
Park Road 30
Park Street 2, 9, 20
Park Street Corner 119
Parker, Philip 47
Parker, Sarah 47
Parkhurst, Henry, wheelwright 71, 73, 74, 94
Patching, George 70, 75
Patching, John (1) wheelwright 70, 72
Patching, John (2) 50, 104
Patching, John (3), carpenter 68
Patching manor court 27, 83
Patching, Mary (née Butcher) 70, 72, 75
Patching, William, wheelwright 70, 84
Path, Ann, schoolmistress 121
Pavey, Pat 82
Pavey, Dot (née Davis) 82
Penfold, Dorothy 61

Penfold, Frances 67, 72
Penfold, Henry, yeoman 64, 68, 71
Penfold, Joan 68
Penfold, John, victualler 61, 72
Penny, Mr, schoolmaster 120
Pephurst, Loxwood 9
Peppercorn Cottage (1 Church View) 7, 24, 50, 53, 54-6, **Pl 16**
    Map 1
    origins 55
Perkins, George 88
Perrin family 40
Pescod, W.H. 58
Pickering, Helen 72
Picton, Hubert 57, 101
pig pastures 1
pigs 9, 28
Pinkhurst farm 29
Pinkhurst Gate 99
Pinkhurst manor 2, 3, 28, 29, 79
    door jambs 49
Pipper, Mrs, housekeeper 57
Pocklington, Joseph 80
Poltick, Ann (née Wood) 64
Poltick, Elizabeth 64
Poltick, Hannah 64
Poltick, John, blacksmith and innkeeper 61, 64
Poltick, William (1) 64
Poltick, William (2) 64
population 7, 12, 17
Portsmouth, Mrs G.G., innkeeper 63
Post Office 20, 25, 63, 85-8, **Pl 31**
postcards of local views 25, **Pl 8, 9, 58**
Potter, James, tailor 64
Pratt, Winifred 69
Pratts Cottages 36
Prosecuting Societies 19
Pulborough, saddlery business 55
Puttock, Caroline 47
Puttock, James, butcher 103
Puttock, John, butcher 103
Puttock, Philip 47
Puttock, Phoebe 105

R
railway 17, 18, 21, 23
Ranfold farm 9, 15, 18, 28, 43
Read, Elizabeth 50
Read, Evangeline 51
Read, George (1), carpenter and joiner 11, 50
Read, George (2) 51

Index

Read, Lewis 51
Reader, Charles (1), innkeeper 63
Reader, Charles (2), tailor 18
Reader, Charles (3) 63
Reader, Mary, innkeeper 19, 63
Rectory
   see also Conkers; Ironwood House
   5, 21, 45, 124, **Pl 57-8**
   Maps 1, 4, 5
   wing demolished 125-6
Red Cottages *see* The Barracks
Red Lyon 61
Redman, Thomas 71, 107
Reed, George, steam sawyer 18
Reed, Thomas, steam sawyer 18
Regency House 13, 18, 26, 55, 57-8, **Pl 3, 19**
   brickwork 36
   Map 1
   origins 57
   shop 18, 24, 25, 57
   slate roof 36
Regency Kitchens 58
Richardson, Emily, schoolmistress 121
Riddles, Henrietta 56, 57
ritual protection 49, 102, **Pl 44,** *Fig 13*
roads
   maintenance 10, 28
   tarred 23
roadside waste 12, **Pl 2**
Robeson, Elizabeth 84
Rock Brewery Company 62
Roman Gate 1, 20, 23
Romans in the Weald 1
roofs 32-3, 35, 36, 52, *Figs 2, 3*
Rose Cottage 62, 66, **Pl 23**
Rosewarne 30
Rowadams 49
Rowfold farm
   16th century 2-3, 46
   18th century 83
   19th century 15, 43, 91, 93
   20th century 26, 82
   Map 3
   Patching manor court 27, 83
   Shop Field 12, 89, 96
Rowfold Lea, Lyons Road 25
Rudgwick 3
   medieval houses surviving 29
   Naldrett House 85, 116
   Southlands 85
Ruse, Nora 21, 26, 82

S
Saddlers (2 Church View)
   7, 14, 18, 50, 54-6, 57, **Pl 16**
   Bier Room 56
   Map 1
   origins 55
Sageman, Reuben, poacher 19
St John family 117
St John, Colonel Edward Francis 30, 108
St John, Major Edward 31, 118
St Peter's Church 113-14, **Pl 51, 52**
   Dedisham Chancel 28
   Dedisham Chapel 113, 114
   demolished 14, 114, **Pl 4**
   Lady of Tregoz 114
   Maps 1, 4-5
   memorials 14, 92
   musicians' gallery 113
   new church 36
   origins 2-3, 26
   recasting of bell 9
   removal of spire 114
Saxons in the Weald 1-2
school *see* Slinfold School
Seamors 61
Shelley family 36, 46
Shelley, William 46, 60
Shipley 1
Shiprods 1
shoe club 15
shoemakers 10, 17-18
Shop Field 12, 89, 96
shopkeepers 11
shops 10-11, 19
   see also Slinfold Stores
Short, Harty 53
slate 36, 89
slaughter house 11
Slinfold
   16th-18th century 5-9
   19th century 12-14
   20th century 21-6
   Canadian troops stationed 23, 107, 110
   development 3-26, 37
   manors 2
   Map 1
   medieval houses surviving 29
   name 3
   open-hall houses 29
   parish of 3
Slinfold Benefit Society 63

Slinfold Chapel 72-4, **Pl 28**
Slinfold Chapel
  19th century 73
  20th century 74
  datestone Pl 27
  origins 14, 74
Slinfold church house 5
Slinfold Fire Brigade 69
Slinfold House 12, 102-7, Pl.1 33, 45, 46
  18th century 9, 103-4, 106
  19th century 26, 104-5, 106
  20th century 106
  Canteen 23, 64, 107
  construction 34, 35, 104
  earth closet 92
  ground plan *Fig 22*
  Map 5
  name 104, 106
  occupants 10, 101, 16
  origins 5, 102-3
  Parish Reading Room 14, 106
  porch 89
  semi-detached 29
Slinfold Inn
  see also Kings Head
  3, 61, *Map 1*
Slinfold Lodge 14, 29, 117
Slinfold Manor 73, *Map 5, see also* Hayes House
Slinfold Mill 3
Slinfold school 14, 108, 119-23, **Pl 55, 56**
  Board School 120
  construction 119
  curriculum 121
  Loan Exhibition 122-3, **Pl 56**
  Map 1
  medical inspections 122
  non-attendance 121-2
  prize days 121
  pupil-teacher system 121
  school bell 119
Slinfold Stores
  see also Rowfold
  19, 20, 25, **Pl 34**
Slinfold Street 12, *Map 1, 6*
Smith, Sylvia 110
Smith, William 9
Smithaw 98
smoke bay houses 5, 34, 40, *Fig 10*
Snelling, John, blacksmith 64, 66
Society for the Apprehension of Felons 19
South Lodge 13, 96, 112, **Pl 50**

  Map 1
Spence, Barney, innkeeper 63
Spring Lane, Rosewarne 30
Stane Street, Slinfold 1, 9, 17, 20, 36
Stanford family 15, 50
Stanford, Alfred, pupil-teacher 121
Stanford, Ann 47
Stanford, Harry 53
Stanford, John 9, 46-7
Stanford, Mary 53
Stanford, Sarah 46-7
Stanford, William, carpenter 63, 68
Stanford House 3, 5, 26, 45-7
  16th century 46, 60
  19th century 46, **Pl 13**
  Maps 1, 3-5, 48
  new brick building 9, 14
  occupants 41
Star Inn *see* Weeping Eye
Station Inn 30
statute labour 10
Steer, Mr 72
Stemp, Alfred George 24, 64, 72, 107
Stemp, Maurice 71-2
Steuart, Miss 47
Stevens, Corelli 51
Steyning 3
stocks 5
Stokes, Wendy 67
Stokes, William 67
Stone Cottages 7, 12, 21, 79, 80-1, **Pl 32**, *Map 3*
The Street 3, *Maps 1, 6*
street lights 21, 23
Stringer, Francis 67
Stringer, John 48, 49, 85, 103, 115
Strood (later Farlington School) 29, 36, 114
Strudwick, Robert, victualler 48, 49
Strudwick, Sarah 55
Strudwick, William, agricultural labourer, parish clerk 55
Sturt, Harry Stanford, grocer 85, 86
Sturt, Mary (née Stanford) 85
Sturt, Sarah (née Patching) 71, 73, 84
Sturt, Thomas
  farming 85
  grocer 19, 71, 72-3
  Old Bakery 84
  owner of Chewton 50, 53, 85
  owner of Church View 85
  owner of Peppercorn Cottage 85
  owner of Saddlers 85

Index

owner of Taylors 12, 75, 85
owner of Weeping Eye plot 55, 56
owner of White Briars 85
Survey of Mr Nyes land called Hayes *Map 5*
Sussex Census of Churches 73
Sussex Congregational Union 73
Sussex Home Mission 72
Sutton, Robert, Rector 125
sweet shop 58
Sweeting, Richard 40

T
tailors 10, 18
Talbot, Rev W. 74
Tanner, Rebecca, schoolmistress 14
tannery 11, 21, 41, 41-2
Tanyard Cottages *see* Collyers
Tanyard House 15, 43
   see also Collyers; Hall Land House
Taylors 24, 75-7
   19th cent 12, 17
   20th cent 26
   granary 82
   Map 1
   origins 70, 72, 75
   late roof 36
Taylors Cottages 71
Tebbit, Miss 79
Thayre, Edward 115
Theale 9
theatre barn 45
Thornden, John 29
Thornden family 29
Thorpe, Ted, innkeeper 63
tile-works, Itchingfield 1
timber yard, Stane Street 17, 18, 21
timber-framed buildings 32-5, *Fig 1-6*, 15
Tithe Map 2, 11, 42, 55, 65, 71, 89, 104
title deeds 27
tobacconists 58
Torrington, Sid, signwriter 64
trades and tradesmen 10-11, 15-20
transhumance in the Weald 1
transport 9, 20-1
Trotman, Barbara 72
Trotman, Eric 72
Turner, Matthew 46
turnpikes 10, 20

U
United Brewery of Horsham 62
United Reformed Chapel 14, 75

V
Vestry Minutes 10
Vickress, Thomas 73
village green 26
Village Hall
   14, 92, 106, 107-10, **Pl 3, 19, 27, 48, 49**
   Map 1
Village Shop 65, **Pl 33**
village stores *see* Slinfold Stores
Village Stores and Post Office 51, 55, 83-8
Vincent, Rev Frederick, Rector 51, 53, 114, 124-5

W
F. & C. Wadey 24
Wadey, Annie 95
Wadey, Charles 64, 94, 95
Wadey, Charlotte 94
Wadey, Frank (1), wheelwright and smith 68, 74, 94, 96, **Pl 40**
Wadey, Frank (2) 94-5
Waller, Mr 88
Waller, William 25, 67
walls 33, Fig 4
Walpole, Horace, on Sussex roads 10
war memorial 30, **Pl 9, 49**
Warnham 3, 15
Waterland 85
Waters, Lena **Pl 6**
Waters, Leonard 111
Waters, Mary 110
wattle-and-daub 33, *Fig 4*
Weakford, Ada 79, 86
Weakford, Charles (1) 55, 63, 79, 85-6
Weakford, Charles (2) 86
Weakford, Walter, civil servant 86
Weald
   bad roads 9
   commons 2
   early settlement 1-2
   manorial control 28
   outliers 1-2, 28
   transhumance 1
Weale, Thomas, tanner 11, 41
weavers 10
Weeping Eye alias the Star Inn 11, 48-50, 52-3, 54, 55

17th century 48, 52
20th century 20
occupants 53
origins 7
plot 54, 55, 56, 57, 59
Wensley, James 65
West, John Capon 55, 86-7, 111
West Lodge 112
West's Stores 55, 86
Wey and Arun Canal 21, 36
wheelwrights 10, 11, 19, 24
wheelwright's workshop 11, 19
White Briars
  18th century 53
  alehouse 7, 11, 49, 50, 51-3
  butchers 20, 21, 25, 53-4
  carpenter's marks 33
  construction 32, 33, 35
  ground plan *Fig 12*
  Map 1
  occupants 106
  origins 52, **Pl 15**
  outbuildings *Fig 14*
  ritual protection marks *Fig 13*
White, Cliff: *Horsham, The War Years* 106
White, Lois, postmistress 25, 87, 88
White, Nurse 111
Whittington, George, agricultural labourer 75
Whittington, William 71
Wickham, George, innkeeper 63
Wiggonholt Manor 2, 115
  court 27
Wild Harrys 18, 46, 79
Williams family 47
Williamson, Albert 71
Williamson, David (1) 71
Williamson, David (2), journalist 71, 72
Williamson, Esther 71
Williamson, Frederick 71
Williamson, William (1) 71, 72
Williamson, William (2) 71
Windalls
  17, 21, 30, 43, 83, 89-92, 108, **Pl 36-7**
  bay windows 91, **Pl 38**
  Map 1
  origins 12, 89
  porch 89
  slate roof 36, 89
Windalls farm 2, 3, 12, 14, 15, 98, 103
  see also Clapgate Cottage
  Map 3

Winters, C.W.R.: *The Queen Mary* 106
Women's Institute, scrap book 17, 73-4
Wood, Edwin 77
Wood, Janet 77
Woodlands 82
Woodman, Matthew, Rector 123
Woodman, Richard, martyr 123
workhouse 84
working men's club 31
World War I 23
  war memorial 30, **Pl 9, 49**
World War II 23
Worsfold, David (1), cordwainer 10, 104
Worsfold, David (2), cordwainer 104
Worsfold, Thomas, cordwainer 104

Y
Ye Olde House 29, 49
York Cottage 20, 25, 36, 79, 86, **Pl 31**, *Map 1*
Yorke, Colonel 44
Youngman 17